A CONCISE
HISTORY OF THE
FRENCH REVOLUTION

A CONCISE
HISTORY OF THE
FRENCH REVOLUTION

SYLVIA NEELY

ROWMAN & LITTLEFIELD PUBLISHERS, INC.
Lanham • Boulder • New York • Toronto • Plymouth, UK

ROWMAN & LITTLEFIELD PUBLISHERS, INC.

Published in the United States of America
by Rowman & Littlefield Publishers, Inc.
A wholly owned subsidiary of The Rowman & Littlefield Publishing Group, Inc.
4501 Forbes Boulevard, Suite 200, Lanham, Maryland 20706
www.rowmanlittlefield.com

Estover Road, Plymouth PL6 7PY, United Kingdom

British Library Cataloguing in Publication Information Available

Library of Congress Cataloging-in-Publication Data
Neely, Sylvia.
    A concise history of the French Revolution / Sylvia Neely.
        p.   cm. — (Critical issues in history)
    Includes bibliographical references and index.
    ISBN-13: 978-0-7425-3411-7 (pbk. : alk. paper)
    ISBN-10: 0-7425-3411-1 (pbk. : alk. paper)
    1. France—History—Revolution, 1789–1799. I. Title.
    DC149.N44 2008
    944.04—dc22

                                                                2007029526

Printed in the United States of America

♾™ The paper used in this publication meets the minimum requirements of
American National Standard for Information Sciences—Permanence of Paper for
Printed Library Materials, ANSI/NISO Z39.48-1992.

CONTENTS

ILLUSTRATIONS

MAPS

FIGURES

ACKNOWLEDGMENTS

This book has benefited from the expert assistance of many people to whom I wish to extend my thanks. I want to thank Erin Greb of the Gould Center for Geography Education and Outreach at Penn State University who created the maps. The Department of History at Penn State and its head, Prof. Sally McMurry, provided assistance for the maps and illustrations. The staffs of the Cornell University Division of Rare and Manuscript Collections, Cornell University Library (especially Evan Earle and Laura Linke), and of the Penn State University Special Collections (Sandra Stelts and Curt Krebs) aided me in selecting illustrations for this book. The College of the Liberal Arts at Penn State University provided a reduced work load one semester so that I could devote myself to this book. I want to acknowledge the support of Prof. Donald Critchlow, who was editor of this series when the book was commissioned, and Susan McEachern, editor at Rowman & Littlefield.

I am especially grateful for the help of Prof. Barry Shapiro of Allegheny College, who generously read the manuscript and offered many important suggestions for improvement and correction. As always, I appreciate the help of Mark Neely, who provided invaluable advice and edited with a vengeance.

Introduction

UNDERSTANDING THE
FRENCH REVOLUTION

Revolutions are not made; they come.

—Wendell Phillips, 1852

In 1989, France celebrated the bicentennial of the French Revolution with big parades and fireworks. But in the midst of the celebration, a nagging question kept intruding: Exactly what were they celebrating? The American Revolution, whose bicentennial was celebrated without soul-searching in 1976, is no longer controversial. Nobody seems to believe that the thirteen American colonies should have remained part of Great Britain. But the French Revolution has a more complicated legacy. Traditionalists deplore the attack on the king and the church. Some people embrace parts of the legacy of the Revolution while rejecting others. And some radicals believe the promises of the French Revolution have never been fulfilled. In the twentieth century, Russian revolutionaries saw themselves as continuing the French Revolution. Will the discrediting of Communism and the collapse of the Soviet Union force us to revise our understanding of the French Revolution?

The French Revolution was a complex event with repercussions in not only French government and society, but in all of Europe and even the rest of the world. During the nineteenth and twentieth centuries, writers and politicians constantly referred back to the Revolution as a way of understanding the changes taking place in their world. What lessons did it teach? What should be retained from it? What should be discarded? Understanding the French Revolution is essential for making sense of the history of the nineteenth and twentieth centuries. And it still has relevance for our own times.

The French Revolution bequeathed to us the very notion of revolution as something with profound and far-reaching effects on society. Previously, the word "revolution" (which is derived from the verb "to revolve") had referred to the motion of heavenly bodies. In the political realm it had been applied to the Glorious Revolution in England in 1688. A change in a ministry might be called a revolution. This limited meaning of the word revolution can be shown by its use in the diary of Arthur Young, an English visitor to Paris in the summer of 1789. After the Estates General was called, the Third Estate insisted that all three orders should meet together. When the king finally accepted this demand, the three estates met together as the National Assembly. On June 27, the English visitor commented: "The whole business now seems over, and the revolution complete."[1] In fact, it had hardly begun. The Bastille had not even fallen yet. Thomas Paine, the British writer who became famous in the American Revolution as the author of *Common Sense*, noted the changing meaning of what was occurring:

> What were formerly called Revolutions, were little more than a change of persons, or an alteration of local circumstances. They . . . had nothing in their existence or their fate that could influence beyond the spot that produced them. But what we now see in the world, from the Revolutions of America and France, are a renovation of the natural order of things, a system of principles as universal as truth and the existence of man, and combining moral with political happiness and national prosperity.[2]

Modern revolutions, Paine believed, were bringing about deep-seated changes, not just surface alterations. And it is this meaning of the word that we continue to use when we call something truly "revolutionary."

The comment by the visitor from England can teach us something very important about the French Revolution. Nobody knew that the French Revolution was going to occur. Nobody expected it. No revolutionary groups were plotting or conspiring to bring it about. The government was not making contingency plans to keep it from occurring. The way it began was a surprise, and the way it developed was an even greater surprise. This point is worth making at the beginning because the choices taken at the time sometimes seem foolish or dangerous. Why, we often want to cry out, would you make that decision? Don't you see it will lead to more trouble? But, of course, the individuals making the crucial decisions did not know what we now know, that the changes begun in the late 1780s escalated into revolutionary upheavals that disrupted people's lives, caused hundreds of thousands of deaths, remade the map of Europe, and challenged many long-cherished political, religious, and moral ideals.

It is hard for us to remember the unplanned nature of the French Revolution because we have come to think of it as a specific set of events that had a beginning and an end. Historians have carefully mapped out its stages, its winners and its losers, and the lessons to be learned from it. Historians have often given the events of the French Revolution an air of inevitability, as if the trajectory it took was the only one that could possibly have occurred. But this air of inevitability is the result of the way the story has been told, and not of the events themselves. Revolutionaries in the nineteenth century tended to assess their activities in the light of whether they were living up to the great French Revolution. They consciously tried to copy the Revolution that had inspired them. They planned and acted and followed what they believed was the model of revolutions. So we have too often fallen into the habit of assuming that the Revolution itself could have evolved only in a certain way.

A recent historical event can shed light on this subject. The breakup of the Soviet Union and the demise of the Soviet empire were neither planned nor expected. Political commentators can now see the signs of its demise, but at the time those were not visible to most observers. Revolutionaries did not cause the fall of the Soviet empire. Political repression had prevented the formation of an organized opposition. When the troops retreated, Eastern European countries found that they had no organized political groups to lead them in the new circumstances. And yet, even though the change had come about without a great struggle, the fall of the Soviet empire led to widespread revolutionary changes in both domestic and foreign politics. When the monarchical government of France collapsed in the late 1780s, the result was desperate improvisation to figure out what would take its place.

Writers along the entire political spectrum have helped to reinforce the impression that the French Revolution was bound to occur, either because there was a conspiracy to bring it about or because the laws of history dictated it. Conservatives at the time, overwhelmed by the losses they had suffered, appalled by the new political system, and unable to believe that the old institutions were bad enough to warrant such wholesale destruction, charged that the Revolution was the result of deliberate actions taken by evil men inspired by new and dangerous ideas. Uninformed by the abstractions of political science (the term itself had only recently been invented), conservatives naturally sought explanations in the motives and actions of particular people. At the other end of the political spectrum, the Communist theorist Karl Marx (writing in the 1840s) explained that the Revolution was caused by the demands for change from a rising "bourgeoisie" whose relatively low status in society no longer matched its increasing economic wealth. To take its rightful place in the country, the bourgeoisie, according to Marx, overthrew the nobility and the monarchy and established a system more congenial to the needs of capitalism. In Marx's theory, this struggle was the inevitable result of the workings of economic laws operating throughout the eighteenth century and culminating in the Revolution.

Recent historians have concluded that neither of these explanations satisfactorily accounts for the origins of the Revolution. Another reinforcement of the idea of the inevitability of the French Revolution came in nationalist histories of the nineteenth century. Nationalist theory taught that peoples naturally divided up into nations. Nationalists interpreted the Revolution as the inevitable victory of the "divine" people of France, who had thrown off the Old Regime and created a new kind of nation. They assumed that the French Revolution was merely the first in a series of struggles in which European nations would overturn the structures of the Old Regime.

This book is an introduction to the French Revolution. My intention here is to acquaint the reader with the most important events, the most prominent people, and the essential terms. Armed with those, you will then be able to read with profit others of the thousands of works on the subject. Interpretations cannot be left out of the story, however, because the French Revolution was, from the very beginning, a controversial event. And it has continued to be controversial. Thomas Paine, as we saw above, believed that the French Revolution had enormous moral implications—that it was bringing about freedom, prosperity, and happiness by doing away with despotism. But to many people in the nineteenth century, the French Revolution was used as an example of unspeakable evil, of destruction of kings, and of attacks on religion. To them, it had the same meaning as the Holocaust does nowadays, an instance of moral depravity so awful that one needed to constantly guard against its recurrence. Debates over morality and values pervade the speeches of the revolutionaries and the books that describe them. It is not surprising, then, to find that no single, agreed upon interpretation of the French Revolution exists.

This book will introduce you to the events and the major interpretations of the Revolution. Because chronology is essential in making sense of what occurred, this book provides a timeline of events. To understand the events, we need constantly to keep in mind what preceded them. People make decisions based on what they believe, what they have learned about the past, and what experiences they have lived through. French revolutionaries invoked classical examples (that they had learned in school), they referred to the history of France and other European countries (especially Great Britain), and they occasionally compared events in France to those that had recently occurred in the American Revolution. But the historical examples they invoked did not always fit because nothing like the French Revolution had occurred in France or any other European country. The French Revolution was itself a learning experience. As events evolved, things that had seemed totally out of reach and things that nobody had ever thought of suddenly became possible. To understand the Revolution, we must never lose the sense of amazement that both the revolutionaries and their enemies had as they tried to make sense of the totally unexpected events.

ENGLAND

AUSTRIAN
NETHERLANDS

English Channel

FLANDERS
AND HAINAUT

BOULONNAIS

ARTOIS

Douai

METZ AND
VERDUN

LE HAVRE

PICARDY

LORRAINE

Rouen

ÎLE-DE-FRANCE

Metz

NORMANDY

CHAMPAGNE

TOUL

Paris

Nancy

Rennes

LORRAINE

ALSACE

BRITTANY

MAINE

ORLÉANAIS

ANJOU

Dijon

Besançon

TOURAINE

NIVERNAIS

FRANCHE
COMTÉ

SAUMUROIS

BERRY

POITOU

BURGUNDY

BOURBONNAIS

AUNIS

MARCHE

SAINTONGE

LYONNAIS

ATLANTIC
OCEAN

LIMOUSIN

AUVERGNE

Grenoble

DAUPHINÉ

Bordeaux

GUYENNE
AND
GASCONY

PROVENCE

Toulouse

Aix

Pau

LANGUEDOC

BÉARN

COMTAT
VENAISSIN

ROUSSILLON

Mediterranean
Sea

COMTÉ
DE FOIX

SPAIN

CORSICA

France in 1789

Pays d'états

Pays d'élections

Internal customs barriers

Province boundaries

ANJOU Province name

o Seat of a parlement

0   100   200 mi

1

THE ANCIEN RÉGIME, ITS
CRITICS AND SUPPORTERS

The French Revolution began because of a financial crisis. The debts and expenses of the French government far exceeded its ability to pay them. Yet France was a prosperous country, the largest in Europe, with a population of around 28 million. Its economy, based primarily on agriculture, was expanding during the eighteenth century, especially in the lucrative area of overseas trade. After 1770, several years of poor harvests caused distress, and the Revolution itself coincided with a severe downturn in the economy. But the government's inability to pay its debts cannot be explained by looking only at the immediate economic pressures. We must also explore the nature of eighteenth-century French government and society, what the revolutionaries who dismantled it called the Ancien Régime (the Former or Old Regime).

THE ANCIEN RÉGIME

When Louis XVI came to the throne in 1774, the power of the king of France appeared secure. For many generations, starting with the reign of Hugh Capet in 987, a male heir had been born to the king. This ensured the transmission of the title reign after reign. However, in 1328, the king died without a direct male heir, and the conflict between the two claimants (one French and one English) resulted in the Hundred Years' War. When the French contender won, royal lawyers explained that the English contender (whose claim came from his mother's side) was excluded because of the Salic Law, an ancient law of the Salian Francs that excluded women from inheriting noble titles. Therefore, they concluded that the French sovereign must always be male and descended through males. The Salic Law was one of the fundamental laws of the kingdom, in fact the only one nearly everybody could agree upon.

The territory ruled by the king of France had expanded outward from the Ile de France (the area around Paris), eventually encompassing the important provinces of Brittany and Burgundy. By the beginning of the sixteenth century, the unifying principle of the French monarchy was "*un roi, une loi, une foi.*" France was united under "one king, one law, and one faith," but the Reformation and the Wars of Religion challenged the unity of the Roman Catholic faith in France in the sixteenth century. French Calvinists (known as Huguenots) fought to wrest control of the country and the crown from the Roman Catholic party. In 1589, Henry of Navarre (or Henry of Bourbon), the head of the Huguenot party, inherited the throne. Knowing that he needed the support of the staunchly Catholic city of Paris if he was to reign, Henry reputedly stated, "Paris is worth a mass," and converted to Roman Catholicism. With Henry IV, the Bourbon line of kings began.

At first, the kings exerted little control over the great lords in France, but the chaos of the wars of religion of the sixteenth century caused some political thinkers to argue that it would be better for the country to have one strong leader who had the authority to make laws and enforce them. Taking advantage of this desire for order, the royal governments of the seventeenth century consolidated their power, developing what came to be called "absolutism." With Louis XIV (who ruled from 1643 to 1715), absolutism in France reached its peak. He built a magnificent palace at Versailles, surrounded by gardens, showing that the king no longer needed a castle to defend himself from rebellious nobles. A throng of courtiers attended the king and participated in daily rituals that emphasized his power and glory. Great lords (formerly powerful because of the troops they could gather) now had to be content with honors and high position in society. Louis XIV had developed a professional army so that he did not have to rely on the lords' troops. The power of the king was summed up in the phrase Louis XIV was supposed to have uttered: "*L'état c'est moi*" (I am the state). His position rested on tradition, armed might, and religion. He was called "the most Christian king," and the theory of the divine right of kings asserted that his authority to govern came directly from God, not from the people he ruled.

As the power of the king's government grew, so did its complexity. In theory, absolutism meant that the king was the source of all authority. But he was not a despot, even in theory. He was supposed to rule according to the precepts of the Christian religion. His power was limited as well by tradition and by practical realities, such as difficulties in travel and communication. At the end of the eighteenth century, a courier might take eight days to ride between Paris and the south of France, and the trip could be interrupted by weather or other hazards. Regular schedules for travel became possible only with the advent of railroads in the nineteenth century. Therefore, royal officials on the local level exercised a great deal of autonomy. Twentieth-century dictators might realistically aspire to total control of their country and its people, but absolutism in the eighteenth century did not mean the same thing as totalitarianism. A traditional agricultural economy could not be organized, controlled, and planned as the economies of twentieth-century totalitarian countries were. The central government did not even have a reliable census of the population.

The structure of society (called "corporate" by historians and political scientists) also limited the power of the king. In contrast to modern Western societies, which tend to treat all individuals as equal, individuals in French society belonged to a variety of groups known as corporations, each of which had certain privileges (privilege means literally "private law"). Some had more privileges than others, but most individuals belonged to some collective group. Trades (from cobblers to carpenters) were organized into guilds, each with its own rules and privileges. For example, masters could decide who entered a guild. Many parts of the government were corporate entities. Judges and tax collectors were granted a certain status and privileges (exemption from taxes, for instance). The church enjoyed a special corporate identity, as did the religious orders. Towns and cities were also considered corporations, each having won special dispensations from the king over the years. Cities generally did not pay the tithe and other taxes, and each one was organized and governed differently. Each province, as it came under the king's jurisdiction, had been guaranteed its privileges and special institutions (judicial courts, for example), which might differ from those of other provinces. Other examples of collective identities will make their appearances as this description continues, because the notion of collective identity was central to the Ancien Régime, and privileges were the principal means by which the government conferred rewards on those it valued or on those it needed to placate. Because corporations held on fiercely to their privileges (guaranteed by law and often the subject of lawsuits), even an absolutist government was limited in what it could demand of its subjects.

One historian of the Ancien Régime has likened the governmental structure of France to a large palace to which rooms and wings were added over the years without any overall plan. Some institutions dated back to the Middle Ages, others were more modern, but none were ever destroyed.

Obsolete institutions were not eliminated, in part because tradition was an essential element of the Ancien Régime. When each king came to the throne, he pledged to preserve the mutual obligations and privileges that existed at the time. Unlike modern governments, in which candidates campaign for office by promising to bring about change or introduce a "new deal" or a "new frontier," the French kings got the support of the important people in the kingdom by promising to preserve their power and privileges, not change things. As the area ruled by the king expanded to incorporate more territory, each province brought its own habits, laws, systems of weights and measures, and other institutions. Over time, the royal government had created a central government with more uniformity, but a great deal of local particularism still existed in the late eighteenth century. Attempts by the royal government to make changes in this traditional system could always be expected to encounter the opposition of important people.

The royal governments of the Ancien Régime did not aspire to do as much as modern governments do. At the court of Versailles, the king governed with the help of advisers, called ministers, who were brought together in the king's council to deliberate and come to decisions. The king appointed them, and each minister was in charge of a department. Under Louis XVI, there were six ministers: the chancellor (the head of the judicial system), the secretary of state for foreign affairs, the secretary of state for war, the secretary of state for marine (in charge of the navy and the colonies), the secretary of state for the king's household (which included many internal policy matters), and the controller-general of finances. The office titles make it obvious that the king's government focused primarily on foreign policy, war, and the means to pay for them.

The country was divided administratively in various ways. The provinces were old divisions, usually corresponding to previous feudal territories that had originally been ruled by a duke or other nobleman. Now incorporated into the kingdom, each province was headed by a governor, generally somebody from the old military nobility. During Louis XIII's reign, new officials (intendants) were created to oversee administrative districts called intendancies or generalities. The intendants had vast duties and were expected to rule their area not only in the name of the king, but according to the directives of the royal government. They really governed the country. But in a process typical of the Ancien Régime, when their offices were created, the governors were not abolished. Because of their power, the intendants were called "the thirty little kings" (in the 1780s, they actually numbered thirty-four).

For purposes of organizing the church, all of France was divided into parishes, and these parishes were grouped into dioceses, each headed by a bishop. The church was in many ways an extension of the government because the king appointed the bishops, and the church performed crucial services in the life of the kingdom. The concept of separation of church and state was not known. The church supported the monarchy, and the king's right to rule came from God.

The territory of France was also divided into the jurisdictions of the courts. The highest courts (called "sovereign courts," each with lower courts under them) oversaw finances and taxes and tried judicial cases. Emerging originally as specialized wings of the medieval court of the king, they had become separate institutions with their own structures and rules. The most important of the sovereign courts for the history of the French Revolution were the parlements. These should not be confused with the British parliament. The parlements were courts of law, not representative legislatures. The power of the magistrates in the parlements to serve as judges derived from the power of the king, who was the ultimate judge. The parlementaires dispensed justice in the name of the king.

In 1789 there were thirteen parlements, all in theory equal to each other, though the jurisdictions they covered were not of equal size. In fact, the Parlement of Paris was the most important because the king resided in its jurisdiction, many of the great lords were automatically members of it, and its jurisdiction covered a large and important area that included Paris and Versailles. Parlements were primarily judicial bodies, trying cases brought to them on appeal and overseeing the lower courts. But each one had administrative and political functions as well as judicial ones. The administrative duties included control over education, maintenance of good order, censorship, and regulating the market place. Because other authorities (such as intendants) might also have power in these areas, many conflicts over jurisdiction arose. This confusion can be understood if we remember that no separation of powers existed in the government of the Ancien Régime. All of the royal courts and officers held a bit of the sovereignty of the king, and, as an absolute monarch, he functioned as legislator, executive, and judge.

The parlements exercised a political function because all edicts and ordinances issued by the king had to be sent to the parlements for registration before the judges could enforce the law. If a parlement thought a law was ill-advised, the judges could ask the king to reconsider. This request was called a "remonstrance." If so challenged, the king usually made changes in the law. But if he did not want to do so, he could force the parlement to register the law in a ceremony called a *lit de justice*. The king appeared in person, sat under a special canopy (originally he sat on cushions, hence the name *lit* meaning "bed," as in a canopied bed), and forced registration of the law. The parlement had to give in because its authority to judge derived from the king. It had no independent power from which to challenge his decision.

In the eighteenth century, the Parlement of Paris, which received the royal edicts first, sometimes questioned the kings' decisions and thereby stimulated and led a public debate on the policies of the government. The politics of the royal court at Versailles had always been private. It was hard for outsiders to know why certain things were decided or why certain ministers were appointed or dismissed from office. The parlement, by challenging the decisions of the royal government, brought political questions out into the open and thus contributed to the coming of the Revolution. The government felt compelled to respond to justify its actions, and the resulting exchange of views brought what had once been strictly court matters into the view of a wider public. Other parlements also indulged in debates with the government. The parlements presented themselves as the guardians of French liberty, as the only institutions that could protect the French people from a tyrannical government, and they won widespread public support for that position.

The parlements took on this role in the eighteenth century in the absence of an institution like the British parliament, a representative body that had won the right to vote on legislation and approve taxation. An institution similar to it had once existed in France, called the Estates General, which had originated in the Middle Ages with the king's practice of calling people together to advise him. In England, the practice had grown and the institution had developed into the Parliament with a House of Lords (whose members sat by virtue of inheritance) and a House of Commons (whose members were elected). The French Estates General, made up of three parts or estates (the clergy, the nobility, and the commons or Third Estate) had last met in 1614, during the minority of Louis XIII. The nobility traditionally forced the calling of an Estates General when the monarchy was weak, as was the case when a child inherited the throne. The increasing power of the king in the seventeenth century meant that the consent of the country through representatives was not needed and was not sought. However, the lack of this institution proved ultimately to be a liability for the royal government. When it tried to solve the serious financial problems of the 1780s, no institution existed to give consent to taxation, and without that consent, the government was accused of despotism.

THE TAX SYSTEM

The divisions of the Estates General reflected the old view of the proper ordering of society. The clergy prayed, the nobles fought, and the rest of the population worked. At the end of the eighteenth century, the clergy numbered approximately 130,000 (or around 0.5 percent of the population). The number of members of the nobility has been estimated at between 1 percent and 1.5 percent. The other 98 percent or more of the population constituted the Third Estate. These designations were legal categories and brought with them both duties and privileges. Nobles had been able to acquire special privileges and exemptions from taxation. But nobles were not the only ones who had been able to gain privileges. The church and townspeople, for example, did not have to pay some taxes. Those at the lowest level of society, unable to obtain exemptions, bore the brunt of the tax burden. This unequal distribution of taxes was one of the reasons for the financial crisis. It was impossible to raise taxes any further on the poorest people, and the richer people refused to accept greater taxation unless they had more of a say in the running of the government. The financial crisis, then, threatened the very structure of absolutism with its hierarchical system of orders and privileges.

French people paid a bewildering array of taxes to the national government. In addition, they owed feudal obligations to their local lords and taxes and fees to support the church. The types of taxes and their amounts had been increasing during the eighteenth century, so that the tax system was both complicated and inefficient and the unequal distribution of taxes caused resentments among taxpayers. Tax evasion was rampant. In order to understand why the system proved so difficult to reform, we will need to look closely at its main features.

The royal government perennially fell short of funds and over the years had given up long-term revenue and control over the tax system in return for immediate and short-term gains. The royal taxes can be divided into two main groups, what we would call direct taxes and indirect taxes, though they did not use those terms. The most important direct tax was also the oldest: the *taille*. Dating from the Middle Ages, it was originally considered the equivalent of military service. Nobles were exempted because they contributed through service. The clergy had been able to gain exemption as well by offering to contribute a *don gratuit* (free gift) in place of the *taille* when they assembled at a national meeting every five years. Merchants in towns, government officials, students, and others were also exempted. The *taille*, then, was a sort of land tax paid by the rural masses, except that the amount to be paid was not determined exclusively on the value or product of the land. In some areas of the country the *taille* was personal, that is, based on the status of the individual. If you became ennobled, you did not have to pay. In other areas it was called "real," that is based on property. In those areas, noble land was not taxed, even if a commoner had purchased it, and non-noble land was taxed, even if a nobleman owned it.

The *taille* tended to be "real" in provinces more recently attached to France where the provincial estates still survived. These areas were called *pays d'état*. Similar to the Estates General (but limited to the province), provincial estates had been abolished in most provinces, and those still in existence had few powers. Their most important function was to negotiate with the government to determine the tax for the province and then to allocate the taxes throughout the territory. In other parts of the country, called *pays d'élection*, the *taille* was collected by royal officials called *élus* (which means "elected ones," so called because once upon a time the office had been elected, but it had long ceased to be so). These officials, appointed by the royal government, determined the amount of taxes that each district was to pay, and that amount was then divided among the various parishes. Ultimately, each parish was responsible for the *taille* and for seeing that all taxpayers contributed to the collective obligation. The unequal distribution of the tax obligation led to frequent discontent and disputes.

Because rich and influential people could get out of paying the *taille*, the government in the eighteenth century tried to increase revenues through new kinds of direct taxes and through raising indirect taxes. The *capitation* (or head tax), a new kind of direct tax introduced during the reign of Louis XIV, was originally pegged to professions as a sort of income tax, graduated according to one's ability to pay. This tax marked a departure from the traditional hierarchical structure of the monarchy because everyone was now being taxed, both privileged groups and commoners. In practice it was not quite universal: in exchange for making a one-time payment, the clergy managed to gain exemption altogether. The *capitation* also differed from the *taille* in that each individual was responsible for the tax, rather than each parish.

Louis XIV, desperate for money to support his wars, introduced another universal tax equivalent to one-tenth of each taxpayer's income (the *dixième*). In 1749, it was converted into the *vingtième* (or one-twentieth of income). Because of the expenses of war, another *vingtième* was added on top of that, and for several periods yet a third *vingtième* was levied. The last *vingtième* was due to expire in 1786, and the need to replace it was one of the causes of the financial crisis that brought on the Revolution. Based on old registers of landed worth that underestimated the income of nobles, the burden of the *vingtième* fell most heavily on the Third Estate. Although the tax burden of the nobility rose during the eighteenth century because of these new taxes, their tax burden was still considerably less oppressive than that of the commoners, who had to pay the *taille* as well.

During the course of the eighteenth century, direct taxes became less important as a proportion of all taxes collected. Just before the Revolution only 35 percent of government income came from direct taxes. Indirect taxes, on the other hand, amounted to 47 percent of income. Another source of funds for the government was the income from the royal domain. Direct taxes were collected by government officials, but indirect taxes were not. With only a rudimentary government structure, early royal governments had found it convenient to "farm out" the collection of taxes. A "tax farmer" negotiated a contract with the government, agreeing to pay a fixed amount for the right to collect all the indirect taxes in a particular area. The advantage to the government was that it received a steady income, even if times were bad, and received it in advance.

In the eighteenth century, because the economy and the population were expanding and the tax rates were increasing, the tax farmers profited. From 1726 on, a syndicate of investors called the Farmers-General negotiated leases (renewable every six years) to manage and collect the indirect taxes. The largest tax-collecting area, known as the "Five Great Farms," encompassed Paris and the center of the kingdom. Although government officials might have done this work, the governments depended so much on the loans they received from the Farmers-General that they were never able to do away with the system. This was especially true after mid-century, when the government owed the Farmers-General large amounts of both long-term and short-term debts. The Farmers-General, who were getting rich at the expense of the taxpayers, were universally resented. Taxpayers assumed incorrectly that the financial problems of the government were caused by the greediness of the tax farmers.

The indirect taxes were of various kinds and not at all uniform throughout the kingdom. Salt, an essential commodity for preserving food and for some industrial processes, was heavily taxed. The collection of this *gabelle* (salt tax) varied widely by region. In the largest area, called the *grandes gabelles* (equivalent to the Five Great Farms), the salt trade was a royal monopoly, and the price included a huge tax. Consumers were required to buy a minimum quantity of salt annually, and salt bought beyond that minimum was also heavily taxed. In some areas prices were lower and there was no forced purchasing. In other areas, salt was free from taxes. This situation led to widespread smuggling of salt from the free areas (especially Brittany) into the adjacent *grandes gabelles* region, where the price might be twenty-five times higher. To prevent smuggling, the Farmers-General employed large numbers of guards, and smugglers were severely punished on dreaded prison ships called galleys.

The guards of the Farmers-General also enforced the collection of customs duties. Not only were tariffs levied on goods brought into the country from foreign countries (the kind of tariff we are still familiar with), tariffs were also levied between different sections of the kingdom. A large custom-free zone coincided with the *grandes gabelles*. Goods brought into it from other regions were required to pay tariffs, and goods exchanged among the other regions also paid tariffs. The Farmers-General collected these tariffs as well as royal tolls on bridges and roads.

The most valuable of the indirect taxes were *aides* (equivalent to sales or excise taxes), and the most lucrative of these was the tax on wine. Other taxes (called *entrées*) were imposed on a wide variety of goods as they were brought into certain cities and towns. The taxes levied in Paris were especially burdensome. Because the growth of the city was making it easier for people to smuggle untaxed goods into the city, the Farmers-General decided to build a large wall that would ring Paris, with sixty-six tollgates where the entry taxes could be collected. Construction started in 1783 and was so resented that when the Revolution began in the summer of 1789, Parisians first attacked the tollgates before turning to the more famous attack on the Bastille.

The system of tax-farming meant that the government did not have access to all of the indirect taxes collected in its name by the Farmers-General. But even the direct taxes, collected by its own officials, were not really under the control of the royal government because the royal officials owned their offices in a system known as "venality of office." Strapped for money, the royal governments of the sixteenth century had begun the practice of selling royal offices in order to raise money. An individual bought an office, and then the government paid him a salary. Many offices (judgeships, for example) conferred the right to collect fees, which were a further source of income for the office holder.

At first, offices reverted to the crown when the owner died, so that the king could sell them again. In the early seventeenth century, the practice developed of permitting an office holder to pay a yearly fee (called the *paulette*) that gave him the right to pass on the office to his heirs. The fee provided a regular source of income for the government, but at the price of losing control over its own officials. As more and more offices became eligible for this arrangement, a permanent group of office holders was created who owned their offices by inheritance and could not be removed. They had paid for their position and it was their own private property. The king could not remove them unless he bought back the office, but there were roughly fifty thousand of them, and the government never had enough funds to do that. Venal office holders were therefore somewhat independent. This independence made it possible for the venal judges in the Parlement of Paris, for example, to challenge the decisions of the royal government with relative impunity.

Tax collection was affected by venality because each tax collector (called a financier or accountant), while technically a royal official, owned his office and hired his own staff. He was required to pay into the government, at designated times, the taxes that he collected. To avoid needlessly moving money around, the financiers paid pensions or other obligations of the government directly from the taxes they collected. But until the time came to pay out the funds, the financier could do with them whatever he wanted. He kept the funds in his own account, called a *caisse* (meaning box or fund). He usually invested the money and tried to make a profit. He could lend it to others. Often the government borrowed money from these financiers. In essence, then, the government was borrowing and paying interest on its own money for short-term needs. And the decentralized nature of tax-collecting meant that it was difficult for the government to know what its resources were or to make changes in the system. No central bank or fund existed in which all the money on hand could be gathered and managed.

The tax collection system does not seem logical or fair, but taxes seldom are. What is surprising is that reform was not necessarily a popular measure. Taxpayers held on tenaciously to their privileges because the complicated tax system seemed mysterious and beyond anyone's control. They suspected that attempts to change the tax system were merely intended to extract more money. After all, taxes had increased dramatically in recent years. Between 1705 and 1781, the tax rate rose 50 percent. Most of this increase occurred after 1760. People naturally resisted paying more taxes to a government that seemed unable to balance its budget, even with increasing taxation. Yet, as we have seen, the costs of running the tax system, the lack of control over it, and the antiquated nature of many of the taxes meant that despite the increasing wealth of the country, the royal government was not able to tap those resources.

Taxpayers did not sufficiently understand the nature of the debt, which derived first from the escalating costs of foreign policy and war. The debt had tripled between 1780 and 1786, so that 50 percent of the annual expenses went for the interest on the debt. The only way to reduce that expense would be to reduce the debt, but the government was having trouble paying interest on the debt and could not manage to decrease the principal. The next largest expenditure was for the armed forces, which the international climate of the late eighteenth century made dangerous to cut. Only about 7 percent of annual expenses were truly discretionary, going for such things as pensions, court expenses, and welfare. The lavish expenses of the court were resented, but even if all of them had been eliminated, the problem of the deficit would not have been solved.

THE NOBILITY AND THE BOURGEOISIE

The society of the Ancien Régime was hierarchical, in an order believed to have been created by God. The king was at the apex and below him were his subjects divided into three estates or orders. Orders are not the same as classes. They do not derive from economic status or a sense of self-identity. Orders are legal categories. You had to prove noble status to enjoy the privileges of the nobility. The church had to certify your status as clergy. Everybody else was of the Third Estate. The French Revolution would challenge this ordered conception of society and replace it with the ideal of a nation of equal citizens.

The nobility, or Second Estate, was the wealthiest and most powerful part of the population. Nobles (constituting about 1 to 1.5 percent of the population) enjoyed the highest status in society, but not all nobles were the same. Some were very rich, while others (especially nobles eking out an existence on a small amount of property) were quite poor. Whatever his wealth, a nobleman clung to certain symbols of his status, the right to wear a sword and have a coat of arms, for example. More valuable economically were the many exemptions from taxes, such as the *taille* and the *gabelle*. Nobles were supposed to live nobly off the proceeds of their landed property or investments. If a nobleman engaged in commerce or manual labor (occupations considered demeaning and sordid), he would lose his status as a nobleman. This loss of nobility was called *dérogeance*. Increasingly in the eighteenth century, this stigma against commerce was losing its force, and some nobles were taking part in wholesale and maritime commerce without loss of status (though retail trade was still considered below their dignity). However, in the popular imagination a noble was still seen as somebody who had inherited through the blood a sense of honor and family pride and who thought of himself as naturally superior to those who were not noble.

Nobles who could trace their ancestry back to the Middle Ages were considered greater than those of more recent vintage. Only about one-twentieth of the nobility had titles that dated back several hundred years. They were called the *noblesse d'épée* (nobility of the sword) because originally nobles had been vassals of the king who provided troops for him when danger threatened. Although the king's army was now a royal army (not dependent on feudal levies), nobles still served as the officers in that army. Nobility was either inherited or conferred by the king for special service to the crown. In order to raise money, the kings of France had begun to confer nobility on those who were willing to pay for it. Of the roughly fifty thousand venal offices in the royal bureaucracy, four thousand conferred hereditary nobility. Judges in the parlements and in other important courts were nobles, as were some officers in municipal governments. Magistrates who were nobles were known as the *noblesse de robe* (nobility of the robe, because of their judicial robes).

Most venal offices that conferred nobility did not do so immediately. A man who had gotten rich through commerce would invest in land, begin to live nobly, and buy an expensive venal office that conferred nobility. Although he was not yet considered a nobleman, after two or three generations his descendants would be noble. Somebody who had bought an office that conferred nobility, but who had not yet attained that status, was called an *anobli*. A family in this situation would take on the trappings of nobility and assume all the privileges of nobility that they could get away with. A few extremely expensive offices with no duties attached (*secrétaire du roi*, for example) conferred nobility immediately. Perhaps as many as 6,500 families acquired nobility during the eighteenth century. The nobility, then, was an open, not a closed elite, with about one-fourth of its members being very recently ennobled.

These statistics on recent entries to the nobility are compelling evidence against the essentially Marxist interpretation of the origins of the French Revolution that dominated histories during most of the twentieth century. This theory posited that the French Revolution was the result of a class struggle during the eighteenth century pitting the nobility against the bourgeoisie. During the Middle Ages, when the only source of wealth was land, the nobility had constituted a landed aristocracy. But with the growth of a capitalist economy, according to the Marxists, a new class had arisen that possessed economic wealth but that was excluded from positions of political power. The nobility jealously guarded its status and refused to share power with the bourgeoisie. In the French Revolution, this interpretation argues, the bourgeoisie fought the nobility for control of the government and for dominance in society and won.

The Marxist interpretation of the French Revolution has been convincingly refuted by recent scholarly research. As we just saw, rich merchants were buying their way into the nobility. Many new nobles were being created, though perhaps not as many as there were newly rich people who aspired to nobility. Still, the relations between these groups do not give the impression of a struggle between antagonists, but rather of an elite continuously recruiting new members.

Another argument against the Marxist interpretation is that neither of these supposedly antagonistic groups was really a homogeneous class. The members of the nobility, though sharing that legal status, were otherwise quite diverse. A special gulf separated the country nobles from those of the court. Country nobles who lived off their own lands had more modest fortunes. Some were even desperately poor. They held to their privileges not out of exclusiveness, but because those privileges were all they had to sustain them. The court nobility, on the other hand, were enormously rich. In addition to their family fortunes, they received pensions and positions from the king. They dominated the government offices, the army, and the upper hierarchy of the church.

Most country nobles could not afford the cost of maintaining residences and servants in Paris and Versailles (as well as a country estate), attending balls and receptions, and living the lavish life expected of a court noble. If the family fortune no longer allowed such expenditures, a noble family might arrange a marriage between a noble son and the daughter of a rich merchant whose dowry would help replenish their wealth. Nobility was handed down through the father, so such a marriage did not threaten their noble status. Rich noblemen and rich commoners living a sophisticated urban life in Paris obviously had more in common with each other than did a rich court noble and an impoverished country noble who had never been to the big city.

Also part of the sophisticated urban world of Paris were the nobles of the Parlement of Paris. Although their nobility dated back only to the seventeenth century, the Parlement of Paris magistrates were nonetheless definitely identified as nobles. The great sword and robe families were often allied by marriage. For example, one of the sons of the Noailles family (one of the oldest and most important of the court nobility) had married a daughter of the Chancellor d'Aguesseau, a prominent jurist under Louis XV. And the *noblesse de robe* was also likely to arrange marriages with the rich families in Paris.

The other side in this supposed class conflict also seemed to lack the characteristics of a self-conscious class. It is difficult to define the term "bourgeoisie." It was not a legal category, like the nobility. In the eighteenth century the term generally referred to a non-noble resident of a city who, as we have seen, enjoyed certain privileges under the Ancien Régime, including exemption from some taxes. Marx used the term to mean a class of capitalists, owners of the means of production, who were comfortably well off and definitely above the working class (the proletariat). In this Marxist definition of the term, the bourgeoisie was not large in the eighteenth century, because France's economy was still predominantly agricultural. On the eve of the Revolution, 78 percent of the population lived in the country and most of them lived and worked on farms.

Whereas rich commoners were getting richer during the eighteenth century, they still had not eclipsed the wealth of the nobility. Nobles still owned between a quarter and a third of the land. Because noble values set the standard for everybody, men who made their fortunes sought to live "nobly" even if they did not acquire noble status. They invested in land, purchased fine houses, and retired from active business. There was, in other words, no notion of class solidarity among the bourgeoisie. Although they might resent the arrogance of the nobility, they sought to join them, not eliminate them. Before the French Revolution hardly anybody had advocated doing away with the nobility. It was considered an enduring and essential part of the kingdom.

One of the pieces of evidence cited in the argument that the nobility was becoming more exclusive in the eighteenth century was the Ségur Ordinance of 1781, which restricted recruitment of army officers to those who could prove four generations of nobility. But this ordinance was not aimed at commoners. If the ordinance had been intended to prevent commoners from becoming army officers, it could have stipulated only that officers had to be noble. The ordinance was aimed instead at nobles of recent vintage and at *anoblis* (whose nobility was not to begin for a generation or two, but who nonetheless tried to take on all the attributes of nobility). Fearing that rich families who had bought nobility did not have the dedication and sense of duty of the old noble families, the army wished to exclude them to make sure their leaders would be competent and command the respect of their soldiers. Because the demand for purchasing noble offices exceeded the supply, only very rich people could purchase nobility, and the army believed that wealth alone did not qualify a man for command. Nobles, they believed, would have the sense of honor that went with their status. The Ségur Ordinance was also a way to provide employment for impoverished nobles (barred from other professions because of *dérogeance*) by restricting the number competing for officer positions. So the

Ségur Ordinance is an indication of a struggle within the nobility, as well as an example of the desire of the royal government to improve the army.

If the French Revolution was not the result of a class conflict between the nobility and the bourgeoisie, then what was the cause? If the king's position seemed secure and the nobility was not under attack, then why were they eliminated in the Revolution? In order to answer these questions, historians point to several intellectual movements in the eighteenth century that seemed to be undermining the support for traditional ways. Some of the challenges to tradition came from new intellectual ideas. Others came from new social organizations. And some of them came from conflicts within the institutions of the Ancien Régime itself. Although none of these conflicts was strong enough on its own to bring down the institutions of the Ancien Régime, they helped to weaken allegiance to tradition and made it less likely for disaffected groups to defend the old ways with vigor.

THE ENLIGHTENMENT AND PUBLIC OPINION

One of the oldest explanations for the coming of the French Revolution was put forward by unhappy conservatives who could see in it nothing but destruction and chaos. Although they might acknowledge some imperfections in the Ancien Régime, conservatives believed revolutionary changes were much worse than the old problems. It seemed to them as if revolutionaries had been deluded, and they saw the source of that delusion in the new ideas of the Enlightenment. As early as 1790 when the British writer Edmund Burke published his influential *Considerations on the Revolution in France*, conservatives charged that the Enlightenment had led people astray by weakening their faith in tradition and religion and by placing entirely too much confidence in the abilities of human beings to reason and improve the world. In this view, a conspiracy of skeptical and dangerous thinkers had orchestrated attacks on the church and the government and had so undermined morality that the excesses of the Revolution ensued.

The writers who thought of themselves as espousing the new Enlightenment ideas (often called *philosophes*) did not always agree on political issues, but they did agree on the basis of their mission. They believed that the scientific discoveries of the seventeenth century were transforming the way the world could be understood, and they wanted to apply the new scientific ideas to all aspects of life. Isaac Newton's discoveries in planetary motion had proved that the universe functioned in conformity to certain basic natural laws that were uniform and predictable. Nature was like a machine that ran according to the laws that God had written for it. They envisioned a God who was rational and distant, who revealed his purpose through the workings of nature. Frequently God was compared to a watchmaker. If you were to discover a perfectly functioning watch, you would naturally conclude that somebody had made it and set its mechanism in motion. Likewise the Creator had set the world in motion according to his own design and therefore had no need to intervene in it. This view of God is called Deism. Most Deists were not traditional Christians. They were suspicious of revelation, of miracles, and of such notions as the Trinity.

Deists believed that knowledge of God came through study of the nature that he had created. God, they were convinced, had given human beings rationality so that they could understand the world. Influenced by the ideas expressed by John Locke in his *Essay Concerning Human Understanding* (1690), they emphasized the similarity of human beings at birth. Locke wrote that human beings learn through sense experience. "Human nature" was everywhere the same, but human beings varied because of the environment in which they were raised. By studying people in other cultures and looking beneath the merely surface differences, Enlightenment writers hoped to determine what that human nature consisted of, what the rules were that governed people's actions, and how a better society could be created in conformity with those rules. Cosmopolitan (rather than nationalistic) in outlook, they intended to learn from other cultures and deplored passionate commitment to nation or religion. Reason was preferred over passion.

In political terms, their most potentially corrosive notion was to question the reasonableness of existing institutions, most of which had been created long before the new discoveries in science. Institutions handed down from the past that had developed by chance were not necessarily in conformity with scientific laws. Just because an institution had lasted for a long time did not mean it should continue. The ideal of the *philosophes* (seldom uniformly applied) was to subject everything to critical examination. They believed they could do better. They could improve society and life on earth. They especially criticized institutions that they thought were interfering with reason and science: the church, priests, censorship.

Voltaire, the most famous of the *philosophes*, was also the most active in fighting the power of the Catholic Church. Despite their name, *philosophes* were not philosophers in the modern sense of the term. They were popularizers of the new scientific way of looking at the world. After a trip to England in 1726 (he was forced to leave France after a brush with the law over insulting a nobleman), Voltaire wrote books praising the ideas of England's great thinkers, Isaac Newton and John Locke. He admired the openness of British society. Voltaire wrote voluminously in every genre (novels, plays, short stories, essays, histories, and always many letters), and his witty style ensured that his works sold well. He exposed the plight of Protestants in France, whose religion had been forbidden by the revocation of the Edict of Nantes in 1685 (see below for more on this subject) and whose marriages were therefore not considered valid. His campaigns to eradicate injustices against Protestants targeted the Catholic Church and brought into question the intimate connection between the monarchy and the church.

Voltaire espoused ideas that were radical for his time, but he was no democrat. Most people, he believed, lacked enlightenment: "The thinking part of mankind is confined to a very small number."[1] The reforms that he wanted were not likely to come from ordinary people, but rather from those who were enlightened and educated, and they were in the minority. He advocated, then, reform from above, what is often called "Enlightened despotism." Only rulers would have the intellect to understand the new ideas and the power to battle the entrenched interests holding back reform. When Frederick II of Prussia invited Voltaire to give him advice on ruling and writing, Voltaire eagerly accepted his invitation to the Prussian court. He hoped that leaders might be enlightened, but it would take a lot longer before ordinary people could shake off the weight of the past and the prejudices of religion and think rationally. Religion, *philosophes* tended to believe, was still needed as a means of restraining ordinary people who were incapable of reasoning for themselves.

Voltaire's interest in Enlightened despotism was not common among other *philosophes*, but it does indicate the degree to which educated people of the eighteenth century assumed the superiority of aristocrats over ordinary people. Voltaire even called himself "de Voltaire" to give the impression (falsely) that he was a nobleman. Although the church condemned his writings and the government forbade their publication, they were printed clandestinely and sold well. By 1778, when he finally returned to Paris after living in the country away from the reach of the police and the church, he was celebrated as the greatest writer of the century. The excitement apparently proved too much for someone of his advanced age (he was eighty-three), and he died in the midst of his triumph.

The most famous achievement of the *philosophes* was the publication of the *Encyclopédie*. Edited by Denis Diderot, it brought together contributions from a stellar array of *philosophes*. The first volume was published in 1751, and others appeared until 1772, eventually numbering around thirty large volumes. Intended to be a compendium of all knowledge, it made no

Figure 1.1.   Agriculture. In the eighteenth century, a vast majority of French people lived in rural areas and earned a living by farming. This illustration of peasants at work plowing (*labourage*) appeared in the *Encyclopédie*. The authors' interest in tools and techniques of production can be seen in the detailed drawings of the plows. Courtesy of Special Collections Library, Penn State University.

pretense to objectivity. By the choice of subjects and by the sly use of cross-references, the *Encyclopédie* hammered home its message. The *Encyclopédie* also revealed the practical bent of the *philosophes*, who were not interested in learning for its own sake, but rather for its utility for society. The *Encyclopédie's* eleven volumes of plates illustrated scientific features and demonstrated manufacturing and agricultural processes and tools. The interest in technology and the latest methods spread throughout the country as literary and scientific societies sprang up in urban areas. These societies sponsored essay contests, published journals, and disseminated discoveries in agriculture.

The rigid government censorship of the Ancien Régime raised difficulties with the publication of the *Encyclopédie*. However, these difficulties were overcome in part because it was sold by subscription, and the rich subscribers who had paid for the work in advance clamored to receive their volumes. Furthermore, the royal censor at mid-century, Malesherbes, proved sympathetic to the enterprise. He could not give the work an official permission to publish, but he could turn a blind eye to its appearance. This administrative ploy (called "tacit permission"—neither condemnation nor approval) was increasingly used by the government as it dealt with works of a questionable nature. Malesherbes believed that it was best to save the punishment of censorship for truly outrageous publications and ignore those the government could not endorse, but had no compelling reason for stopping. His successors reintroduced rigor in the control of the book trade, but without much success. Books were published abroad and smuggled into the country. The increasing demand for new books, the development of newspaper readership, and the growth in the publishing business made it impossible for the government to pretend any longer that it exercised control over what people read and thought.

It would be wrong to overstate the reach of the Enlightenment before the Revolution. Although the literacy rate was rising throughout the century, just before the Revolution 63 percent of the population could neither read nor write. And even among those who could read and could afford to buy books and newspapers, the best sellers were not the works of the *philosophes* but rather religious books. Ideas, of course, do not spread only by means of the written word. The provincial academies sponsored discussions, and the aristocratic salons of Paris aired new ideas. But there is no reason to believe that French people had become revolutionaries by reading the *philosophes*. In fact, the new ideas in circulation were not necessarily revolutionary (as Voltaire's example proves). And even if they had been, the new ideas became most influential only after the government had collapsed because of the financial crisis it was unable to solve. Once that happened and French people began to contemplate what kinds of changes were required in their institutions, they searched the writings of the *philosophes* for new ideas. In this sense it has been suggested that the Enlightenment did not cause the French Revolution but rather that the French revolutionaries, by embracing and popularizing Enlightenment ideas, caused them to seem more important in retrospect.

More recently some historians have stressed that the significant change before the Revolution was not so much intellectual as cultural. What helped to bring on the Revolution were not radical ideas, but rather that more and more people were now discussing public policy and taking a lively interest in political and governmental matters. Instead of government being the exclusive province of a few nobles at court, public issues were being debated by a wider circle of informed individuals. There had been created, in other words, something that can be called "public opinion."

Though not at all what we mean by the term nowadays, as the people who took an interest in these questions were still only a small minority of the population, this new development posed a threat to absolutism because people now questioned and debated the decisions of the king. They began to expect that their views would be considered. And the king's government realized they too had to influence this opinion. Challenges to absolutism can therefore be said to have arisen from within the structures of the Ancien Régime itself. When the parlements protested government measures and printed their remonstrances, and the government responded and published their responses, both sides were attempting to get public opinion on their side. The parlements justified their challenges by arguing that, in the absence of a Parliament on the British model, they were defending France from becoming despotic. They were all that stood in the way of the arbitrary actions of a government that otherwise had few checks on its power. Especially resented by critics of the royal government was the king's power to imprison people by *lettres de cachet*. On his own authority, without recourse to courts or trials, the king could have somebody put in prison indefinitely.

The fear of despotism (widespread in eighteenth-century France) could be seen in many areas. It showed up in legal cases in which the complainants accused each other of "despotism" and in which nobles were pictured as arrogant and arbitrary, taking advantage of the weakness of those of lesser ranks. Although the charge of being despotic was applied rather indiscriminately to all sorts of people in positions of authority, it was especially significant in the coming of the Revolution because the royal government appeared to be threatening traditional ways of doing things. Thus, attempts at reform (that we might see as positive) were interpreted quite differently in the eighteenth century. The way in which the government tried to impose reforms gave rise to fears that monarchy would degenerate into despotism.

The contrast between despotism and liberty is central to the ideas of Montesquieu, a magistrate of the Parlement of Bordeaux, who wrote one of the greatest works of the Enlightenment and one of the most influential studies of political systems. *De l'esprit des lois* (*The Spirit of Laws*) was published in 1748 and exerted enormous influence on French revolutionaries (as well as on the founders of the American republic). Montesquieu hoped to develop a science of government by comparing and classifying different types of regimes throughout history. Ultimately he wanted to figure out the natural laws that governed political organization and to determine what arrangement was most conducive to liberty.

Montesquieu classified governments into three types: republics (suitable for small city-states), monarchies (appropriate for the Europe of his day), and despotisms (needed for large empires). Each had its own characteristics. Republics, he believed, rested on the virtue of the citizens who ruled themselves, monarchies were based on honor, and despotisms depended on fear. He greatly admired the British system of government and believed that its structure created a separation of powers: executive (the king), legislative (the Parliament), and judicial (the courts). With each balancing the other, power could not be concentrated and thus freedom was guaranteed. Another feature of the British system that he admired was that Parliament was divided into two houses: the House of Lords and the House of Commons. The British government therefore was a mixed government, including aspects of monarchy (rule by one), aristocracy (rule by the few), and democracy (rule by the people). Fearful that monarchy could degenerate into despotism, Montesquieu believed that noblemen were essential in a monarchical system. The nobility would keep the king from trampling on freedom, something that ordinary people might not be strong enough to do. The principles of separation of powers enumerated by Montesquieu were widely influential. His defense of nobility, on the other hand, was soon ignored in the French Revolution.

A younger Enlightenment figure became even more influential during the radical phase of the Revolution. Jean-Jacques Rousseau, who had been born in Geneva, was an outsider in Parisian social circles. A typical *philosophe* in that he wanted to improve society, he parted ways with many *philosophes* by arguing that society had caused the corruption of mankind. He praised the simplicity of nature over the artificiality of civilization. Rousseau believed that human beings at birth were good, and society corrupted them. *Emile*, a novel he published in 1762, described raising a child in isolation in a natural environment. Children should learn by experience, Rousseau urged, and his fictional hero was not introduced to book learning until he was about thirteen years old. The child learned to love God through the beauties of nature. This charming picture of education (which has had an influence on modern progressive education) was not carried over into his view of the way to raise girls. Their education was confined to domestic skills.

Rousseau was much more egalitarian than other *philosophes*. His *Discourse on Inequality* (1753) decried the foundation of private property as the beginning of usurpations and wars. Although Rousseau yearned for a simpler time, he did not really believe that one could go back to a state of nature. Instead he searched for a way that men in society could be free and equal. He thought he had found the solution in what he called *The Social Contract* (1762). His views contrasted with those of the British political thinker John Locke, who in the late seventeenth century had written that society had been founded by a contract between the governed and the governor. Human beings, Locke argued, willingly gave up some of the freedoms they enjoyed in nature in order to secure the protections of government. According to Locke, governments were instituted to protect the rights of life, liberty, and property. The only way governments could take away any of those rights was through the consent of the governed given by their representatives. Thus, taxes (taking away your property) could not be levied unless the representatives approved. This notion was the basis of the American revolutionaries' cry of "No taxation without representation." In Locke's ideal society, the majority ruled and people agreed to abide by the will of the majority.

Rousseau's contract was quite different from Locke's. He wanted to figure out how a society could be created in which individuals would benefit from the safeguards of society, but remain as free and equal as they had been in the state of nature. Rousseau's answer was the "social contract." Unlike Locke's contract (a pact between the government and the governed), Rousseau's social contract posited an agreement between the individual and the collectivity. Each individual gave himself absolutely to the entire community; therefore all members of the community were equal and were equally participants in the social contract. Because all members of the collectivity were equal, nobody would have an interest in oppressing people because they would, in the process, be oppressing themselves. The people were sovereign, and what was best for the people in this society he called the "general will."

One of the difficulties inherent in understanding Rousseau's thinking is that it is not clear how the general will was to be determined. An individual (as an individual) might have interests that differed from those that the individual had as a member of the collective society. Therefore Rousseau thought that majority rule (adding up individual wills) might not necessarily yield the general will. Individuals might be mistaken, might be selfish, or might be led astray by an evil conspiracy to vote contrary to the general will (what was good for the society as a whole). Rousseau hoped that proper institutions could regenerate human beings because ultimately a society of free individuals had to be founded on virtue. Only by participating in the community and abandoning merely private and selfish motives could an individual truly be free. In a famous but puzzling formulation, Rousseau wrote that "whoever refuses to obey the general will shall be compelled to do so by the whole body. This means nothing less than that he will be forced to be free."[2]

Rousseau has been accused of offering a justification for totalitarianism in his theory of the general will. He seems to put much more emphasis on the good of the community than on the rights of the individual. Dictators could too easily declare that they were carrying out the general will, that they knew what was best for society. Rousseau assumed that good people placed in a good society where all were equal would have no reason to fear each other. They would cooperate and the freedom of all would result. But when his ideas were most influential during the French Revolution, the result was a Reign of Terror that, in attempting to institute a Republic of Virtue, created a society where liberty was absent and suspicion was rampant. Ultimately Rousseau's political system rested on the assumption that human beings were naturally good, a vision of human nature that differed profoundly from the traditional Christian view of flawed and fallen human beings in need of redemption.

THE CHURCH AND JANSENISM

The Enlightenment writers would have been surprised to find out that they were later blamed for causing the Revolution, because they saw themselves as a beleaguered minority struggling to make headway against powerful and entrenched interests. They tried to popularize political ideas that challenged the foundations of absolutism, but without any real means of putting their ideas into practice. Historians more recently have pointed out the way challenges to absolutism came from institutions that were intimately associated with it. The idea of the divine right of kings naturally provided a major role for the Catholic Church in France. The king and the church inevitably buttressed each other. However, because it was disciplined and hierarchically organized, the church enjoyed a degree of autonomy and could negotiate with the government. Furthermore, struggles within the church itself led to criticism of the monarchy that provided another source of debate about and a challenge to absolutism.

It would be hard to overemphasize the importance of the Catholic Church in eighteenth-century France. The great Gothic cathedrals that had been built in the Middle Ages still dominated the cities, and each town and village had its parish church. Painting and music were devoted mainly to religious subjects. The church was a rich institution, holding from 6 to 10 percent of the land, from which it derived a large income. In addition, the church received income from tithes, taxes that supported the church. Its wealth could be justified because of the important services it rendered the state. In addition to celebrating regular religious ceremonies, the church baptized, married, and buried people. All marriages and births were registered in the church; civil registers of births and deaths did not exist. Catholic religious orders provided charity and education.

Every five years, the General Assembly of the Clergy of France met. At that time they granted the king a *don gratuit* (free gift) in lieu of the taxes levied upon the rest of the population. The royal governments permitted this extraordinary national meeting and special arrangement for taxation because the wealth of the church made it possible for them to borrow money at better rates than could the royal government and because the church was a crucial support of the monarchy.

The French king had exercised enormous power over religion since the Concordat of Bologna of 1516, when Francis I had granted the pope income from the French bishoprics in return for the right to appoint bishops and abbots. Some have argued that France did not become a Protestant country in part because the king had already received control over religion within his kingdom and had no incentive to adopt Protestantism in order to create a national church. The church in France was called the Gallican Church (the term derived from the ancient name of Gaul).

When Henry IV adopted Catholicism in order to be king, the official religion continued to be Roman Catholicism. But in order to pacify the Protestants, Henry issued the Edict of Nantes in 1598, which allowed Protestants some freedom to worship and control over some fortified towns. During the course of the seventeenth century, Protestants lost their privileges, and in 1685, Louis XIV revoked the Edict of Nantes entirely, ordering Protestants to convert to Catholicism. In creating an absolutist monarchy, the king could not allow an entire group of people to escape his authority. The result was that many Huguenots fled the country. Those who stayed were eventually tolerated, but they suffered because their marriages were not recognized and they were excluded from public life.

Protestantism may have been defeated, but Louis XIV faced a division within the Catholic Church that took on political implications in the eighteenth century. Jansenism was a movement within the French Catholic Church that built on the ideas of St. Augustine. Jansenists emphasized predestination and preached strict morality and austerity. Although sharing some theological positions with Protestantism, Jansenists insisted that they were good Catholics, that they believed in the importance of the sacraments, and that they were within the historical traditions of the church. However, their enemies, especially the Jesuits, accused them of being Protestants. The Jesuit order (the Society of Jesus) had been created in the sixteenth century to fight Protestantism. Taking a special oath of obedience to the pope, Jesuits had close ties to the papacy and also powerful positions within France as teachers and confessors to important people in the government and aristocratic society. Jansenists accused the Jesuits of mollifying the consciences of their powerful patrons by promising that adherence to the ceremonies of the church could earn them salvation, while paying insufficient attention to morality and God's grace.

Jansenism appeared to be dying out, but then in 1713, at the request of Louis XIV and his Jesuit confessor, the pope issued a bull entitled *Unigenitus* that condemned a series of propositions of a Jansenist writer as heretical. When the bull was sent to the Parlement of Paris to be registered, the magistrates refused to do so, arguing that the pope was interfering in the affairs of the Gallican Church. To get the support of lay people against this perceived encroachment on the Gallican Church, the Jansenists began publishing a periodical called the *Ecclesiastical News*. With the involvement of the wider public, these religious issues took on political significance. The more the king's government sided with the Jesuits and the pope on the theological questions and demanded religious conformity, the more the Jansenists argued against the king's absolute power. Jansenists advocated church councils that would limit the power of the pope, and thus, by implication, criticized absolutism in whatever form.

Although Jansenism was not a widespread religious movement, these debates had important political implications because Jansenists had allies within the Parlement of Paris. When the bishop of Paris declared that Christian burials would be given only to those who had confessed and received communion from a priest who had endorsed the *Unigenitus* bull, the church hierarchy was accused of despotism. And if the king was on the side of the hierarchy, then he was guilty of despotism, too. The Parlement of

Paris declared the church's policy on burials against the law, thus coming into direct conflict with the royal government over religion. In these struggles the parlement and the Jansenists began to call for reform in the government so that it would be more responsive to the will of the people. They used arguments about the rights of citizens and invoked the notion of a contract between governor and governed. They endorsed national sovereignty and councils to fight what they saw as the despotism of the king and the pope. The parlement began to assert that its powers were as ancient as those of the king and not derived from him. The struggle between the Jesuits and the Jansenist sympathizers culminated in 1764, when the Jesuits appealed a case dealing with money to the Parlement of Paris. The parlementaires took the opportunity to declare the entire Jesuit order "despotic" and prohibited its operation in France. Louis XV reluctantly suppressed the Jesuits in order to quiet the controversies within the country. With many enemies, the Jesuit order was soon being suppressed in other countries as well, until the pope dissolved the order entirely in 1773.

Because church and state were so closely connected in an absolutist system, it was impossible to oppose the church hierarchy without also opposing the monarchy. The church hierarchy was criticized because the bishops (appointed by the king) were almost exclusively noblemen. Between 1743 and 1788, only one commoner was named a bishop. So no matter how hard-working and accomplished a young clergyman might be, he could not aspire to promotion unless his father was a nobleman. The dioceses differed in size and wealth, but the bishops could supplement their income by being named abbots of great monasteries. Holding more than one ecclesiastical appointment meant that a clergyman could not adequately carry out the duties expected of him. He merely collected the incomes. The gap between the wealth of the upper hierarchy and the poorly paid parish priests caused discontent in the eighteenth century. Like the Second and Third Estates, the First Estate was not really a unified order at the time of the Revolution. The lower clergy yearned for reform in the church to make advancement easier and to make the church more responsive to the needs of the faithful.

Religious devotion seemed to be waning in the late eighteenth century. Bequests made to religious organizations when a person died were declining and so were the number of candidates for the priesthood. Fewer religious books were being published while, at the same time, Freemasonry was spreading. Utilitarian notions made some people question the usefulness of monasteries to society. New notions of toleration brought an end to the exclusive status of Catholics within the country. In the late eighteenth century around 2 percent of the population was Protestant, and a much smaller number of Jews also lived within the kingdom. Hemmed in by limitations on where they could live and how they could earn a living, Jews were considered a separate corporate group (almost a "nation with the nation"), granted certain privileges by the authorities. Although these religious groups were rarely persecuted, their existence was precarious and always subject to local discrimination. Louis XVI, noted for his pious devotion to Catholicism, nonetheless conformed to the prevailing feelings of humanitarianism by approving an edict of toleration for non-Catholics in 1787 that improved the status of Protestants. But it is important to remember that before the Revolution nobody called for doing away with the Catholic Church. The prevailing opinion was more anti-clerical (critical of the church hierarchy) than anti-Catholic. However, many people (including members of the clergy) recognized that the French church was in need of reform.

CONCLUSION

In the eighteenth century, new ideas challenged absolutism and new social practices accustomed increasing numbers of people to take an interest in political questions. Although discontent prompted criticism, the parlements and the church obviously did not intend to overthrow monarchical government. Indeed, the king's power seemed strong and secure. Nonetheless, the arguments in public debate with the king weakened the basis of his power. Because France lacked a national representative body and elections to choose representatives, opponents of the government's policies could not challenge them in a serious and organized fashion. People could talk about policy, but there was precious little they could do about decisions until the government invited them into the process. That invitation came, not because there was a revolution against the government or out of benevolence on the part of the government, but rather because the acute financial problems that the government faced could not be solved by the traditional means. The institutions and expediencies by which the royal governments had managed to pay their bills no longer sufficed. Indeed, the reforms now proposed to bring in more money threatened the essentially corporatist nature of society. Once the government began to ask others for help in paying the bills, it discovered that the country would not agree to further taxes unless the government promised to consult them in the future. The struggle over who should be consulted and how the government should function in the future brought on the French Revolution.

2

THE FINANCIAL CRISIS

The growing expense of war in the eighteenth century made it difficult for the French government to pay its bills, and the attempt to solve the ensuing financial problems exacerbated tensions within the country. The authority of the crown was weakened when the king's ministers seemed unable to govern effectively. Lack of success in foreign affairs also undermined royal authority. The king's reputation depended on maintaining a strong position among the powers of Europe, and France's foreign policy failures caused discontent among noble army officers and other prominent people whose loyalty the crown needed to retain.

FOREIGN POLICY AND WAR

At his death in 1715, Louis XIV had left France in debt from the many wars he had fought. After a period of peace during which the country was able to recover economically, France went to war again in 1740. The War of the Austrian Succession began when Frederick the Great of Prussia invaded Austrian Silesia. France joined with Prussia in fighting their traditional enemy, the Austrian Habsburgs. But this war put a special strain on French resources, because, in addition to the cost of armies on the continent, France was also fighting Great Britain in far-flung colonial areas. This world war therefore also required an expensive navy. Great Britain, protected by the sea that surrounded its island, could concentrate most of its resources on its navy, without the expense of a large army, but France could not. It had to maintain strong forces at sea and on land. The war ended in 1748 without France having gained anything and without much hope that the conflict was really over. A new direct tax, the *vingtième*, was now a permanent part of the tax system, justified on the grounds of military necessity and the need to pay for the debts contracted during wars that, according to the government, "justice and honor made indispensable."[1]

When war resumed, Austria was still trying to get Silesia back from Prussia and France was still competing with Great Britain for colonial possessions. But the alliances had changed. In the Seven Years' War (1756–1763), Great Britain and Prussia were allied against France and Austria. This change in French foreign policy (often called "the diplomatic revolution") proved to be unpopular in France, where people since the sixteenth century had been accustomed to thinking of the Habsburgs as the enemy. Marie Antoinette, whose marriage to the young man who would rule as Louis XVI was a part of the diplomatic settlement, suffered from association with the hated alliance and from suspicion that she was in France as the spy of the Austrian government. The diplomatic change actually made sense. Austrian power was on the decline. A Bourbon rather than a Habsburg king now sat on the throne of Spain. The real threat to France's position as a great power came from Great Britain rather than Austria. France hoped by this change to free itself from having to fight the Habsburgs in Europe in order to turn its attention to colonial matters. It hoped as well to be rewarded by the Habsburgs with the Austrian Netherlands, located on the northeastern border of France.

The chances of success seemed promising. In addition to Austria, Spain (in what was called the "family compact" of the Bourbons) and Russia were allied with France. On the continent the allies had a combined population of around 70 million, while Prussia had a population of only 3.6 million. But the war turned out to be a disaster for France. The French lost an ignominious battle against Frederick II of Prussia at Rossbach in 1757 (despite numerical superiority) and were beaten by the British in Canada, the Caribbean, and India. By the Treaty of Paris (1763) France gave up all its possessions in North America. Many French people blamed their country's fall from power on the Austrian alliance. France fought Austria's battles, according to this complaint, but got nothing in return.

What the complainers failed to appreciate was the changing nature of the state system in Europe and the more hostile environment in which France had to operate. Since the time when Louis XIV dominated the continent, Great Britain had become richer and stronger. In addition, two new powers had joined the system of great states: Prussia and Russia. France was still a populous and prosperous country, but it now faced formidable competition. Even if a state remains rich and has a large army, its relative position vis-à-vis other powers will decline if those powers are getting richer and stronger faster. And that was what was happening to France in the eighteenth century. Furthermore, France's traditional allies in Europe (Sweden, Poland, and the Ottoman Empire) were also declining in power. If the king of France hoped to maintain his position in Europe, he had to make sure his interests were respected and that he had an army and a navy large enough to enforce his goals. It would be wrong, however, to blame the foreign policy dilemmas on warmongering or excessive ambition on the part of the French kings. Louis XV, in fact, did not particularly like war, having taken to heart his great-grandfather's dying injunction to "avoid making war as much as you can; it is the ruin of peoples. Do not follow the bad example I have given you in this. I have often undertaken war too lightly and pursued it out of vanity. Do not imitate me, but be a peaceful prince . . ."[2] Louis XVI was even less of a warrior and less vain about his own glory. But he operated within an international system that forced him to stand up for the interests and honor of his country or suffer dire consequences. In an attempt to reduce the risks of war and to promote better conditions for French commerce, Louis XVI's foreign minister Vergennes negotiated at least sixteen treaties or agreements with other countries.

Rulers at the time were expected to promote the interests of their own country and keep other countries from becoming stronger. They aspired to a "balance of power" in which no country became so strong that it dominated the whole continent. This term unfortunately gives the impression of a static condition in which all the powers are peaceful and contented. But in practice, balance-of-power ideas tended to promote rather than to prevent wars. Because each state was independent and in competition with all the others, when one country conquered more territory, for example, the others demanded compensation in order to maintain the balance of power. Even minor incidents could therefore escalate into war if a king felt his honor had been impugned or that another king threatened his power. Constant competition meant that no state could feel secure or satisfied for long, and no agreement on what was just and fair (i.e., what would be a real balance) was possible.

Under these circumstances, the king of France could not consider the Treaty of Paris of 1763 a final arrangement, but must try to restore his honor by gaining back what he had lost. He obviously could not do so immediately because the cost of the war had seriously undermined finances. The Seven Years' War not only lasted longer than had been anticipated, it also cost more than twice as much per year as the previous war. Before the war, 30 percent of revenues had been expended to pay interest on the debt.

Immediately after the war, the cost of meeting debt obligations amounted to 60 percent of revenues. A second and a third *vingtième* had been imposed and indirect taxes had been increased, but most of the costs had been met by loans. The debt had also increased because those in charge of finances were not very competent and relied on expensive life annuities (*rentes*) to borrow money. In 1770, the Controller-General Terray had been forced to put through what was called a "partial bankruptcy," that is, he lowered interest on some debts and suspended payments on others. But that was the last time this expedient would be tried. From then on, governments assumed that even a partial bankruptcy would undermine the regime and make future credit more expensive. Louis XVI, in particular, held steadfastly to the notion that he would not write off any of this debt. And so the debt continued to grow and eventually did undermine the regime.

REFORM AND THE MAUPEOU REVOLUTION

The French were accustomed to paying extra taxes during wartime, but they expected those taxes to end with the coming of peace. The debt forced the government to maintain some of the war taxes and to begin a survey of the value of land (called a *cadastre*) with the objective of assessing taxes more accurately. Protests from the parlements forced them to abandon the *cadastre* project, but the debate over these issues became heated, as calls for reform were heard from many quarters. Stung by the humiliating defeat in war, the French now began to realize the seriousness of the government's financial problems. The parlements resisted new impositions without more detailed information about the government's finances. But the government refused to reveal any specifics of its operations. In the absence of accurate information, most commentators assumed incorrectly that the main problem was that money collected was not reaching the government because of a corrupt and expensive system of tax collection.

The noblemen of the parlements, who doubtless hoped to protect their own privileges, justified their right to review government proposals by arguing that they were standing up for the people. By using terms such as the "nation" or the "people," they suggested that the interests of the king and his subjects were different. They asserted that the role of the parlements in the history of the French constitution was as ancient as that of the king and presented themselves as the protectors of the "liberties of the French" against the encroachments of ministerial oppression. The parlementaires lacked confidence in the king's ministers, who were appointed and fell from office subject to the whims of factional disputes at court, rather than ability and performance. They did not believe Louis XV would stand firm on an unpopular policy.

Quarrels begun in Brittany led to a major crisis. When a bitter dispute erupted over taxes, the government ended up exiling the Parlement of Rennes, the chief city of Brittany in 1765, and setting up a new court. When the Parlement of Paris came to the defense of its fellow magistrates, Louis XV responded on March 2, 1766, with a famous statement asserting his view of absolutism:

> It is in my person alone that sovereign power resides . . . it is from me alone that my . . . courts hold their existence and their authority . . . public order in its entirety emanates from me, and my people forms one with me, and the rights and interests of the nation, of which people are daring to make a body separate from the monarch, are necessarily united with mine and repose only in my hands.[3]

Despite the extreme words, the government actually backed down and reinstated the Rennes Parlement in 1768. But this did not bring peace, because the parlementaires now brought charges against the provincial governor, the Duc d'Aiguillon, who had suppressed the parlement. Accused of illegal actions, the duke wanted to clear his name and asked that he be tried by the Parlement of Paris acting as a court of peers. Instead of quickly exonerating him as d'Aiguillon had rather unrealistically hoped, the Parlement seemed about to find him guilty. Fearing that such an outcome would be an indictment of the government's policies as well as a spur to future parlement obstruction of the government, Louis XV was persuaded to put an end to the proceeding with a *lit de justice* proclaiming d'Aiguillon's innocence. Now parlements throughout the country protested this royal interruption of ordinary court proceedings.

The ministry responded in November by arresting some parlementaires and by declaring that the parlements were forbidden to correspond with each other. The parlements were told that they must accept without further remonstrances the decisions taken in *lits de justice*. The Parlement of Paris responded by accusing the ministers of trying to change the basic constitution of the country. In January 1771, Chancellor Maupeou (the minister in charge of the judiciary) arrested the members of the Parlement of Paris and sent them all into exile. He then set up new courts staffed with appointed salaried judges rather than venal judges. When the other parlements around the country protested, they too were abolished. Lawyers at first refused to argue cases in the new courts, but by the end of 1771, they went back to work. Without the obstruction of the parlements, the government was able to put through new taxes, and the financial circumstances improved considerably by 1774.

The "Maupeou revolution" unleashed a flood of pamphlets and transformed the public debate about the royal government. No longer was the government merely bullying the parlements in order to get them to accept their proposals. By doing away with the parlements entirely, the government seemed to have moved to outright despotism. The parlements had claimed that the ancient constitution of France gave them the role of protecting the country against arbitrary actions. The "Maupeou revolution" showed that this claim was hollow, that no institution could check the government's power.

Despite the protests, as long as Maupeou had the support of Louis XV, the reorganization would be maintained. The notoriously undependable Louis XV did not, in this case, back down, but he was stricken with smallpox in 1774 and died. His successor, his grandson Louis XVI, decided to undo the "Maupeou revolution" and bring back the parlements. He did so, he said, because he wanted to be popular. Some historians have argued that this was a fateful decision, that it once again allowed an elite to block fundamental reforms that threatened their own self-interest. Had they not been brought back, according to this view, changes could have been made and the Revolution could have been prevented. But the restored parlementaires were more docile than before, and Louis XVI's ministers prudently worked with them in a less confrontational manner. For more than a decade, the parlements did not stand in the way of reform because the government did not propose sweeping reforms. Substantial changes might undermine the social system of the Ancien Régime and threaten what were considered the ancient liberties of the nation. It was only in the late 1780s when France once again had to deal with a serious fiscal crisis that the parlements blocked the measures brought forward by the government.

The real significance of the "Maupeou revolution" was that it revealed that the parlements, despite their rhetoric about their role as protectors of the liberty of the nation, offered no guarantee against the potentially despotic power of the government. In the absence of a genuinely representative legislature, the nobles in the parlements had tried unsuccessfully to assume that role. If the parlements could not be depended upon to protect the interests of the people, then some Frenchmen began to believe that the Estates General should be called. The government, too, recognized that changes required the support of the country, and they began to experiment with other ways of consulting the country and getting its approval. Without an established institution that could speak for the country (some kind of representative body), the government found itself increasingly accused of despotism and unable to justify new taxation.

The "Maupeou revolution" hurt the king's cause in another way. When the popular parlements were reinstated, those men who had risked opprobrium to stand by the king, to enforce the unpopular measure, and to take places on the new courts now felt betrayed. These men might have formed the nucleus of a "king's party," but now they would hesitate to support the king in the future.

LOUIS XVI AND MARIE ANTOINETTE

When the nineteen-year-old Louis XVI came to the throne in 1774, his reign was greeted with enormous optimism. In contrast to his old grandfather, whose private moral failings had considerably undermined respect for him, the new king was young, well-meaning, and conscientious. Louis XVI had not had a happy childhood. His older brother, his father, and his mother all died before he was thirteen. He had two surviving younger brothers (the comte de Provence and the comte d'Artois) and two younger sisters. Having received a good education from his tutors, Louis was shy, pious, and moral. He loved to read history, especially the history of Britain, and was taken with the story of the unfortunate English king Charles I (beheaded in 1649), whose mistakes he vowed to avoid. Louis was good at mathematics and geography, and he avidly pursued the royal sport of hunting. He also enjoyed practical pursuits like carpentry and locksmithing, which would not prove particularly useful to him as the heir to the throne.

In 1770, at the age of sixteeen, Louis was married to the Austrian princess Marie Antoinette, then only fourteen. Though not well educated, Marie Antoinette loved and promoted music and the theater. The primary duty of royal princesses was to bear an heir to the throne, and Marie Antoinette was unpopular for not doing so. The fault was not hers, but her husband's. Louis XVI apparently suffered from a physical condition that made sexual relations uncomfortable. The abandoned princess consoled herself with frivolous pursuits at court: gambling, fancy dress balls, and novels. The childless couple caused consternation not only in France but also among Marie Antoinette's family in Austria. Her brother Joseph arrived for a visit and his advice (some believed he persuaded Louis to undergo an operation) finally solved the difficulties. Marie Antoinette gave birth to a daughter in 1778. Three years later the continuity of the dynasty was assured by the birth of a male heir, followed in 1785 by the birth of another son.

VIme Cahier de   *Costume François*

Figure 2.1.   Marie Antoinette in court dress. The queen was criticized for extravagance, but she could not ignore the etiquette of the court, which required elaborate costumes. The queen's exaggerated hairstyle and sumptuous jewels contrasted sharply with the modest attire of ordinary people and with the simple dress adopted by revolutionaries at the height of the Revolution. Courtesy of the Division of Rare and Manuscript Collections, Cornell University Library.

Louis began his reign with hopes that he could reverse the demoralized condition of the country. He elevated the moral tone of the court by remaining faithful to his wife, in contrast to his grandfather's notorious sexual habits and many mistresses. Ironically, without mistresses to talk about, court gossip now became more damaging to the royal family, as it focused on Marie Antoinette. At court, factions had gathered around Louis XV's mistresses, who used their closeness to the king to promote their candidates for office and to enrich their families by pensions and positions. The factions of the "reigning" mistress and the queen tended to alternate in power. But in Louis XVI's court, without a faction around a mistress, such alternation was not possible. Marie Antoinette alone was criticized for her supposed power over the king and for her extravagance and haughtiness. She became the subject of scurrilous and pornographic pamphlets. Abetted by the king's brothers, who had lost their places as next in line to the throne, rumors circulated that Louis was not the father of her children. Marie Antoinette hurt her own popularity and the cause of the monarchy by surrounding herself with a few favorites and excluding many of the old court families that had traditionally served the king. No longer having access to power and positions and with no hope of getting back into favor at a future time, some of these old noble families became supporters of reform and were prominent in the early years of the Revolution.

French people especially resented Marie Antoinette because they assumed she used her influence over the king to promote the cause of Austria. It is true that when they were first married the teenage princess had tried to follow her mother's instructions to further the alliance with Austria. But at that time Louis XVI carefully prevented her from having any say in public policy decisions. It was only in the late 1780s, as his problems became overwhelming, that Louis turned to her for help and support. As he sank into despair and his ordinary indecisiveness became a crippling inability to take action (his irresoluteness probably amounted to clinical depression), she was forced to make more decisions, even though she was even less prepared than Louis to govern. Once she and Louis had children, she no longer listened to her foreign relatives but instead strove to protect the power of her husband and the heir to the throne. In the early days of the Revolution, she counseled the king against compromising and set herself resolutely against change.

Marie Antoinette became the subject of scurrilous political pamphlets that corroded her popularity. They pictured her as insatiably dissolute, with both male and female lovers, as an agent of Austria within France, and as a spendthrift who caused the financial problems of the government (she was labeled "Madame Déficit"). A particularly glaring incident, which showed the loss of the traditional respect in which the queen was held and which further hurt her reputation, occurred in 1785. The Affair of the Diamond Necklace involved the Cardinal de Rohan, a member of a powerful French family. His immorality (despite his clerical status) and his poor reputation while ambassador to Vienna led Marie Antoinette to shun him entirely. Wishing to win her favor, he became embroiled in a plot hatched by a woman named Madame de Lamotte along with her husband and her lover. They convinced Rohan that Lamotte was a close friend of Marie Antoinette's and that she could arrange a meeting with the queen. Lamotte and her accomplices found a prostitute who looked like the queen, and hired her to impersonate Marie Antoinette and meet with Rohan in a thicket in the dark, giving him instructions to purchase a fabulous diamond necklace for her. Rohan went to the jeweler, gave him a deposit, and showed him an order supposedly signed by the queen. Rohan then delivered the necklace to Lamotte, who was to give it to Marie Antoinette. Needless to say, she never saw it. When the jeweler wrote to Versailles seeking the next installment on the payments, the whole story came out.

Louis XVI was furious and ignored his advisers' recommendation that the matter be hushed up. The king believed that Rohan knew the signature on the order was a forgery and, rather than being a dupe of the conspirators, was himself in on the plot as a way to make money. Louis wanted Rohan to be punished for the gross injustice done to his wife. But when Rohan came to trial in the Parlement of Paris (the court of his peers) charged with disrespect for the royal family, he received support from those in his political faction, as well as from those under the influence of his prominent family. The trial briefs presented by the lawyers for the various defendants were published in the thousands and were eagerly snatched up by the public. Madame de Lamotte was found guilty and punished by flogging, branding, and incarceration. Her punishment contrasted sharply with the fate of the powerful cardinal. His exoneration seemed to suggest that the parlement believed it was understandable for Rohan to expect the queen of France to act in such a disreputable way. The traditional respect due the queen had been undermined by the pamphlets written about her. Behind much of this criticism of the queen (which would become even more vicious during the Revolution) lay a fear of women controlling power behind the scenes and corrupting the virtue of the government.

LOUIS XVI'S GOVERNMENT

Louis XVI chose his first ministers for their integrity and ability. He brought back as an adviser an old man who had been exiled from court in 1749. Maurepas helped persuade Louis XVI to restore the parlements. "It may be considered politically unwise," the king commented, "but it seems to me to be the general wish and I want to be loved."[4] The king's appointments reflected his desire to create a good government. Vergennes was put in charge of foreign policy and Turgot in charge of finances. Turgot's appointment attracted a great deal of notice because he was a member of a group of economic reformers known as physiocrats, who included the Marquis de Mirabeau (father of the famous Mirabeau of the Revolution) and Samuel Dupont de Nemours (whose son later emigrated to the United States). The physiocrats, whose ideas influenced the thought of Adam Smith, were inspired by the Enlightenment and believed that all wealth came from the soil. They advocated a single tax on the products of the soil that would replace the bewildering array of taxes.

Although Turgot did not propose such a reform when he came into office, he believed as other physiocrats did that political science could be studied with the same precision as the physical sciences and its conclusions could be as definite. Convinced that the laws of economic science dictated that free trade would bring prosperity, Turgot wanted to dismantle the restrictions on commerce that were commonly followed by all the governments of the time. The economic ideas of the eighteenth century that Adam Smith later labeled "mercantilist" emphasized that prosperity should be promoted by tariffs to encourage people to buy locally rather than importing goods, by controls on production that would assure quality, and by monopolies that would ensure the availability of essential goods. In order to prevent bread riots in towns (bread being the principal food of most people), the French government controlled the price of bread and supervised the trade in grain. In September 1774, soon after coming to office, Turgot liberalized the grain trade hoping that this would lead to more abundance. This experiment unfortunately coincided with a bad harvest. Riots and violence against the new measures and the government's suppression of the disturbances were so serious that they were called the "flour war."

Turgot further attacked the corporatist structure of the Ancien Régime's economy by dismantling the traditional guilds of Paris. When the parlement protested that the guilds helped to maintain order in the city, the decree eliminating them had to be forced through with a *lit de justice*. Another measure, replacing the *corvée* (work on the roads undertaken by peasants) by a tax to be paid by all landowners, seemed dangerously to undermine the privileges of the nobility. By attacking those who benefited from "monopoly," Turgot made more enemies, including the Farmers-General. Turgot (and therefore his policies) did not last long when Louis XVI began to fear that his finance minister was attempting to make himself a prime minister. Turgot's dismissal was also hastened by developments in foreign policy. In 1776, as the relationship between Great Britain's American colonies and the mother country deteriorated, Vergennes, operating under the traditional balance of power assumptions, hoped to take advantage of the situation to weaken France's enemy. Turgot counseled against preparations for war on financial grounds. In May 1776, the king dismissed Turgot and rescinded his reforms.

NECKER AND THE AMERICAN REVOLUTION

Louis XVI hoped to elevate the moral tone of foreign policy as well as domestic policy, but the prospect of recovering the position lost in the Seven Years' War proved too tempting. To split the British Empire by helping its American colonies become independent would enhance France's position in Europe. However, Vergennes and the king knew that they could not engage the British in war until their armed forces had been built up, especially the navy. While that rebuilding was taking place, the French government aided the rebels covertly by sending them arms and money. The American cause was popular in France and illustrates the strange friendships that foreign policy can create. Louis XVI's government certainly did not endorse the principles of the American Revolution with its calls for "no taxation without representation" and its crusade against monarchy. The French goals were entirely in conformity with the customs of eighteenth-century diplomacy, which was not ruled by ideological or religious concerns.

The war was popular mainly because the French people wished for revenge against the British. They followed with interest the careers of the French soldiers who fought in America, especially the dramatic exploits of Lafayette. Lafayette came from an old noble family in Auvergne. Left an orphan at the age of twelve, he was immensely rich as he had inherited great fortunes from both sides of his family. His relatives promoted his career by arranging a marriage to Adrienne de Noailles, a member of a prominent court family, and he took his place among the circle of young people at court. He was made a captain in the Noailles dragoons, but government attempts to reform the army and save money placed him in the reserves in 1776. Fired by enthusiasm for the American revolutionaries fighting the British (his father had died in battle against the British) and wishing to distinguish himself militarily, Lafayette wanted to join the Americans. The government, not yet wishing to support the Americans openly, forbade him to go, but his wealth allowed him to purchase a ship and set sail for America in 1777 anyway. The Americans were delighted to have somebody so well connected in their army and made him a major general. He was nineteen years old. Lafayette's subsequent association with George Washington had a lasting impact on his political views and goals. He hoped that France could follow the American example and create a government based on freedom and rights. Although most French soldiers who fought in the New World did not share Lafayette's commitment to the new political ideas of the Americans, the American Revolution played a major part in bringing on the French Revolution because the enormous costs of waging war left the French government in even worse financial shape than before.

The French concluded a formal alliance with the Americans in 1778 and contributed money and men. In addition, they persuaded their Spanish allies to join the effort and got the Dutch on their side as well. The French contribution to the victory was especially significant in the battle of Yorktown (1781) when the French navy kept the British navy from rescuing Cornwallis's army, bottled up on a Virginia peninsula, long enough for the combined American and French armies to defeat it. Although Yorktown marked the end of major combat in America, the treaty ending the war was not signed until 1783 (another Peace of Paris).

The French had achieved their major goals of splitting the British Empire and avenging the loss in the Seven Years' War, but the peace was otherwise not very encouraging. Although it conformed to the king's stated goals of "morality" in foreign affairs by providing no territorial gains for the French in either America or Asia, the other benefits that might have come along with the peace were not forthcoming. The anticipation that increased trade with the United States would help the French economy proved to be a vain hope. The friendship between France and the United Provinces of the Netherlands (Holland) led to an alliance in 1785, thus removing the Dutch from their accustomed alliance with Great Britain. But the war so undermined France's finances that when an incident occurred in the United Provinces in 1787 the French were unable to intervene to protect their ally, thus once again demonstrating the pitiful position France had been forced into in foreign affairs because of lack of money. The financial difficulties resulting from the American Revolution left the king unable to act forcefully in foreign policy to protect the honor of the throne and keep promises that he had made. This foreign policy failure in the Netherlands weakened his position both at home and abroad. In the area considered the special province of the king, Louis XVI was found wanting.

Jacques Necker, the man selected to supervise royal finances during the American war, was and still is a controversial figure. He was a native of Switzerland and a Protestant, and thus not eligible to be controller general. He was instead called director general of finances, but he had all the powers of previous controllers general. Necker had made his fortune as a banker. He had married Suzanne Curchod, a daughter of a Swiss pastor, whose charm and intelligence quickly established her salon as an important fixture of the Paris social and literary scene, and certainly helped her husband in his political ambitions. The devoted couple had only one child, known to us by her married name, Madame de Staël. She wrote important political and literary works, and her fame would eclipse her father's.

The king, who prided himself on his mathematical abilities, was probably responsible for the appointment of Necker. The finance director and the king seemed to agree that both bankruptcy and new taxes were out of the question. Necker's ties to the world of international finance made it possible for him to finance the American war through borrowing without raising new taxes. In hindsight, this decision seems strange, because war was the one emergency in which extraordinary taxes might be considered justified. It would be much harder to raise taxes once France was at peace. Necker tried to improve the financial system by focusing on reforms in the administration of finance. To get more control of the tax system, he renegotiated the contract with the Farmers-General when it fell due. The collection of the *aides* was assigned to salaried government officers rather than having them farmed out. In the collection of direct taxes he sought to replace venal officers with salaried ones. Some considered these reforms dangerous, because the financial establishment provided loans to the government. Instead of relying on them, Necker sought to found government credit on the willingness of the moneyed interests to lend to a government in which they had confidence. Britain's credit was better than France's, he believed, because their institutions provided a way for the country to be involved in supporting the government. Because Parliament approved taxes, bankers were confident that loans would be repaid and they were willing to lend the British government money on much better terms than they would to the French government.

To provide a way to channel public support to the government in France and make it possible to reform the collection of taxes, Necker proposed the creation of provincial assemblies made up of landowners. These assemblies would be in charge of raising taxes in the *pays d'élection*, thus bypassing the intendants and undermining the contention of the parlements that they represented the interests of the nation. Necker explained: "It is preferable to allow each province to determine how it can best raise the quota of tax revenue assigned to it by the royal government."[5] The assemblies he envisioned would maintain the distinction of orders, but the number of Third Estate members would be equal to the number of the other two orders and the discussions and voting would be held jointly. Instead of being elected, some members would be appointed by the government and they would in turn select others. Necker started slowly with plans for four assemblies, two of which were actually founded and survived his fall. He argued that his assemblies would not undermine the power of the king because the members would not enjoy the independence of venality (like the parlementaires) and because the king, having made the assemblies, could also put an end to them.

An essential part of Necker's plan was openness about the workings of the government. Shortly before being dismissed from office in 1781, he wrote and published a report on finances entitled the *Compte Rendu au Roi* (*Report to the King* or *King's Accounts*) in which he asserted that part of the reason for Britain's better credit was that its budgetary affairs were out in the open. Necker's strategy to bring the force of public opinion into the government was greeted with delight by those previously excluded from participation. His book became a best seller, and he became a hero to many for showing that France had a surplus in ordinary government accounts of 10 million livres per year. Informed critics immediately pointed out that this surplus did not exist, that it was arrived at only by considering "ordinary" accounts, and that the expenses of war fell into the "extraordinary" category and were not included. Necker apparently was using these figures to bolster the country's credit, but the result was that many people remained convinced that when he left office a surplus existed in the royal budget. He seemed a hero as well because of his willingness to pull the veil away from the workings of the government. To traditionalists, including the king and Vergennes, this bold maneuver threatened to undermine the structure of the French monarchical government and to lead to a kind of British system. Necker's self-serving writings earned him the enmity of many prominent people, from members of the parlements to intendants, and they were not sorry to see him leave.

When Joly de Fleury replaced Necker in 1781, he managed to get a third *vingtième* approved by the parlement, a measure scheduled to last until three years after the peace. He worked with Vergennes in attempting to impose limits on the amounts spent by other ministers and to bring coherence to the government's decisions about finances by creating a Financial Council. He especially hoped to rein in the spending for the army and navy, departments headed by Ségur and Castries (members of another faction), who fought this intrusion into their areas of responsibility. Although Joly de Fleury brought back the venal officials that Necker had tried to eliminate, he was forced (like Necker) to continue a policy of borrowing money.

The rapid turnover in ministers meant that no policy was pursued persistently or effectively. Indeed, Joly de Fleury lasted less than two years and his replacement only a few months. In November 1783, when Calonne took over the finances, he recalled that "All the funds were empty, all public stocks were low, all circulation was interrupted; alarm was general and confidence destroyed."[6] An elegant man with all the airs of a nobleman (even though his father had been ennobled), Calonne had been a crown lawyer and a bitter critic of Necker's *Compte Rendu*. His plan for reviving confidence involved a program of public works, including creating a naval fortress at Cherbourg. This ploy worked for a while as the country's economy boomed. But the recovery was short-lived.

Matters were made worse when the truce between the government and the parlement came to an end. The government found it impossible to manage the parlement effectively because of factional strife among the ministers. Each minister feared that the others were trying to hasten his fall from power and sought support among groups within the parlement to bolster his position. The parlement now once again began to block decrees brought to it. In December 1785, the king resorted to a *lit de justice* to force the registration of Calonne's measure to adjust the amount of gold in the coins. The king scolded the parlementaires for making their remonstrance public. The parlement's role in the Affair of the Diamond Necklace (see above) had demonstrated that it would not be led by the throne. Calonne now persuaded the king that the financial situation had reached a crisis and that it could not be solved by business as usual. It was time to try something entirely different.

THE ASSEMBLY OF NOTABLES

Unlike Necker, Calonne decided that gradual reforms would no longer be sufficient. In August 1786 he presented a memorandum to the king outlining a broad plan of reform. He told the king:

It is impossible to increase taxes, disastrous to keep on borrowing, and inadequate merely to cut expenses. Under present circumstances, with all the ordinary measures inoperable, the only effective remedy, the only alternative remaining, the only way to bring real order into the finances, is to revitalize the entire state by reforming all that is defective in its constitution.[7]

His memorandum ranged widely in criticizing the complexities of Ancien Régime governance, the hindrances to commerce and industry, and the inequities of the tax system. He thought that a country

where certain areas are totally freed from burdens of which others bear the full weight, where the richest class contributes least, where privileges destroy all balance, where it is impossible to have either a constant rule or a common will, is necessarily a very imperfect kingdom, brimming with abuses, and one that it is impossible to govern well.[8]

The heart of his plan was to do away with the *vingtième* taxes and replace them with a land tax that would be levied on all products of real estate without exception. In order to be fair to all parts of the country whose land varied greatly in productivity, land would be assigned to four categories and the tax would be levied in kind, not in cash. Paying in kind (that is, in produce rather than money) had the advantage that if there were a bad harvest, the tax would automatically be lowered. Another key part of his proposal was the creation of a series of assemblies in the *pays d'élection* (the *pays d'état* would keep their provincial estates). Unlike those established by Necker, Calonne's assemblies were to be elected by landed proprietors. Parish assemblies would choose district assemblies, who would in turn choose provincial assemblies. These assemblies were to be consultative bodies working under the direction of the intendants. Distinction of orders would be eliminated. To encourage the economy, Calonne followed the ideas of the physiocrats (Dupont de Nemours worked closely with him on the plan) to propose freedom of the grain trade and elimination of internal customs barriers. The *gabelle* was to be made more uniform throughout the country, and the *corvée* was to be commuted to a money tax on those who paid the *taille*.

The timing of Calonne's proposal was not an accident. The *vingtième* that had been approved during the American war was about to expire, and the government desperately needed to make up the lost revenues. Calonne wanted to revive confidence in the government so that he could continue to borrow while the reforms were taking effect. But he knew that the parlement would be unlikely to pass these measures easily or quickly. He came up instead with the idea of nominating an Assembly of Notables, made up of prominent and distinguished people from throughout the country who could be expected to endorse the necessity of a reform program. With their backing, the parlement would no longer have any justification for rejecting the plan. The last time an Assembly of Notables had been called was 1626.

The list of 144 notables was carefully crafted to include what Calonne called "people of substance" who were "dedicated to the service of the king, well intentioned and removed from all intrigue and partiality."[9] On February 22, 1787, the king opened the meeting. In an attempt to maintain control over the deliberations, the government decided to divide the members into seven committees, each chaired by a prince of the blood, to discuss the proposals before a final meeting together to endorse the program. At least, that was what Calonne intended to have happen, though things did not work out as he had planned. The Assembly did not automatically reject the proposals. They approved freedom of the grain trade and replacing the *corvée* with a money tax. They supported the idea of provincial assemblies, but they were not happy that the distinction of orders was to be done away with in the assemblies. The members of the clergy especially objected to the challenge to their separate status. The Assembly worried that traditional privileges of some provinces were being destroyed contrary to law by the new tariff regulations. Although most agreed that taxes needed to be made more equitable and were willing to consider giving up tax privileges, they raised objections to the details of the plans. Paying the land tax in kind, they pointed out, would set no limits to the amount the government could raise, which went against the traditional view that taxes should be levied only for the actual needs of the government. They remained unconvinced of the necessity of such a wholesale reform, demanding that Calonne show them the accounts to prove that indeed there was a deficit of 112 million livres. Only six years earlier, when Necker had left office, they argued, there had been a surplus. Calonne insisted that Necker's figures were wrong, but the Assembly thought he was blaming Necker for the shortfall he himself had caused. They hesitated to provide the very people who had caused the deficit with more money to squander.

Some of the objections to Calonne's plans stemmed from factional disputes. Shortly before the session opened, Vergennes had died, leaving Calonne without strong support among the remaining ministers. Some in the Assembly (especially the Archbishop of Toulouse, Loménie de Brienne) were hoping for Calonne's failure so that they might replace him as minister. The king, as he had promised, continued to support Calonne. But Calonne made a mistake when he paid too little attention to the objections that the Assembly of Notables had raised. In a speech on March 12, he said that the king was "pleased to find that in general your opinions agree with his basic ideas," and he characterized their objections as having "to do mostly with form."[10] The Assembly then became recalcitrant. Calonne made another mistake by deciding to appeal to public opinion. He published a pamphlet accusing the Assembly of lack of patriotism and unwillingness to give up their privileges. This tactic backfired by inflaming opinion and forfeiting the little amount of confidence that the Assembly had in him to begin with. Calonne now found his enemies working to persuade the king to dismiss him, which Louis did reluctantly on April 8, 1787. On the same day, one of Calonne's opponents, the Keeper of the Seals Miromesnil, was also dismissed, to be replaced by Lamoignon (a leader in the Parlement of Paris).

The king, genuinely distressed at the failure of Calonne's plan and refusing to call Necker back to office as public opinion seemed to prefer, turned to Loménie de Brienne (the queen's candidate), whose stature in the Assembly of Notables might make it possible to salvage something from the wreckage and restore the shaken credit of the government. The Assembly was shown the figures proving the existence of the deficit. Although they could now confirm the reality of the crisis and although the king had backed down on some of the parts of the program they considered most troubling (the composition of the provincial assemblies and the open-ended nature of the land tax, for example), the Assembly of Notables still refused to endorse the additional taxes. Influenced by new political theories (ultimately derived from Locke) that stipulated that new taxes had to have the consent of the people through their representatives, many members of the Assembly of Notables, which had been appointed by the government, not elected by the people, now argued that only an Estates General could approve new taxes. They also declared that the king must promise to reorganize the Financial Council. The king replied only vaguely to this resolution. It was time to dismiss the Assembly of Notables, which had failed to accomplish what the government had hoped. Instead of providing an easy endorsement of the need for reform to smooth the way through the parlements for the legislation, they had put even more obstacles in its path. But before they disbanded, one of the Notables, Lafayette, called for the convening "of a truly national assembly."[11] This proved to be only the first of many calls for the convening of the Estates General.

LOMÉNIE DE BRIENNE

Loménie de Brienne and Lamoignon embarked on a wide program of reform to make changes that would save money, inspire confidence, and bring to fruition the parts of Calonne's program that the Assembly of Notables had endorsed most enthusiastically. Brienne set up a central *caisse* as a depository for taxes so that the government could more easily keep track of its money. The extravagant system of royal pensions was cut back, and expenses at court were reduced. When some prominent court favorites found their superfluous offices done away with, they reacted with outrage. Reforms in the military led to more serious repercussions.

A War Council was created, and under the inspiration of Colonel Comte de Guibert—a man already famous as a writer and as the author of the influential *General Essay on Tactics* (1770)—began to transform the military. The French army had too many officers. Guibert estimated that the "total of 1,261 generals, lieutenant generals, and brigadier generals constitutes a greater number of general officers in France than in all the armies of the rest of Europe combined; hence the lack of respect for these distinguished ranks and the disgust reflected in the lower ranks . . ."[12] The military reformers set about eliminating these positions as they became vacant by retirement. The King's Military Household was cut back. They did away with civilian contractors who supplied the army with rations and clothing at enormous expense, and assigned those tasks to the army itself. They maintained the rules that officers should be noble, as had been stressed in the Ségur Ordinance of 1781. However, in order to open opportunities to all nobles and to make sure that competence was taken into consideration in promotions, young court nobles were no longer allowed to become colonels without any experience. And officers were now expected actually to serve with their troops. One historian, T. C. W. Blanning, wrote that "Of the 1,132 colonels, only about 200 actually served with their regiments on a permanent basis, while of the total officer corps of around 35,000, fewer than 10,000 can be described as 'serving.'"[13] The drastic changes in the army profoundly disconcerted many officers, who were already demoralized by France's apparent decline as a power, a decline demonstrated vividly by the Dutch crisis of 1787.

Two parties in the United Provinces of the Netherlands vied for power. The Stadholder, William V, was supported by the British. The French, who had concluded a defensive alliance with the Netherlands in 1785, supported the Patriots, convinced that they would prevail. In 1787, when the Stadholder's wife tried to enter Holland to restore his power, she was arrested and insulted. This event had international ramifications because she was the sister of the king of Prussia, Frederick William II, who now came to her defense. On September 13, 1787, a Prussian army entered the Dutch Republic. According to the treaty of alliance, France was obligated to help the Dutch. But Brienne, in the middle of a struggle with the parlement over France's financial problems, decided that finances should take priority. France could not afford war, especially not a wider war should Britain decide to back up the Prussians. Indeed, the problems within France probably emboldened the Prussians to take action, assuming that the French would not intervene. And so the French abandoned their ally, and the army felt the humiliation. Some at the time argued that intervening, by rallying the country around military glory, would have brought support for the king without worsening the financial situation. It was generally easier to raise taxes in wartime, and the Dutch would have helped to subsidize the French army. As it turned out, the army, buffeted by reforms, cost-cutting, and loss of status, would waver in loyalty during the crucial events of the early Revolution.

Brienne and Lamoignon made changes in other aspects of French society that had nothing directly to do with the financial crisis they faced. Protestants were granted civil status in November 1787. Lamoignon appointed a group to revise the civil and criminal laws. Several exceptional courts were abolished, and the structure of trials and appeals was streamlined. These ministers, genuinely devoted to change, worked to solve the problems that they believed the country faced. Sometimes we tend to believe that revolution results when the government is unresponsive, and people feel compelled to rise against their oppressors. Far from maintaining the old ways intransigently, this government worked assiduously to institute the kinds of reforms that writers on questions of public policy had been advocating. What their experience teaches us is that the process of making changes (even when they are needed) can be dangerous, because it creates uncertainty and inevitably antagonizes groups who benefited from the old ways. And we can see as well that there is a difference between the content of reform and the means of carrying it out. If the king forced through reform measures (as absolutism in theory certainly gave him the power to do), many Frenchmen now believed that such action was tantamount to government tyranny. The reforms might be needed and reasonable, but what would prevent the ministers from becoming more tyrannical and more oppressive in the future?

Brienne held special hopes for the beneficial effects of provincial assemblies in the *pays d'élection*. The Assembly of Notables had been in favor of their creation, and Brienne followed the Notables' suggestions to organize them according to orders, with the Third Estate having half the members ("doubling of the Third") and in which each individual would have one vote (voting by head, not voting by order). Brienne had originally thought of giving the Third Estate even more influence with two-thirds of the votes, but settled on one-half. An edict in June 1787 stipulated their method of election: elected municipal assemblies would choose district assemblies that finally would choose provincial assemblies. Working closely with the intendants, they were to allocate and collect taxes, be in charge of public works, and supervise charities. Brienne envisioned that, in the future, representatives from each of the provincial assemblies along with delegates from the estates in the *pays d'état* would be able to send representatives to the king. This body, far superior to the Estates General in Brienne's point of view because it would represent more equitably the landowners of the country, would then be able to approve taxation. He confidently expected that with representative bodies to consent to taxation, collection would be both more plentiful and more equitable. But it would take a while for this new institution to become established. In the meantime, Brienne had to face the financial problems.

CALLING THE ESTATES GENERAL

The Parlement of Paris registered without incident many of the reforms endorsed by the Assembly of Notables, including (surprisingly) the provincial assemblies that might threaten their claim to speak for the nation. But when Brienne sent them a stamp tax and a land tax in July they refused to register them, arguing that only an Estates General had the authority to consent to a new permanent tax. On August 6, 1787, a *lit de justice* was held to force their registration. The next day, the parlement declared that the registration was "null and void" and they were determined to continue discussion. The intransigence of the parlement evoked rapturous acclaim in Paris, where large crowds cheered the parlementaires as they left the building. Fearing that serious incidents might result, the government exiled the entire parlement to Troyes. From there, the parlementaires tried to rally other courts to their side, and soon other courts also joined in denouncing the imposition of the new taxes. It was in the midst of this stalemate, with violence increasing in Paris, that the crisis in the Netherlands came to a head, and the French did nothing.

Hoping to gain time, Brienne offered to compromise by dropping the new taxes and merely extending the *vingtième* taxes for five years. By then, he expected that finances would be in order and the government would be in a much stronger negotiating position. And he now finally promised that the king would call the Estates General sometime in the future, at least by 1792. The parlement, eager to come back to Paris from their enforced idleness in the provinces, accepted this compromise. On November 19, a special meeting of the Parlement of Paris was called to register the decrees. Louis XVI was present as were the princes of the blood. Not technically a *lit de justice*, all were allowed to express their views, but whether they were expected to vote or not was unclear, though it was likely that the measure would have passed had they voted. At the end of the long day's deliberations, when the king ordered that the edict be registered, his cousin, the Duc d'Orléans, objected that a vote should be held. The king, taken aback by this interruption, stammered out that what he was doing was legal: "it is legal because I will it."[14] Offended at this seeming act of despotism (rule by one man, rather than by law), the parlement refused to register the decree. That night the Duc d'Orléans received a *lettre de cachet* sending him into exile in the provinces, and two men assumed to be his confederates were arrested and put into prison. The king then brought the parlement to Versailles and forced them to accept the tax measure.

The debate between the government and the parlements now became even more heated. The fight against the actions of the ministers spread to provincial courts and animated public discussion throughout the country over the winter of 1787–1788. The parlements saw themselves as the custodians of the rights and traditions of the nation. They accused the government of "ministerial despotism" for riding roughshod over the accepted customs and guarantees of the past. In the spring of 1788, they published a protest regarding the November session in which they declared that the

> sole will of the king is not a complete law; the simple expression of that will is not a national form of law. . . . The right to verify the laws is not the right to make them; but if the authority which makes the law could hinder its verification or arrogate that function to itself, then . . . the will of a man could replace the public will and the State would fall under the hand of despotism.[15]

The government began to make plans in great secrecy to reorganize the system of justice. Knowing that something was about to befall them, the Parlement of Paris decided to preempt the attack by declaring on May 3, 1788, that there existed in France certain fundamental laws that could not be transgressed. Some of these (like the Salic Law) were undisputed, but others they had developed more recently in the heat of debate. They listed "The right of the Nation to accord subsidies freely through the organ of the Estates General convoked regularly and composed correctly," and "The irrevocable tenure of the magistrates." They condemned as well the use of *lettres de cachet*, the favorite weapon of the government against recalcitrant magistrates.

In a dramatic scene on May 6, two leaders of the opposition in the parlement were arrested in the halls of the parlement, and on May 8, a *lit de justice* was held to register what became known as the "May Edicts" that transformed the system of justice. To do away with the obstructions of the parlements, the government now reorganized the courts. They were deprived of many of their judicial powers as well as their political role. A new court made up of high nobles and government officials (similar in composition to the Assembly of Notables) was to be created to register laws. Because the functions of the parlementaires had been so reduced, their numbers were to be reduced as well. An explosion of discontent now swept the country. Huge demonstrations took place, all the parlements printed remonstrances, and hostile pamphlets appeared accusing the government of despotism.

Many commentators have found it puzzling that the obstructions of the parlement to the needed reforms should have been supported by so many people. After all, the noble judges were motivated in great part by the selfish desire of not wanting to lose their tax exemptions. But the focus of the debate had shifted from who was to pay taxes to how the reforms were to be put in place. The parlements, by standing up to the ministers, seemed to be saving the entire country from "despotism." They appealed both to those who favored maintaining the traditional forms of the French system and to those who wanted to create a more liberal government based on the rights of the people. And by publicizing their views, the fight between the parlements and the ministers spread these ideas on proper governance to a wider population who would take more and more interest in public affairs.

The government's situation was not hopeless. They still commanded a great deal of power, as their troops were able to put down the violence and maintain order. Had they been able to hold on, the crisis might have dissipated (as it had after the Maupeou Revolution). Brienne still hoped that he could get the country on his side by continuing to set up provincial assemblies that could give consent to taxation and would serve as counterweights to the power of the parlements. But establishing them would take time. In the summer of 1788, time ran out for Brienne because the fiscal crisis got worse. The government depended on "*anticipations*," that is, borrowing on the promise of future tax receipts. But the political crisis of 1788 coincided with an economic downturn. Five of the major financiers who collected taxes and lent money to the government went bankrupt, and the credit of the government completely dried up. Fearful of the soundness of the government credit in the midst of the tumult over the parlements, even bankers and financiers who had money now refused to advance any to the government. At the beginning of August, Brienne was informed that the government coffers were empty. Hoping to stimulate credit, he announced that the Estates General would meet on May 1, 1789. He stated that the government would in the meantime meet its financial obligations by paying in treasury bills (thus forcing creditors and vendors to accept a promise of future payment, which was in essence a forced loan). With his enemies trying to persuade the king and queen to dismiss him, Brienne resigned on August 25, 1788, to make way for Necker to resume office. Lamoignon soon followed him into retirement.

Necker's return was greeted with joy, as many still saw him as a wizard who would be able to salvage the situation. But the demonstrations since May had alarmed Necker, who now believed that the country was about to descend into civil war. In order to prevent that, he did not propose any extraordinary measures. Instead he put all his hopes in the meeting of the Estates General. The royal government, in other words, had no more ideas about how the fiscal crisis would be solved under the traditional means available to absolutism. They would wait for the Estates General. But the taxpayers, through their representatives in the Estates General, would provide money only on their own terms. They expected to be consulted and demanded changes in the government. Calling the Estates General spelled the end of absolutism. Something new was to take its place, but nobody knew what it would be.

CONCLUSION

By the time the Estates General met, one delegate wrote in his journal: "The king is carried along endlessly from one policy to another, changing them, adopting them, rejecting them with an inconceivable capriciousness; exercising force, then weakly retreating. He has entirely lost his authority."[16] The royal governments had limped along by one expedient after another, without a settled policy of reform to tackle the serious problems that they faced. The history of those attempts shows how difficult it was to make meaningful changes, especially when the tax reforms threatened to undermine the fundamental corporate character of the Ancien Régime. Royal governments had faced fiscal crises before and had always managed to get through them by borrowing and bullying. In 1788, traditional methods no longer worked because the royal government now had to deal with the widespread belief that the only valid taxes were those consented to by the people through their representatives. A government acting without that consent was called despotic. Some important reforms were instituted, especially rights for Protestants, reform of the military, and abolition of torture. But fundamental fiscal problems had not been solved.

In the summer of 1788, when Necker returned to office as a caretaker, the Ancien Régime finally collapsed. The struggle over what would replace it now took center stage, and the competition over who would control the Estates General and thus shape the new institutions brought to the surface tensions and hostilities that had been held in check under the Ancien Régime. Now a more open political climate allowed and even helped to foment the expression of hatreds and suspicions that would be defining features of the French Revolution.

3

THE ESTATES GENERAL
AND THE NATIONAL ASSEMBLY

Many things had changed in the 175 years since the last meeting of the Estates General. Brienne, in anticipation of a meeting some time in the future, had asked the municipalities and provincial assemblies in July 1788 to forward information on previous practices and had invited suggestions on how the Estates General should be organized. Brienne obviously did not believe that the old procedures would be acceptable any longer. When the king issued the official order of convocation in September, he merely stated that he intended to call the Estates General, but did not provide details of its election or organization. In the fall of 1788, the method of election and the form that the Estates General would take became issues of intense debate.

CALLING THE ESTATES GENERAL

Having given up attempts to solve the financial crisis under the institutions of absolutism, the government also gave up the changes that had been made in the judicial system in May. In September 1788 the parlement returned to Paris, and its first item of business was to register the decree calling for the convening of the Estates General. Now completely convinced of the danger of ministerial despotism, afraid that the government intended to control the new provincial assemblies, and suspicious of the call for suggestions for transforming the Estates General, the parlement decided to forestall any new government manipulations by stipulating that the Estates General would meet "according to the forms observed in 1614."[1]

Continuing their role as custodians of tradition, the parlement by this statement probably meant to prevent the merging of the three orders and control of the elections by the provincial assemblies. Yet, their statement demonstrated how little they had considered the question. In 1614, the members of the parlement had sat with the Third Estate. In 1788, the parlementaires (had they thought seriously of the matter) would not have endorsed a "form" that excluded them from the nobility. In 1614, the three estates had met and voted separately by order, so that the Third Estate could be outvoted by the privileged orders 2–1. The parlement's statement of September 1788 provoked cries of indignation throughout the country at what seemed to be an effort to stifle the Third Estate, and all of the good will that the parlement had built up in its quarrels with the ministers melted away.

Necker decided to reconvene the Assembly of Notables and submit the issue to them. The Assembly met from November 6 until the middle of December against a backdrop of intensifying public interest in the outcome. Without the restraint of government censorship (which had originally been lifted in the summer to allow for comments on the Estates General), pamphlets poured forth debating the questions, and various groups and clubs began to organize. The Third Estate constituted an overwhelming numerical majority in the country, and its supporters especially opposed voting by order. They demanded that the Third Estate have twice as many delegates as either of the other two orders ("doubling of the Third") and that the votes of individuals determine the majority (vote by head, not by order). They were confident that enough nobles and priests would side with the Third Estate to give them the majority. During the fall, many petitions presented these ideas, along with demands that only non-nobles be allowed to represent the Third Estate and that all deliberation be in common.

This program had a precedent. In the summer of 1788, Jean-Joseph Mounier had led a movement in the province of Dauphiné calling for the reinstatement of the parlement and the revival of Dauphiné's provincial estates. Seeking and gaining the collaboration of members of all three orders, the estates of Dauphiné were organized with double representation for the Third Estate and voting by head. Though the attempts to create estates in other provinces had led to conflicts and acrimony, the example of this amicable cooperation among the orders in Dauphiné was frequently cited by those hoping to achieve the same arrangement for the Estates General.

Those who wanted representation on the basis of the individual rather than the group (or corporation) began to call themselves the Patriots or the National party. They argued that France did not have a constitution, and they insisted that one should be written for the whole nation. At the time of the Second Assembly of Notables, a club with these ideas (later called the Committee of Thirty, though it had consisted of around fifty members) began to meet in Paris at the home of a liberal counselor of the parlement named Adrien Duport. The Committee of Thirty included able pamphlet-eers (Condorcet, Dupont de Nemours, Abbé Sieyès) and eloquent jurists (Target, Pierre-Louis Lacretelle, Roederer), as well as liberal nobles (Lafayette, Mirabeau, Destutt de Tracy, La Rochefoucauld). Nobles domi-nated the group. Of the known members, 42 percent were sword nobles of ancient lineage and 43 percent were robe nobles. Hoping to influence the Assembly of Notables to double the delegates of the Third Estate and to endorse voting by head, their pamphlets countered the view that France had a constitution that prescribed a meeting of the Estates General accord-ing to the old rules with separate orders. Just because something had been done a certain way in the past, they argued, did not mean it should be con-tinued. They asserted that the people were sovereign and that the rights of the nation should come before the interests of privileged groups, no mat-ter how ancient. One of the members (a military officer named Mathieu Dumas, who would later have a large role in military reform) recalled the heady anticipation of their hopes for change:

> We talked about the establishment of a new constitution for the state, as [if it were] an easy job, a natural event. In the ecstasy of those days of hope and celebration, we scarcely cast a glance at the obstacles to be overcome, before laying the first bases of freedom, before establishing the principles rejected by the spirit of the court, the privileged Orders, the great corporations, and the old customs.[2]

The pressure of this group and of others had no effect on the Second Assembly of Notables, most of whose members were more committed than ever to maintaining the separate status of the nobles and the clergy, which now seemed threatened with extinction. The Assembly of Notables was willing to go along with making all people subject to taxation, but they re-jected the doubling of the Third Estate by a vote of 111 to 33.

The parlement, distressed at having lost the goodwill of the nation by their September decree, "clarified" their position in early December, saying that they had not intended to make any pronouncements on the number of each order's representatives. They meant only that the elections should be organized by local judicial districts (known as *bailliages* and *sénéchaussées*), rather than by province or generality. But by the time this statement ap-peared, the damage had been done, and the parlement discovered that they could no longer provide leadership on political questions. Their statement did make it possible for Necker to persuade the king to approve doubling of the Third and to align himself with sentiment throughout the country that favored the Third Estate. The decision, taken at a council meeting on December 27, 1788, did not satisfy any side. It decreed doubling of the Third, but said nothing about voting by head or by order. Therefore, the clash between the Third and the privileged orders was bound to continue. The journalist Mallet du Pan noted the increasing bitterness: "The public debate has changed complexion. No longer a question, except secondarily, of the king, despotism, or the constitution, it is a war between the Third and the other two Orders."[3]

Newspapers and pamphlets now poured forth from the presses to debate the issue. Newspapers were an invention of the eighteenth century. The increase in literacy rates and in wealth in that century meant that some people now were able to subscribe to newspapers. Like modern newspapers in that they often provided practical information on public matters such as markets and theaters and often printed advertisements, they differed from modern newspapers by making no pretense of journalistic objectivity. The news often was little more than an extended editorial, much more like modern weblogs than like a large modern metropolitan newspaper. Newspapers had been carefully censored under the Ancien Régime, but in the first few years of the Revolution with the lifting of press censorship, hundreds of newspapers of various shades of opinion were founded. Pamphlets proved especially useful in the political debates because they could be easily produced and could focus on one topic. Many speeches were also distributed in pamphlet form.

The most famous pamphlet in the "war between the Third Estate and the two other orders" appeared in January 1789: *What Is the Third Estate?* The author, the Abbé Sieyès, was the son of a government official from the south of France. Wishing to rise from his modest circumstances, he pursued a career in the church, even though he held no deep religious convictions. Indeed, he was an avid reader and supporter of the *philosophes* and shared their dislike of religion. Dependent on the patronage of others for advancement, he was frustrated at his lack of progress. Because only nobles might realistically hope to attain the higher positions in the church, Sieyès came to resent the aristocrats who blocked his rise. In 1788, he eagerly joined the debate on representation by writing pamphlets that made him a celebrity. His fame would win him election to the Estates General as a representative of the Third Estate of Paris.

Vigorously argued, Sieyès's *What Is the Third Estate?* set out to convince his readers that the demands of the Third Estate were reasonable and modest. He posed three questions:

1. What is the Third Estate? Everything.
2. What has it been heretofore in the political order? Nothing.
3. What does it demand? To become something therein.

His argument was based on utility, nationalism, and arithmetic equality. The Third Estate, he argued, did almost all of the useful work in both the private and the public realms. Nobles dominated the "lucrative and honorary" positions, but those could be easily dispensed with. The Third Estate, then, had "within itself all that is necessary to constitute a complete nation." A nation, by his definition, lived under a common law. But the privileged orders lived under a different and separate law and were therefore not really part of the nation. And yet he noted that despite the overwhelming predominance and usefulness of the Third Estate in the nation, they demanded only equality of representation with the other orders and vote by head. Sieyès did not think that was sufficient. The general will, he concluded, could be determined only by consulting the views of individuals who made up the nation. If, he wrote, the constitution of the country really provided "that 200,000 or 300,000 individuals out of 26,000,000 citizens constitute two-thirds of the common will," then one might as well say that "two and two make five." Even with vote by head in the Estates General, one would be declaring that "the wills of 200,000 persons may balance those of 25,000,000." The Third Estate, he argued, represented the nation and should declare itself the National Assembly. As to the privileged orders, he thought their influence "must be *neutralized*." This radical argument, intended to make the point as forcefully as possible that the Third Estate should have much more of a say in the political system, had within it some dangerous propositions of exclusion from the nation that, when taken up and interpreted literally by revolutionaries with other purposes in mind, would lend weight to the Terror later in the Revolution. His call for a National Assembly proved to be influential (or perhaps forward-looking). That path was the one eventually taken by the Third Estate. But much was to happen before that change took place.[4]

ELECTIONS AND *CAHIERS*

The king's order calling for the elections to the Estates General was issued on January 24, 1789. Providing for a wide participation (almost all adult males could take part), it created an electorate much larger than had ever been seen in Europe. The document assured everybody "from the extremities of the kingdom and from the most obscure settlements" that "his wishes and claims" would receive the king's notice.[5] By including so many people, the election ensured that the entire country would invest enormous hope in the outcome of the meeting. The electors were instructed to draft a list of their concerns, called a *cahier de doléances* or notebook of grievances, which their representatives would bring to the king. They therefore expected that their problems would finally be taken seriously. Elections were held from the end of February into April. Because of its size, special electoral procedures had to be prepared for Paris, and because those were issued late, Paris had not yet chosen its delegates by the time the Estates General opened at the beginning of May. The government made no attempt to influence who was elected and continued its policy of waiting for the Estates General to solve the problems of the country.

The First and Second Estates chose around three hundred delegates each, while the Third Estate sent around six hundred deputies to Versailles. The elections were arranged by judicial districts called *bailliages* (a name more commonly used in the north) or *sénéchaussées* (more common in the south) and generally conformed to the following pattern. Each order selected its own delegates to send to Versailles. Delegates for the first two estates had to choose members of those estates, but the Third Estate could be represented by someone from any estate. All nobles who owned a fief in the *bailliage* and who were at least twenty-five years old were to meet to select delegates to the Second Estate and to draft their *cahier*. A woman who owned a fief could send a man to represent her at the meeting. Nobles were allowed to participate, either in person or by proxy, in every *bailliage* in which they held a fief. The Third Estate was not accorded the same privilege of multiple voting.

Because all the members of the Third Estate in a *bailliage* could not meet in one place (there were too many of them), the elections for the Third Estate were held in stages. Primary meetings in each parish gathered all men listed on the tax rolls who were at least twenty-five years old to write *cahiers* and to elect delegates to go to the next level. Depending on the population, there might be yet another election (or perhaps even two) before the final delegates were chosen who would go to Versailles. The *cahiers* prepared at the primary level were consolidated into a general *cahier* of the Third Estate for the *bailliage*.

The elections for the First Estate provided for each religious community (including orders of women) to choose delegates to attend the *bailliage* meeting. They, along with all the parish priests and the church hierarchy in the *bailliage*, gathered to elect the delegates of the First Estate and to draft the *cahier*. The method of voting gave the advantage to parish priests and brought about a reversal in the normal power of the church hierarchy in which bishops (chosen from the nobility) controlled affairs. Of around 300 clerical deputies, 192 parish priests were elected and only 46 bishops, a considerable diminution of the bishops' traditional dominance in making decisions for the clergy. Priests, who were recruited from among commoners, used their votes to express their resentment against the bishops and others in the upper hierarchy for their wealth and power. The publicists promoting the cause of the Third Estate urged priests to side with them against all those who were privileged. The religious orders were under-represented, with only 3 percent of the delegates being members of religious orders (although their total numbers in the population were equal to those of priests).

The nobility was over-represented in the Estates General as a whole. The delegation of the First Estate included eighty-five nobles (who were also clergymen), and fifty-eight nobles represented the Third Estate (out of more than six hundred delegates). One-third of the approximately 1,200 delegates to the Estates General were nobles. The most famous instance of a nobleman who represented the Third Estate was Mirabeau, whose fiery speeches would earn him the devotion of the crowds.

Historians skeptical of the Marxist interpretation of the coming of the Revolution with its emphasis on a class struggle point to the lack of solidarity in the nobility and the bourgeoisie and the conjuncture of interests and points of view among an elite of nobles and rich commoners in the country. However true this picture of society may have been for the eighteenth century, the differences between those chosen to represent the nobility and those chosen to represent the Third Estate were substantial and made agreement between them difficult. The delegates of the nobility were overwhelmingly great nobles of ancient lineage and quite rich. Only 6 percent had been newly ennobled in the eighteenth century. Four-fifths had been or still were soldiers. One-half actually lived in Paris, although most sought election from provincial areas where they owned property and enjoyed ancestral ties. The delegates of the nobility, according to historian Timothy Tackett, were "a corps of extremely wealthy, aristocratic soldiers."[6]

By contrast, the legal profession dominated among the delegates of the Third Estate. There were 218 magistrates (most from *bailliage* courts) and 181 lawyers. The noble deputies were considerably wealthier than the deputies of the Third Estate, and their experience as soldiers also set them off from the bulk of the commoners. The delegates to the Estates General have often been criticized for lacking political experience and therefore being prone to error and misjudgment. But many had acquired, by the time the meeting opened, considerable experience in public affairs. Almost 20 percent of the Third Estate delegates held municipal offices. At least half of the Third Estate delegates had taken part in provincial assemblies.

Neither nobles nor commoners came to the Estates General with well-developed agendas and political ideas, let alone ones derived from the Enlightenment. However, the prevalence of Enlightenment ideas in the society at large meant that many members of both groups had imbibed the Enlightenment's contempt for religion. The nobles, who were less aggressively anti-clerical than the Third Estate, included many more fervent Catholics. Contrary to the frequently heard assertion that Masonic clubs taught Frenchmen to be revolutionaries, previous participation in Masonic clubs or other groups before the Revolution proved not to be a good predictor of the deputies' political choices. The experience in the Estates General itself was to have a profound effect on the political positions the deputies took. From the very beginning, the First and Second Estates were locked in combat over the organization of the Estates General.

The *cahiers* written by the electoral assemblies offer an invaluable source for understanding the views of the French population at a time when public opinion polls or other measures of public opinion were not available, but they must be used with caution. France was an overwhelmingly agricultural country, and most voters were peasants (that is, individuals who lived in the country and made a living from agriculture). Their views were reflected in the preliminary *cahiers*, but tended to be lost as the elections proceeded. The delegates chosen for the succeeding stages of election came from the richer and more educated portions of the population. Very few peasants were chosen as delegates to Versailles, and those few were comfortably well off. The general *cahiers* of the *bailliages* reflected this by either downplaying rural concerns in favor of larger national issues or by adding so many other issues that the interests of the rural districts were comparatively understated. The views of artisans in towns were likewise lost sight of as the preliminary *cahiers* became consolidated into the general *cahiers*. No artisans were chosen as delegates.

The *cahiers* of the three orders reveal that all voters were worried about taxes, but the peasantry were overwhelmingly concerned with the burdens of taxation. Of the most commonly listed items in local *cahiers*, ten of the top thirteen dealt with taxes. They demanded relief from taxes and equality of taxation. The general *cahiers*, which reflected the views of the leaders of the Third Estate, focused especially on the procedures of the coming Estates General (vote by head), on the need for provincial estates, on measures that impeded commerce (such as internal tariffs), and on the need to get rid of privileges (for example, tax exemptions and limitations on career opportunities). The nobles, doubtless reflecting the recent struggles in the parlements against an absolutist government, were more likely to stress the importance of guarantees of liberties, of regular meetings of the Estates General, and of power for the Estates General and the provincial estates.

The sentiments expressed in the *cahiers* make clear that the population was still devoted to the king and hopeful that the problems of the country were going to be solved. They generally assumed that because the king was asking for their suggestions for change, important reforms to solve the country's problems would be made. But there was great variety in the way the *cahiers* were drawn up and in the issues they chose to highlight. None of the *cahiers* anticipated the extent of the revolutionary changes about to occur. Most assumed that, in the future, the Estates General would be called upon to consent to taxation and that only taxes that received the endorsement of the Estates General were legitimate. But even in *cahiers* that stressed more power for the Estates General, the king was still expected to continue his position as sovereign and to have the dominant voice in shaping laws. The justifications in the *cahiers* for creating or reviving a better structure of government appealed to the history and traditions of France. Ringing calls for revolution based on abstract principles of Enlightenment political theory or demands for natural rights were exceedingly rare.

From the evidence of the *cahiers*, it appears that most people expected nobility and the seigneurial system to continue without interruption, though with some modifications. The rural *cahiers* demanded reforms, especially the abolition of such things as the exclusive privileges of the nobles to raise pigeons, and they wanted to reduce the fees they were required to pay, but they did not imagine the abolition of nobility itself. For peasants, the issue of taxation was more important than the seigneurial system. Although there were calls for reform in the church, the role of the church in society was generally not disputed. From his study of the *cahiers*, historian George V. Taylor concluded that no single *cahier* "enables one to predict the full range of the Revolution of 1789. . . . The only possible conclusion is that the revolutionary program and its ideology were produced and perfected after the voters had deliberated in the spring and that the great majority of them neither foresaw nor intended what was about to be done."[7] The men who participated in the series of electoral assemblies learned as they went along, and their views would continue to evolve after they arrived at Versailles.

MEETING OF THE ESTATES GENERAL

Not all delegates had arrived in Versailles when the proceedings of the Estates General began in early May 1789. The elections in Paris were not yet completed, and other delegates were still on their way. On May 4, a magnificent procession of delegates preceded the celebration of the opening mass. The First and Second Estates were resplendent in colorful garb, while the Third Estate followed in drab black, all prescribed by the strict etiquette of the court. On the next day, the delegates gathered in a large hall to hear the king's greeting followed by a speech on finances from Necker that lasted three hours. When Necker's voice gave out, somebody else had to complete it for him. The boring speech, long on details, offered no plan of action. The issues on everybody's mind, the method of voting and rules for discussion in the Estates General, were left unaddressed. Instead, the delegates were instructed to meet separately by order, with each order verifying the credentials of its delegates. Most of the Third Estate delegates, inspired by the harmony among the orders in the provincial estates of Dauphiné, hoped that the three orders would be able to work together. They worried, though, that if the three orders met separately to carry out the verification, that would be tantamount to acquiescing to the idea that the orders would discuss and vote separately as well. They therefore demanded that credentials be reviewed in a joint meeting of deputies from all three orders.

Absent any leadership by the government, the Estates General now came under the influence of its own leaders. Those in favor of doubling the Third, led by the Committee of Thirty during the winter, had helped to create feelings of resentment against the nobility, who seemed to be obstinately refusing to compromise. The noble *cahiers* showed a willingness to accept equal taxation and equality of careers, but they wanted to hold on to their separate status. The conflict between the nobles and the Third Estate had become particularly bitter in Brittany, where the nobles resented attempts by the government to reform the Parlement of Rennes. The discord culminated in pitched battles in the streets of Rennes in January 1789. The nobility and the upper clergy eventually decided to boycott the elections. The Third Estate delegates from Brittany were particularly anti-noble in their point of view and insisted that verification should be in common.

When the delegates arrived at Versailles, those who knew each other already from provincial assemblies and elections to the Estates General began to meet in provincial caucuses. The two most important caucuses centered around the delegates from Brittany and those from Dauphiné. They both began to invite other delegates to join them. The leaders of the Breton Club urged that no official business be conducted until the question of organization was decided. Mounier, the most prominent member of the Dauphiné delegation, on the other hand, suggested unofficial meetings between the orders so that a compromise might be found. The Third Estate agreed to Mounier's proposal on May 7. On May 13, the first two orders, who in the meantime had been verifying the credentials of their members, proposed the creation of a "conciliation commission." Although the Bretons recommended against this, they were defeated in the Third Estate by a vote of 320 to 66. This vote shows that many members of the Third Estate were still hoping to work with the other two orders and thought the Bretons were too extreme.

The clergy were deeply divided, as we can see by the close vote in their order on a motion to verify credentials with the other orders. It was defeated 133 to 114. But the bishops were able to organize effectively and win back the support of many members of the lower clergy by persuading them that the Third Estate's plans would be detrimental to the church. The Second Estate, on the other hand, was much more united. Despite a sizable percentage of liberal nobles (perhaps as many as one-quarter of the delegates), the bulk of the nobles were adamantly opposed to vote by head. They were willing to accept equality of taxation, but they wanted to give up their privileges themselves and not have the deprivations imposed by anybody else. Even some nobles who were at first sympathetic to the goals of the Third Estate became concerned about what they saw as that order's increasing radicalism. On May 28, the Second Estate passed a resolution stating that vote by order was essential to the constitution and the monarchy. The Third Estate interpreted this vote as "a declaration of war."[8]

After a month of this stalemate, a transformation had taken place in the delegates of the Third Estate. Meeting separately, the delegates had developed a feeling of solidarity. They had gotten to know each other and to share a sense of purpose, and they had become resentful of the intransigence of the nobility. They now unanimously endorsed the idea of vote by head. As they listened to the views of their talented speakers, the Third Estate delegates began to understand the more advanced political arguments and to accept many of the new ideas. One deputy wrote, "For me our sessions are like a school. . . . In it I see universal reason establishing its empire."[9]

Some early customs developed that would have profound effects later on. Most crucial for the future was the support that the public offered the members of the Third Estate. Beleaguered and apprehensive, the Third Estate welcomed the cheers of those who attended their gatherings or who greeted them as they moved about Versailles. One member asserted: "Public opinion is our strength."[10] But once the custom had been established that the sessions were open to the crowds and that the audience was free to applaud or jeer, it would be difficult to silence them later on. The nobility, on the other hand, by excluding outsiders from their meetings, gave the impression that they had something to hide and that they were more interested in their own privileges than in the good of the nation.

By early June, the Estates General had been meeting for a month with very little to show for their efforts. Louis XVI scrupulously refrained from interfering in the affairs of the Estates General, merely urging them to resolve the question of how the Estates General was to be organized. The king's usual indecisiveness was made worse by a cruel accident of fate. His oldest son (traditionally known by the title "the dauphin"), who had been in ill health for most of his life, died on June 4. Retreating to the smaller hunting lodge of Marly to mourn his son, Louis was now isolated from the important events occurring at Versailles. During this time of grief, the king refused to meet with representatives of the Third Estate, communicating with them only through ministers. But his doors were, of course, open to his conservative younger brother, Artois, and to other nobles and clergy, who continued to counsel intransigence. It is likely that the Third Estate might still have been willing to compromise, if a compromise had been offered. But in the absence of any proposals and fearful that the king was siding with the nobility, the Third Estate now moved into actions that were clearly illegal.

On June 10, they issued a "last invitation" to the other orders to join them, and they began a roll call of the other orders on June 12. Only three priests answered the roll call. The Third Estate had, as Sieyès put it, "cut the cables" and declared that they would act alone. They discussed how they would organize themselves and what they would call themselves. On June 17, they accepted Sieyès's suggestion that they be called the "National Assembly," thus implying that they represented the nation and could act on their own without the other two orders. Bailly, who presided over the meeting, administered a formal oath in which each delegate vowed to "fulfill faithfully and zealously the functions with which I have been entrusted."[11]

THE STRUGGLE OVER THE NATIONAL ASSEMBLY

On the very day that the National Assembly came into being, Necker had finally convinced the king that it was time for him to take the initiative in the Estates General. They decided to hold a Royal Session on June 23 in which the king could outline a plan. Louis XVI, who deeply resented the failure of the nobility to back him up in 1788, had seemed sympathetic to the Third Estate at first and willing to work with them. Others at court, however, were urging him to side with the nobility. Rejecting Necker's suggestions, the king, following the advice of the queen, his brother, and others (including a deputation from the clergy), decided to offer a compromise program, but to couch it in language that would show he was in charge.

The chances of a happy reception of the king's message were made less likely by the ineptness of the way the event was prepared. Without informing the Third Estate of its intentions, the government ordered that the hall in which the Third Estate met be closed so that it could be prepared for a joint session (it was the only hall large enough to hold them all). When the Third Estate deputies arrived on the morning of June 20 and found the hall locked, they reacted with fear and anger. Why was the hall being closed so early? What was really intended? Why had they not been informed? In a fever of suspicion, the delegates of the Third Estate (now calling themselves the National Assembly) met in an indoor tennis court and vowed to stay at their posts "until the constitution of the kingdom is established and consolidated upon firm foundations."[12] The Tennis Court Oath made attempts at compromise even less likely to succeed.

Ignoring this dramatic gesture, the government continued its preparations for the Royal Session. In his speech, delivered on June 23, the king finally addressed the question of voting by head or by order. He insisted that "the former distinction of the three orders of the State" was "essentially inherent in the constitution of" the realm. He also annulled the actions taken to create the National Assembly. But he recognized formally that no taxes would be raised without the "consent of the representatives of the nation." He promised equality of taxation, provincial estates in which half of the delegates would be from the Third Estate, reform of the *taille* and other taxes, and abolition of internal customs and *lettres de cachet*. On the method of voting in the Estates General, he proposed that the three orders "deliberate in common upon matters of general welfare," but matters regarding the "ancient and constitutional rights of the three orders, the constitutional form to be given the next Estates General, feudal and seigneurial property, and the useful rights and honorary prerogatives of the first two orders" would not be determined in common. Privileges could be revised only with the consent of the privileged orders themselves. And he specifically ordered that religious matters must have the "special consent of the clergy."[13] The king's long and inclusive presentation (a sort of compromise between what Necker had recommended and what more conservative advisers wanted) might have been greeted with genuine enthusiasm at the beginning of May, but it was now too late. The members of the National Assembly were offended by the paternalistic tone and the king's concluding threat to proceed on his own to bring benefits to the nation should they "abandon" him. He then ordered the three estates to adjourn and to resume meeting separately the next day.

The Third Estate refused to move. They had already been joined by many more members of the clergy and had no intention of giving up the main points in contention, joint meetings of the three estates and the creation of the National Assembly. When the Master of Ceremonies ordered the Third Estate to leave the hall, Mirabeau thundered back, "I declare that if you have been ordered to make us leave you must seek orders to employ force, for we shall not leave except by the force of bayonets!"[14] Once again, the king's unwillingness to follow through meant that his initiative was thrown away. He did not order the expulsion of the deputies from the hall. The dramatic scene is now commemorated in a large bas relief that adorns the building where the French National Assembly meets.

Necker had ostentatiously absented himself from the Royal Session, and when it was over, the king discovered that Necker had submitted his resignation. Furious at Necker's disloyalty, the king nonetheless begged him to stay on as threatening crowds demonstrated at the royal palace in support of the popular minister. Necker remained, but the king felt compelled to order more troops toward Paris to guard against the threats of disorder. The Second Estate continued to vote against joining the National Assembly, but on June 25, forty-seven nobles abandoned their colleagues and, hoping to bring about conciliation, entered the hall of the National Assembly. On June 27, Louis XVI yielded and instructed the members of the first two estates who still held out to join the others in the National Assembly.

Celebrations over this outcome broke out in Versailles and Paris as many hoped the stalemate had been broken and the delegates could now get down to work. Arthur Young (an English visitor whose remark was given in the introduction to this book) wrote in his diary on June 27: "The whole business now seems over, and the revolution complete."[15] But, as we know, the Revolution was not over. At this stage, the distinctions between the orders were being preserved: nobles sat together and clergy sat together in the large hall. But many of the nobles were not reconciled to becoming members of the National Assembly. They declared that their electors had instructed them to maintain the separation of orders and they would have to return home to receive new instructions. Many nobles continued to meet as a separate order in the evenings instead of attending the meetings of the committees of the Assembly.

The next few days were filled with fear and uncertainty for the members of the National Assembly, who expected that they might be arrested or even killed. Rumors began to circulate that the government intended to use the troops they were assembling near Paris to shut down the Assembly. It is difficult to know exactly what the government's intentions were, in part because different factions at court recommended different expedients and because those who advocated aggressive measures, knowing how difficult it was to get the king to make a decision, were not sure whether they could convince him to take action. It seems likely that the king would have gone along with a plan to force the delegates to accept his proposals by treating the delegates as parlements had been treated previously. Some would have been arrested, others would have been persuaded to back the government, and the deputies might have been moved to another city. The king then could have put into place the program outlined at the Royal Session. Some opponents of the new Assembly might have wanted to go further than that. Although troops were being gathered for the ostensible purpose of putting down demonstrations in Paris or Versailles, many feared the troops would be used to close down the Assembly. But the actual orders issued to the commander of the troops in Paris were entirely defensive. Indeed, some of the troops were not scheduled to arrive in the area until July 18. The lack of clear purpose and planning is indicated by the fact that the government did not wait until the arrival of those troops to act.

The first step was taken on the night of Saturday, July 11, when Necker and three other ministers were dismissed. The Baron de Breteuil, a protégé of the queen, was named in Necker's place and Broglie became minister of war. Because the National Assembly did not meet on Sunday, the government doubtless hoped to forestall a hasty and intemperate response from the Assembly. On Monday cooler heads might prevail. But by Monday the situation had changed dramatically due to the actions of people in Paris, to the obvious surprise of the government. The news of Necker's dismissal reached Paris at midday on Sunday, July 12. The streets were full of people on their day of rest, and they reacted with violence.

THE FALL OF THE BASTILLE

Paris, with a population of about 650,000, was as large as the next nine French cities combined. The river Seine flowed through it from east to

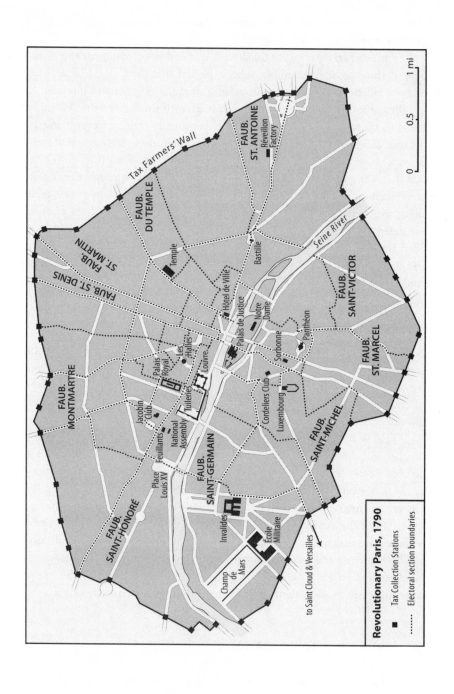

Revolutionary Paris, 1790

■ Tax Collection Stations

····· Electoral section boundaries

Tax Farmers' Wall

Seine River

FAUB. ST. ANTOINE
Réveillon Factory

FAUB. DU TEMPLE

FAUB. ST. MARTIN

FAUB. ST. DENIS

Temple

Bastille

Hôtel de Ville

Palais de Justice

Notre Dame

FAUB. SAINT-VICTOR

Panthéon

Sorbonne

FAUB. ST. MARCEL

Les Halles

Palais Royal

Louvre

Jacobin Club

Tuileries

Cordeliers Club

Luxembourg

FAUB. SAINT-MICHEL

Feuillants

National Assembly

FAUB. MONTMARTRE

Place Louis XV

FAUB. SAINT-GERMAIN

FAUB. SAINT-HONORÉ

Invalides

École Militaire

Champ de Mars

to Saint Cloud & Versailles

0   0.5   1 mi

west, and an island, the Île de la Cité, was the heart of the city, on which were located the Cathedral of Notre Dame, the law courts, and other official buildings. To the north of that, in the half of the city called the Right Bank was the Hôtel de Ville (the city hall) and further to the west the Louvre and the Tuileries, palaces where the kings of France had lived before Louis XIV moved to Versailles. To the south, on the Left Bank, was the university (called the Sorbonne) as well as a fashionable district with fine homes called the Faubourg (or neighborhood) Saint-Germain. Further west were located the military school and its parade ground, the Champ de Mars. The Farmers-General were encircling the rapidly expanding city with a new wall punctuated with gates to make tax collection easier. Trades tended to concentrate in different areas of the city, and the workers in those trades lived nearby, thus giving each area a distinctive character. Market-women lived near the central markets (Les Halles) on the Right Bank. North of that was the chief commercial district with many people who worked at home (such as ribbonmakers). Further to the north were some large textile factories, employing several hundred people. To the east, the Faubourg Saint-Antoine contained many workers in furnishing and woodworking as well as some large factories that made glass products and brewed beer.

In the eighteenth century, few workers were employed in factories. About a third of the male workers in Paris labored in commerce and crafts organized along traditional lines. An apprentice would learn his trade by working with a master. After several years, he would become a journeyman, who generally worked alongside the master for several more years until he could reach the level of master himself, if he had the money and connections to do so. Masters owned their shops, oversaw the workers, and sold the goods produced. The trades were organized into guilds and corporations, which upheld standards and maintained discipline among the practitioners of the mechanical arts (called artisans). Guilds were granted exclusive privileges by the king to carry out their craft in a particular area and set the standards for mastership. The sharp modern distinction between the owner of the factory and the worker did not exist in this system. Journeymen often lived with the master, though this was becoming less common. A source of discontent in the eighteenth century was that access to mastership was becoming more difficult, and journeymen were forced to remain in that status not just for a few years, but frequently for life.

The city teemed with other kinds of workers as well. Many were employed as manual workers for wages (for example, dock workers or porters). A constant stream of immigrants from the overpopulated countryside replenished the population and provided workers. Some of these were seasonal laborers who went home for the harvest and the winter. One example was construction workers from the area of Limoges, whose name (*limousins*) became synonymous with masons. Vast numbers of servants (male and female) were employed by rich nobles and bourgeois, as well as by more modest inhabitants of the city. Peddlers, often women, sold innumerable items on the streets. The very poorest lived off the charity of the city and the church or, when times got tough, turned to begging, crime, and prostitution.

The government feared this urban population could easily turn to violence, so a police system was maintained in Paris, including 150 members of the city watch and around 1,000 men in the Paris Guard. Serious trouble would require calling on the military, especially the 3,600 members of the French Guards, a supposedly elite army unit, which (unlike most of the rest of the army) was not routinely moved from post to post. The French Guards, permanently based in Paris, had over time begun to identify with the people of Paris. The soldiers married Parisian women and, in their spare time, worked at civilian occupations to compensate for poor pay. Attempts to professionalize and shape up the soldiers (common policy in the years before the Revolution) caused resentment among these troops. And they became more restive as they were asked to put down demonstrations by citizens.

The population of Paris had supported the parlement by demonstrations in the fall of 1787. More serious disruptions occurred in the spring of 1788, when the price of bread began to rise dramatically. Riots demanding lower prices for bread were the traditional reasons for urban disorders in the Ancien Régime because bread constituted the most important part of the diet. To make sure that the people of Paris were supplied with bread, the government requisitioned grain from the countryside and regulated the sale of bread. This elaborate system could not withstand the serious disruptions caused by crop failure, which led to higher prices and widespread famine. In 1787 the crops had not been good. In 1788, the crops failed catastrophically. By summer of 1789, much of the supply of grain stored over the winter had already been eaten, and famine threatened everywhere. In the eighteenth century the average worker spent 50 percent of his daily wage on bread. In 1788, the price of bread consumed 58 percent of his wages, and at the height of the famine in 1789, 88 percent. The high cost of bread meant that workers could not afford other commodities, such as wine or clothing or fuel. High bread prices, therefore, contributed to an economic downturn because people did not have money left to spend on anything else, thus causing unemployment in many industries. Many people blamed the economic downturn on the government for signing a treaty with England in 1786 that reduced customs duties between the two countries. The competition from cheaper British goods made unemployment in the textile industry worse, but it was not the main cause of the economic crisis. Contributing further to the plight of poor people, the winter of 1788–1789 was exceptionally cold.

In the spring and summer of 1789, throughout the country perhaps as many as three hundred incidents of attacks on markets, bakeries, and granaries occurred. The most serious event in Paris was the Réveillon riots in late April. Réveillon, the owner of a wallpaper factory, employed around 350 workers. Known as a compassionate employer who paid high wages and who helped his laid-off workers during the winter of 1788–1789 by giving them unemployment pay, Réveillon was frustrated by the economic downturn and the high cost of bread, which forced wages up, further hurting his business. At a meeting of electors, he was supposed to have remarked on the advisability of lowering the price of bread so that wages could also be lowered.

Misunderstanding his remarks and thinking that he advocated lower wages, crowds attacked and looted his factories and his home and those of another factory owner who had made similar comments. Significantly, Réveillon's own employees did not join in these riots. Troops were sent to disperse the widening circle of violence and managed to put an end to the riots at the cost of considerable loss of life. The French Guards had obeyed orders, but resented being blamed for letting the riot get out of control. After the riots, the government began to order more troops to the Paris region to keep order in an increasingly disruptive city.

Hunger, of course, did not abate, and the traditional bread riot became even more serious because it was occurring at a time of political crisis. The elections to the Estates General taking place in Paris in April and May encouraged people to hope that the delegates and the king would work together to find solutions to the many problems. But the disappointing stalemate at Versailles made the people in Paris suspect that the aristocrats were using their power to prevent better conditions and to enrich themselves by high prices in grain. The movements of troops and the dismissal of Necker seemed proof that this was true. Their resentments were further stirred up by political discussions in the city. A center of agitation was a fashionable public area built by the Duc d'Orléans at his palace, the Palais Royal, on the Right Bank. The large open space was surrounded by a grand building with arcaded galleries containing shops of all kinds, bookstores, theaters, and cafés. People congregated there for shopping and amusement, but also to debate the latest news, read political pamphlets, and listen to inflammatory speakers. The groups at the Palais Royal discussing political questions had been growing larger over the summer, and they now tried to get the troops in Paris to side with them and with the Third Estate. Much of this political activity was financed by the immensely wealthy Duc d'Orléans, a descendant of Louis XIV's brother, and thus a distant cousin of the king. His great-grandfather had served as Regent during the minority of Louis XV. Orléans appeared to be planning a similar role for himself as the real power behind the throne should Louis XVI prove incapable of solving the political crisis. Already prominent as an opponent of despotism, the Duc d'Orléans used his money to promote the cause of the Third Estate and to finance the work of political agitators in Paris.

When the news of Necker's dismissal reached Paris at around noon on July 12, crowds gathered at the Palais Royal to listen to speakers urge them to action (one of these was Camille Desmoulins). Demonstrators marched through town with the busts of Necker and Orléans. They forced theaters (considered dangerously aristocratic) to close down. The crowds attacked the hated customs barriers (half of the price of wine was taxes) to burn records and to make the tax collectors abandon their posts. Various rumors circulated that Paris was to be attacked by the army and that the city was mined. That night, crowds ransacked a monastery looking for grain and began to search the city for arms to defend themselves, raiding gun shops and sword makers and grabbing guns at the Invalides (the home for wounded veterans). After the first encounters, the military commander in Paris, Besenval, maintaining his troops on the defensive, had withdrawn the cavalry to the Champ de Mars, and the French Guards had begun to fraternize with and join the crowds.

Unable to count on the authorities to preserve order, those men who had served as Third Estate electors now hurriedly reconvened in their districts and called on Parisians to organize a citizen militia. Delegates from each of the electoral districts created a municipal government that met at the Hôtel de Ville. Those who joined the militia needed arms so the search for weapons continued on the thirteenth. And on the fourteenth, the crowd—still searching for arms—captured the Bastille, an imposing old fortress that served as a prison. The fall of the Bastille became a symbol of the Revolution, and its anniversary is still celebrated in France (equivalent to the American Fourth of July).

Conservatives ridicule the fall of the Bastille for demonstrating the futility of the revolutionaries' aims. The Bastille was scheduled for demolition anyway, and this symbol of despotism actually contained only seven prisoners: four had been jailed for forgery, two were lunatics, and one was an aristocrat whose father had wanted him put away for bad behavior. To conservatives it seems a fitting comment on the delusion of the revolutionaries that the great symbol of the fall of despotism contained only these seven prisoners. For those on the political left, on the other hand, the Bastille symbolizes the entry of the people on the revolutionary scene and the defeat of the despotic power of the monarchy, which could throw individuals into such prisons by *lettres de cachet*. The fall of the Bastille was the first great *journée* (day) of the Revolution, which would be dotted by other days on which the people rose up to keep the Revolution from being defeated.

Who were these people who took over the Bastille? The historian George Rudé, who analyzed the lists of the people who later received medals as "conquerors of the Bastille," discovered that most were inhabitants of the Faubourg Saint-Antoine, just to the east of the Bastille. The guns of the fortress looked out over that neighborhood. Detractors said they were vagrants and criminals, but Rudé identified the people who attacked the Bastille as workers from Parisian workshops. The list included "49 joiners, 48 cabinet-makers, 41 locksmiths, 28 cobblers, 20 sculptors and modellers, 11 metal-chasers, 10 turners, 10 hairdressers and wigmakers, 7 potters, 9 monumental masons, 9 nailsmiths, 9 dealers in fancy ware, 8 printers, 7 braziers, 9 founders, 5 jewellers, 5 goldsmiths, 5 stove-makers, and 3 upholsterers." There were also people engaged in trade and manufacturing, including "11 wine-merchants, 3 café-proprietors, 2 innkeepers, 21 shopkeepers, 9 hatters, 3 manufacturers, 4 businessmen, 6 gardeners, 3 carpenters, and 7 stonemasons." Unskilled workers were in a minority. One of the conquerors was a woman, a laundress from the Faubourg Saint-Marcel. Rudé was unable to ascertain the occupations of all of those who died (fewer than one hundred, though the exact number is not known).[16]

The image of the heroic people saving the Revolution by conquering the Bastille often neglects a key question: How did these artisans and workers manage to overawe a fortress with two walls (the inner one nine feet thick), eight towers, drawbridges, cannon, and a garrison of professional soldiers? The governor of the Bastille, Bernard-René Jourdan de Launey, without clear orders outlining what he should do, tried to negotiate at first and defended the fortress only halfheartedly. Many of those in the crowd were members of the hastily created militia, who had been able to get weapons. But most important was the presence of about one hundred French Guard and regular army troops who had two cannons and who knew how to use them. Instead of holding out, the governor of the Bastille eventually surrendered it to the crowd. He and his garrison were arrested and taken to the Hôtel de Ville. On the way some of them were killed by the crowds, and at the Hôtel de Ville, Launey was murdered and his head paraded on a pike around the city.

The failure of the authorities to use the forces of order effectively is key to understanding the events of the summer of 1789. One observer at the time wrote: "The defection of the army is not one of the causes of the Revolution, it is the Revolution itself."[17] The officers, demoralized by the changes in the army, disappointed by the failures in foreign policy, and out of touch with their own troops, lost confidence in them. The French Guards stationed in Paris had already refused to put down demonstrating crowds in late June and then went over to the crowds in large numbers in July. Troops from distant garrisons had been brought to the Paris area, but they too became infected with revolutionary ideas. Their officers did not trust them to re-establish order, and this in turn demoralized those troops who might have obeyed loyally. Furthermore, it is unlikely that enough men were present to put down a widespread uprising in a city as large as Paris. On the night of July 14, after learning of the fall of the Bastille, Besenval ordered the troops in Paris to retreat to Sèvres.

When Louis XVI learned what had happened in Paris and asked what his options were, Broglie (the recently appointed minister of war) informed him that he could not count on the loyalty of the troops. The only other option was flight, but Broglie again could not guarantee the king's safety, and flight would have led to civil war. In 1792, Louis confessed to a close associate that he had missed his last good opportunity to flee: "Ah, we are in private and can talk freely. I know everybody blames me for weakness and indecision, but nobody has ever been before in a position like mine. . . . I know that I missed my chance on 14 July; I should have left then."[18] The king, who always hesitated to use force against his subjects, gave in and accepted the creation of the National Assembly. He announced that the troops would be withdrawn, went to mass, wrote a last will and testament, and made a visit to Paris on July 17.

By then important changes had occurred in the city. A new Parisian government, organized around the electoral districts, had created a force of citizen soldiers, called the National Guard, to ensure order and protect property. Many members of the French Guards now joined this military force. The new Parisian authorities named Lafayette as the commander of the National Guard. They also chose a new mayor, Bailly, an astronomer who had been elected to the Estates General and who had become famous because he happened to be president of the National Assembly at the time of the Tennis Court Oath. When Louis XVI arrived in Paris, Bailly enigmatically declared that Henry IV had reconquered Paris, and that now Paris had conquered its king. The king reviewed the National Guard and agreed to wear their new symbol, the tricolor cockade, a circle of ribbon bringing

Figure 3.1. Farewell Bastille. During the Revolution, commentary on events was often expressed through cartoons or allegorical images. In this one, as workmen demolish the Bastille, a commoner stands next to a tamed lion, symbolizing the monarchy. Attached to the commoner's leg is a string on which are suspended figures representing the other two estates, the clergy and the nobility. He is forcing them to dance to his tune, played on a bagpipe. Notice the tricolor cockade on the brim of his hat. Courtesy of the Division of Rare and Manuscript Collections, Cornell University Library.

together the colors of Paris, red and blue, with the royal white. From now on Paris would play a central role in events. And royal authority had effectively ended in the city.

THE NIGHT OF AUGUST 4

The events in Paris had immense repercussions throughout the country and transformed the political equation at Versailles. Municipal governments were created in most of the major cities, and support for the National Assembly in the political struggles intensified throughout the country. National Guards were set up in many towns and began to correspond with each other to help preserve order and to stand ready to protect the National Assembly should that become necessary. At Versailles, those delegates who had been considering compromise with the royal government now had no reason to do so. On July 17, the National Assembly renamed itself the National Constituent Assembly, signifying that they intended to write a constitution for France. Necker was recalled to office, and the Comte d'Artois, whose policy had failed and who feared the vengeance of those who had won, left the country, thus becoming the first *émigré*, as those who left the country in opposition to the Revolution were called. The political changes did not bring peace immediately. Hunger still caused suspicion and violence. On July 22, crowds in Paris assassinated two royal officials who were accused of preventing grain from reaching the city. The consequences of hunger were even greater in the countryside because the disruptions there led to what has been called "the abolition of feudalism" on the night of August 4.

Peasants constituted about 80 percent of the population. Great variation existed in their economic status. Between one-quarter and one-third of peasants owned the land they farmed. However, the true measure of your ability to make a living was not the amount of land you owned, but the amount you could rent from noble or bourgeois property owners or from the church. At the top of the economic ladder were farmers who controlled enough land that they could sublet to others and had considerable surplus to sell. Others, known as *laboureurs*, were self-sufficient farmers. They were doing well in the eighteenth century because the booming population meant a rise in agricultural prices. But most peasants struggled to make ends meet. They had insufficient land or worked as sharecroppers on the land of others. And the worst off were those with no access to land, who had nothing to depend upon but their own labor. Agriculture in the south of France still relied on the inefficient two-field system of cultivation, in which one field was planted while another was left fallow to renew its fertility. In the north, the more efficient three-field system prevailed (one field was fallow while two others were cultivated). But nonetheless, this method of agriculture required extensive land.

The rise of population meant not only that prices rose, but that more people competed for employment and wages fell. Some tried to make extra money by cottage industry, but that income was hurt because of the economic downturn in the late 1780s. Desperately poor people then turned to crime. In the famine conditions of the spring of 1789, criminals and beggars added to the numbers of people already roaming the countryside: peddlers, wandering workers looking for employment, and seasonal migrants moving from one job to another. Peasants always feared the people passing through their districts, and in the summer of 1789, they especially worried about the safety of their crops, still in the field and not quite ready for harvest. As early as June 18, an intendant warned about the problem of protecting the ripening crops: "The whole question revolves around the awful fear that the harvest might be pillaged either before it is properly ready or else once it has been gathered. . . . It is all too certain that attacks of this sort have been planned . . . and all the local farmers are in a terrible state of fear—indeed we must prepare to meet this dread eventuality whilst yet pretending to believe that it does not exist."[19] The peasants were defenseless against these criminals because they were not armed. Nobles enjoyed a monopoly of hunting, and therefore guns were not allowed to peasants.

Peasants resented the requisitions that the government carried out in order to supply the populations of the cities, and they (like city dwellers) feared that conspiracies existed to deprive them of the food they needed. Brigands, they thought, had been hired by aristocrats to steal their grain. The peasants, too, had greeted the calling of the Estates General with great hopefulness that the injustices they lived under would be remedied. They had demanded in their *cahiers* that taxes be reduced and that the privileges of the nobles be abolished. When the Estates General did not solve those problems immediately, they believed that aristocrats were pressuring the king to prevent these needed reforms and that the aristocrats were trying to impose their will by starving the country people into submission. Indeed, many peasants assumed that they were no longer obligated to pay taxes. Throughout the country, tax collectors had difficulty doing their jobs in the spring and summer of 1789.

Peasants owed royal taxes, but they also owed various payments to their lords and to the church (the tithe). In some areas, peasants began to attack the homes of their lords to burn the record books where feudal obligations were written down and to recover guns that had been confiscated from them. After the fall of the Bastille, the rumors of aristocratic plots became more widespread. Nobles were hoarding grain, it was widely believed, and brigands in the pay of the nobles would soon come to destroy the peasants' grain before it ripened. The Comte d'Artois and his associates would return from exile with foreign troops, they feared. Peasants believed that the nobles had no intention of cooperating with the Third Estate but were merely biding their time until they could counterattack. As in Paris, then, the disorders in the countryside were caused by a combination of famine and politics—and fear.

All of these problems culminated at the end of July in a strange event called the Great Fear. The news spread quickly from one place to the next that brigands had arrived and were attacking homes and crops. No longer merely anticipating the attacks, people were now convinced that attacks were occurring. Peasants fleeing the supposed brigands spread the rumors even further, and measures taken by authorities for protection lent credence to the belief. The historian Georges Lefebvre traced the path of this Great Fear, as it spread into many (but not all) sections of the country. Unable to verify the truth of these rumors, people believed that brigands in the pay of aristocrats had indeed been let loose on the countryside. The rumors of violence apparently sprang from the attacks the peasants themselves had carried out on the homes of their lords or from gangs of peasants who tried to arm themselves to resist the threatening brigands. Without modern means of communication and verification, people in the Revolution were constantly swayed by unsubstantiated rumors. The peasants genuinely believed they were under attack, and the result was a widespread panic.

Members of the National Assembly (many of whom owned the property and privileges that the peasants were attacking) felt compelled to do something to prevent the country from sinking into chaos. Like the peasants, they were also prey to fears based on rumors and unsubstantiated reports that pictured the situation to be far graver than it actually was. From August 4 to August 5, the National Assembly met through the night in a long session in which they were carried away by mass enthusiasm to reform the system of privilege. The National Assembly tried to calm the violence in the countryside by addressing the issues raised by the peasants in their *cahiers*, but went much further in the process of reform than they had intended to, sweeping away all the vestiges of feudalism.

When they said that they had done away with feudalism, what did they mean? Feudalism, the medieval economic and social system, no longer really existed, but significant remnants of it had important consequences. The word itself comes from the word "fief." In the hierarchical system of the Middle Ages when land was the only source of wealth, a vassal received land from his lord in the form of a fief. The lord enjoyed several kinds of privileges. The French word for lord is *seigneur*, so this system is often called the seigneurial system.

Seigneurial privileges were of three kinds. The first, honorific privileges, refers to symbolic things that indicated the lord's status. He held special pews in church, had the right to erect weather vanes, and could use a coat of arms. The second category can be called jurisdictional rights. Lords exercised judicial authority on the local level, presiding over courts to which local disputes and crimes were brought. The third category is that of "useful" rights, all of which conferred a distinct advantage to the lords and were sources of contention to the peasants. The lord's exclusive right to hunt meant that the peasants found it difficult to supplement their food with game, and they also complained that the lords did not sufficiently keep in check the animal populations that damaged their crops. Also disturbing was that the hunters might trample the crops, which were threatened as well by the pigeons that lords had the exclusive right to raise. The lords enjoyed a monopoly over the village mill, oven, and wine press, which peasants were required to patronize and pay for (these privileges were known as *banalités*).

Another part of the lord's useful rights included dues of various descriptions that were paid either in cash or in kind and that were based on land. A lord, as owner of the fief, did not exploit it all. He controlled only the domain. Peasants held the rest. They owned their land, which they could sell or pass on to their heirs. They were peasant proprietors. But one of the conditions of ownership was that they pay the lord an annual fee called a *cens* (quitrent). If the property changed hands by inheritance or sale, the peasant then owed the lord a fee called *lods et ventes*, which could be a considerable amount. The dues peasants had to pay varied greatly from place to place. Although almost all nobles had fiefs and collected these fees, not all fiefs were in the possession of nobles. Rich commoners had been able to buy noble property and the rights and privileges that went with it. Thus many seigneurial fees were owed to rich bourgeois or to the church.

Most peasants in France, then, were not really serfs. Unlike serfs in Eastern Europe, they could dispose of their property and they were free to move about. Serfdom as it survived in France consisted primarily of some peasants who were under a *mainmorte*. If a peasant under a *mainmorte* died without having a child living at home with him, his property reverted to the lord. This was the kind of serfdom that the National Assembly especially targeted on August 4.

The Assembly's Constitutional Committee had presented a rather limited report on July 27, summarizing the demands of the *cahiers*. But the ideas in the *cahiers* had been expressed long before the momentous changes of the summer. The idea to propose doing away with privileges apparently arose in the Breton Club, whose members believed that if privilege and corporatism were done away with, then the constitution they intended to write could bring about a more decided break with the past. They could thus solve the problem of violence in the countryside and create a basis for a new constitution at the same time. In order to get the Assembly to unite behind this project, the sacrifices would have to be voluntary rather than imposed. They wanted a great landowner to volunteer to give up his seigneurial fees in return for compensation, in hopes that others would then imitate him.

As often happened in the Revolution, things did not go as planned. When the first speaker (actually not the great landowner they had designated, but a nobleman nonetheless) made such a proposal, the Assembly reacted so enthusiastically to the idea, that soon others were coming forward to renounce privileges as well. The session continued through the night, as sacrifices of all kinds were made by people from all over the country and from all three orders. One observer noted that the meeting was "a combat of generosity between the first two orders and that of the commons."[20] Swept away were the tithe, seigneurial rights, seigneurial courts, municipal and provincial privileges, and venality of office. Another observer said the Assembly had been carried away by "patriotic delirium."[21] Privilege as an organizing principle of society was never again revived.

The men who took part in the session of August 4–5 were imbued with a sense of new purpose and patriotism. But as they began to enact legislation to carry out the vast changes that they had so heartily acclaimed, they discovered that they did not always agree and that, in the sober light of day, they had some doubts about how far they wanted to go. The decree passed on August 11, instituting what had been done on the night of August 4, began by declaring boldly the abolition of "the feudal regime entirely." But the decree abolished without indemnity only "feudal and *censuel* rights and dues deriving from real or personal *mainmorte* and personal servitude." It prudently decreed that other feudal dues based on land were property rights, and the owners were to be compensated for their loss.[22]

The most contentious issue was the suppression of the tithe. The clergy tried in vain to save this source of income, but eventually were forced to accept the promise of the Assembly that the nation would support the church. On August 12, the Assembly created an Ecclesiastical Committee.

Figure 3.2.   **Three estates forging the new constitution. Figures representing the nobility, the Third Estate, and the clergy are pictured hammering out the new constitution on a blacksmith's forge. This engraving expresses the hopeful attitude of the early Revolution that the three estates could cooperate. Courtesy of the Division of Rare and Manuscript Collections, Cornell University Library.**

The church, previously a powerful and independent corporation within French society, was losing its special status and becoming subject to interference from others, and the results would ultimately prove to be momentous.

The transformations enshrined in the August decree included responses to complaints frequently mentioned in the *cahiers*, notably, doing away with the nobility's exclusive rights to keep pigeons and to hunt. Seigneurial justice was abolished. Venality of office was to be suppressed, with compensation. They declared that all citizens were eligible for all offices, thus ending the nobility's monopoly over the higher positions in the government and the army. Taxation was to be equal, and special privileges of provinces and towns were annulled in order to create equality and uniformity across the nation. These wide-ranging changes would take some time to organize. Until the compensation amounts were set, people were told to keep paying their dues and carrying out their jobs. But many peasants took matters into their own hands, refusing from then on to pay dues.

Violence over seigneurial obligations continued and eventually led to their complete elimination without compensation. But that decision was still a long way off.

CONCLUSION

The night of August 4 definitely marked the end of the Ancien Régime. The old system of privileges and corporatism had been done away with. The Assembly now had to write a constitution for France based on new principles. The debates over what form the new constitution would take and what those principles would be consumed their attention for the next two years. Nobody had foreseen this outcome when the king initially made the call for elections to the Estates General. The elections themselves, the struggles over the organization of the Estates General, and the violence of the summer of 1789 had transformed the political landscape. The creation of a National Assembly raised the expectations of French people, who now believed that this group would take charge and solve their problems. The people of Paris, convinced that they had saved the Revolution, saw an expanded role for themselves in the future and expected that they would be consulted. The delegates, too, came to endorse the idea that the people had saved them from the hostile designs of the king and his aristocratic advisers. The delegates' sense of purpose had been transformed by their successful creation of the National Assembly and especially by the excitement of the night of August 4. They now had a much larger vision of their responsibilities and of the possibilities for the future. Even more changes were in store over the next two years, as the Assembly tried to carry out its new task and the people became more and more involved in the political life of the nation. Of course, reorganizing the country on entirely new bases proved more difficult than the exultant revolutionaries of August 1789 had expected. Later, one of those revolutionaries, Théodore de Lameth, wrote, "Not a man understood the Revolution nor reckoned its course, nor gave the least thought to the external obstacles it would have to overcome."[23]

4

CREATING THE NEW REGIME

After their fateful decision to abolish the Ancien Régime on the night of August 4, the deputies now faced the considerable challenge of creating a new order to replace it. Imbued with a new sense of mission, the deputies approached their task with confidence that they could do more than merely reform the abuses of the Ancien Régime. They intended to create an entirely new government. By renaming itself the National Constituent Assembly, the Assembly had asserted that its primary purpose was to write a constitution for France. But the debates over what should be included revealed old tensions and resentments in French society that the Ancien Régime had held in check. The struggle over the shape of the new government deepened the divisions among political groups and made success more difficult to achieve.

THE DECLARATION OF THE
RIGHTS OF MAN AND CITIZEN

On July 11, Lafayette, inspired by declarations of rights in American state constitutions, had introduced a plan for a declaration of rights to be put at the head of the French constitution. Immediately objections were raised that such an exposition ought to follow rather than precede the writing of the document. Abstract rights might be dangerous, it was argued, and would limit necessary compromises in creating a constitution. However, many deputies were convinced that an even greater danger had been revealed in July, when it seemed that the Assembly itself might be shut down. They thought it would be wise to publish a list outlining their goals that would survive even if the Assembly did not. The issue of where the declaration would appear and what it would say was referred to the Constitutional Committee. On July 27, that committee recommended that a declaration of rights be placed at the head of the constitution and that it be, in the words of Mounier, "short, simple, and precise" to leave room for necessary modifications. The idea of an accompanying declaration of duties was narrowly defeated on the morning of August 4.

After completing the August 4 decrees, the Assembly took up the declaration again, working to reconcile the many drafts that had been proposed. On August 26, the Assembly accepted provisionally the Declaration of the Rights of Man and Citizen. They intended to return to the Declaration after the constitution had been completed, but by that time, the Declaration had already assumed a symbolic significance in French political life that made it impossible to change. The seventeen articles were reproduced and circulated, they were included in illustrated prints, and they were displayed reverentially in people's houses.

The Declaration of the Rights of Man and Citizen has been criticized as abstract, and therefore dangerous, because it is not rooted in the realities of France's history and institutions. And, indeed, a comparison to the American Declaration of Independence reveals how much more abstract the French Declaration is. Americans listed specific grievances against the king of England and protested that their rights as Englishmen had been violated.[1] The French, of course, launched no invectives against their king because they intended to set up a constitutional monarchy under Louis XVI. The first article seems especially drafted to provide for monarchy and nobility. Instead of saying simply that all men are equal, the first article stated, "Men are born and remain free and equal in rights. Social distinctions can be based only on public utility."[2] They declared that the "natural and imprescriptible rights of man" are "liberty, property, security, and resistance to oppression." Law was defined as the "expression of the general will," and, the document insisted, "all citizens have the right to participate personally, or through their representatives, in its formation." The Declaration insisted also on a separation of powers. It guaranteed that an individual would be considered innocent until proven guilty, that there would be freedom of speech and of opinion, that taxation would be equal, and that all citizens would be eligible for public offices. It outlined a program of national (rather than royal) sovereignty, equality before the law (rather than privilege), and uniformity (rather than diversity) of institutions. Individual rights were guaranteed, and the corporate social order of the Ancien Régime was destroyed. Indeed, the attack on corporatism was so thorough that the Declaration did not even mention the right to assemble peaceably, a key right in the later American Bill of Rights.

By drafting the Declaration of the Rights of Man in terms of the universal rights of man, rather than in terms of the rights of Frenchmen, the National Assembly made the ideas in this document accessible and influential. Anybody contemplating revolution or new constitutional arrangements could find inspiration in it, because it did not claim that these rights pertained only to the French. Yet, despite the seeming universality, much of the Declaration was, in fact, a direct response to the recent history of France. When they declared that "the source of all sovereignty resides essentially in the nation," they were asserting the right of the nation to rule itself, rather than to be ruled by an absolute king. The declaration of "careers open to talent" stood as a repudiation of the exclusion of commoners from positions under the Ancien Régime. The emphasis on imprisonment and prosecution only for breaking a specific law was a response to *lettres de cachet* by which the king could jail people without having to bring them to court. Freedom of speech reversed the system of censorship that had long existed. The guarantees of equality of taxation and consent to taxation were responses to the issues that led to the calling of the Estates General.

The ease with which the deputies came to agreement on the Declaration indicates that these principles were now widely accepted in French society and were not the exclusive goals of one social group or one interest group. The ideas in the Declaration had become commonplace assumptions about the way political life should function. The exception was the question of religion. Some objected to the guarantee of religious freedom, arguing that the basis of all sound society was religion and that the traditional importance of the Catholic Church should be maintained in the new constitution. The clerical deputies, already unhappy at the way the tithes had been swept away, were upset at the anti-clerical pronouncements from those who advocated complete freedom of religion. The anti-clericalism of many of the deputies had been heightened by the struggles over the organization of the Estates General when the First Estate had joined the Second in resisting the demands of the Third Estate. What emerged in Article 10 was a compromise: "No one must be disturbed because of his opinions, even in religious matters, provided their expression does not trouble the public order established by law." Still, the Declaration, though not explicitly anti-religious or anti-Catholic, gave more freedom to other religions than had the Ancien Régime. By downplaying the role of religion, the deputies had inadvertently set the stage for further religious controversy and had alienated many clerical deputies who had previously been supporters of the Revolution.

The stress on order in Article 10 reflected the concern that deputies had in August 1789 with disruptions throughout the country. Indeed, the background of violence in the summer of 1789 helps to explain the emphasis in this document on obedience to law. They did not want declarations of freedom to lead to chaos.

THE DEVELOPMENT OF FACTIONS

The spirit of concord and shared purpose in the Assembly after the night of August 4 did not survive when the deputies began to debate specific provisions of the new constitution. Divisions continued to exist in the country at large as well. The first wave of émigrés to leave the country had followed the Duc d'Artois into exile, but people who shared their hostility to the recent changes still remained inside France. In the countryside, although the violence of late July had subsided and the news of August 4 had been greeted with delight, conflicts arose over dues and tithes when some peasants declined to pay them because they believed they had been completely abolished. The problems of famine had not yet been solved. Although the harvest was in, grain still needed to be ground. The high price of bread continued, and bakers and alleged hoarders were frequently attacked by famished crowds. Political questions and bread riots again threatened to converge as the National Assembly began drafting the new constitution.

Immediately after voting for the Declaration of the Rights of Man, the deputies took up two important issues: whether there would be a two-house legislature, and what the relationship of the king to the legislature would be (the royal veto). Debate over these questions took place in an increasingly acrimonious and chaotic atmosphere. The National Assembly was too large for a legislature, and especially too large for a constitutional convention. The Estates General had not been designed as a deliberative body. It had been envisioned as a broadly representative accumulation of people to give support to the reforms of the royal government and to present petitions to the king. But its size became a problem when it was transformed into the National Constituent Assembly. Speakers had trouble making themselves heard. Because the sessions were open to the public, observers (despite rules forbidding it) applauded, cheered, or jeered as they listened to discussions. Their responses could have a significant impact on the deliberations, as deputies feared to take unpopular positions.

By contrast, the British House of Commons (a much smaller body) met in a room too small to accommodate all of those eligible to attend. The members had no problems hearing or debating in those intimate quarters. The American Constitutional Convention, with only fifty-five members (representing, to be sure, a much smaller population than France's), met in private, and the participants pledged not to reveal the content of their deliberations until the constitution was finished. They also agreed that no part of the constitution would be considered permanent until the entire document was completed, thus allowing members to change their minds or negotiate compromises. The American constitution was finished in about four months. The French labored on their constitution for two years. Compromise became difficult as different groups became identified with certain parts of the document.

Because writing the constitution took so long, the Constituent Assembly had to function not only as a constituent body, writing a permanent founding document that was supposed to represent the will of the sovereign people, but also as an ordinary legislature, making laws that might be changed later. It was difficult to maintain a clear distinction between measures that had constitutional weight and those that were mere laws that could be changed by the legislature. Everything that emerged from the National Assembly, no matter how trivial, took on the aura of the will of the nation, and anybody who opposed a measure might be seen as unpatriotic, anti-revolutionary, or treasonous.

Because the two privileged orders were meeting with the Third Estate, a sizable group of more conservative deputies could make their views felt in the Assembly. No longer sitting according to the Estate by which they had been elected, deputies began to group themselves by political point of view. Radical deputies took up the habit of sitting to the left of the presiding officer's desk. Conservatives distinguished themselves by sitting on the right. These seating arrangements gave the terms "right" and "left" to our political language. On the extreme right were deputies who wanted a return to the Ancien Régime or to the program Louis XVI had given in the Royal Session of June 23. Others, though not that conservative, wanted change to come about slowly.

During August and September, conservatives organized more effectively than radicals. A group known as the "Monarchiens" assumed leadership. The prominent members of this conservative faction were men such as Mounier, Lally-Tolendal, and Malouet, who supported the Revolution but wished to preserve a strong role for the king. Mounier and Lally-Tolendal were members of the Constitutional Committee. The majority of that Committee wanted the new constitution to give the king an absolute veto over legislation, whereas the two radicals on the committee, Sieyès and

Le Chapelier, wanted no royal veto at all. Attempts at compromise (including a meeting organized by Lafayette at the home of the American minister to France, Thomas Jefferson) failed. The Assembly, therefore, had to decide the question when the Committee presented its report at the end of August.

The debate on the veto and the legislature lasted almost two weeks. The Monarchiens, believing that a strong central government was important to prevent chaos and inspired in part by the example of the British system and by the attempted reforms of royal ministers in France in the 1770s and 1780s, wanted a two-house legislature (the upper house to be called a Senate) with a king who would have veto power over legislation. Radicals or Patriots suspected that an upper house would be dominated by the nobility and would become oligarchic and hereditary. They feared giving the king too much power. The Monarchiens, on the other hand, worried that a one-chamber legislature could become despotic. They invoked Montesquieu's ideas of balance in government and argued as well that if a monarchical system was to work, they had to find institutions that the king would accept.

Sieyès advocated "one man, one vote" and continued the arithmetic argument that he had set forth in "What Is the Third Estate?" If fifty men in an upper chamber could block the will of a much larger lower house, then they could be thought of as a privileged group. Likewise, if the king could block the will of the Assembly, then he was also quite privileged. Sieyès argued that the Assembly, chosen by the people, should be the center of the nation's political life, and that neither the king nor the people should interfere with them.

On September 10, the Monarchien proposal to create a two-house legislature was overwhelmingly defeated 849–89 by the votes of those to the left and to the right of them. Radicals had no interest in creating a divided legislature after having just waged a fierce fight to bring together the three orders in the National Assembly. The extreme right feared that an upper house dominated by the king might forge a successful cooperation with the Third Estate, thus leaving the nobility out of power completely. Therefore, they voted for a one-house legislature in the hope that it would fail and that they might salvage something from the wreckage. On September 11, the absolute veto was defeated by a vote of 673 to 325. The compromise that emerged was a suspensive veto that allowed the king to delay legislation. If a law was passed by three assemblies in a row, it would become law over the king's veto. Some argued that a suspensive veto was more advantageous for the king because he would be more likely to use it than the more unpopular absolute veto. But under the system adopted, the king could delay legislation for as much as six years (legislators were to have two-year terms), which in a time of revolution or war might cause untoward delays and lead to serious difficulties. Although the Monarchiens had not prevailed, the radicals were unhappy with the suspensive veto also because the king could substantially affect legislation.

After their defeat on these measures, the Monarchiens resigned from the Constitutional Committee and a new committee was named. But the conservatives still had considerable support in the Assembly. At the end of September, Mounier was elected the presiding officer (a new president was elected every two weeks). The debate over the veto had intensified the factional divisions. Radicals became suspicious that moderates were actually anti-revolutionary. Royalists, on the other hand, became even less willing to go along with the direction that the Assembly was taking, especially since the views of the king were not being taken into account.

The role of Louis XVI in the creation of the constitution was problematic. Louis had insisted since the beginning of the Estates General that the deputies were to give advice but not to pass legislation without his involvement. He assumed that he would have a say in the creation of the constitution and that the people of France wanted him to do so. The members of the National Assembly, on the other hand, had come to view themselves as the embodiment of the general will of the nation. They would write the fundamental document and present it to the king for his acceptance. Louis bridled at his exclusion from the constitutional process. On September 18, he finally sent a message to the Assembly generally approving the August 4 decrees. He pointed out, however, that a few of the provisions would require renegotiating foreign treaties and he could not immediately approve them. Foreign affairs were the traditional province of the king, and Louis XVI intended to maintain his control in that area and uphold the sanctity of treaties. The Assembly replied curtly that he was to promulgate the decrees and not to comment on them. The rift between the two was papered over when Louis agreed to publish the decrees, and the Assembly promised to take his objections into consideration when they enacted the specific laws. But the king delayed promulgating the Declaration of Rights and the first constitutional provisions. At the beginning of October, the people of Paris once again intervened to break a stalemate between the king and the Assembly.

THE OCTOBER DAYS

The radicals in Paris followed the debates at Versailles with keen interest. They feared the king's veto would be used to destroy the Revolution. On

August 30, when the debate over the veto had just begun, a crowd decided to set off for Versailles to bring the king to Paris to get him away from what they believed were the bad influences of courtiers. The National Guard managed to stop the crowd at the outskirts of Paris. Meanwhile, agitation over food continued, with women playing a leading part. Increasingly desperate women tried to find a way of carrying out their traditional duties of procuring food and feeding their families. As the price of bread remained high, they began to attack carts carrying grain and threatened that they would become more involved in political affairs if their acute problems were not solved. The agitators at the Palais Royal, along with the many newspapers that had sprung up in Paris, once again fomented discontent.

Louis XVI responded to the threats of the radicals in Paris by calling troops to Versailles, which had only a small force to defend it. In the middle of September he ordered the Flanders Regiment (almost 1,100 soldiers) to come. Although the army was plagued by desertions during this period, this unit had exhibited good discipline, and its commanding officer had a reputation as a liberal nobleman. Once again rumors began to circulate that the troops were being called to roll back the Revolution by military force. Other rumors asserted that the king was to be spirited away from Versailles to a distant city from which aristocrats could more easily combat the Revolution. The cry in Paris was to bring the king to Paris.

On October 2, news reached Paris that the king's guard had given a banquet for the arriving Flanders Regiment on the previous evening (this was a customary practice when new troops arrived). At this banquet, according to reports, the soldiers drank a toast to the king (but not the nation), cheered the queen wildly, and trampled the tricolor cockade under foot. The soldiers donned the black colors of the Austrian monarchy or the white of the Bourbons instead. Whether the story of the trampling of the cockade is true or not, people in Paris believed it and, encouraged by radicals such as Marat and Desmoulins, interpreted it as evidence of an antirevolutionary conspiracy being hatched at Versailles.

Political concerns once again merged with hunger to produce a march on Versailles on October 5. That morning, a crowd of women (many from the city market, Les Halles) went to the Hôtel de Ville to demand bread. They also sought guns for the men who were with them. They stormed into the building and threatened the officials who, they charged, had done nothing to solve the problems of famine. To deflect them from pillaging the building, one of the victors of the Bastille (a man named Stanislas Maillard) urged the women to go to Versailles where they could ask the king and the Assembly for help. On their way, the women persuaded others to join them, so that when they arrived at Versailles in the evening they numbered close to seven thousand of all social ranks. They immediately entered the Assembly to mingle with the deputies and present their petition for bread and for punishment of the soldiers who had stomped on the cockade. The court, torn between the incompatible tactics of resistance, flight, or compromise, ultimately did nothing. The king had been out hunting when the news arrived of the approach of the crowds. He returned to the palace to meet with his advisers. Carriages were ordered, but the king refused to flee. Mounier, accompanied by a delegation of women, sought an audience with the king, begging Louis to accept the Declaration and the constitutional decrees. The king promised he would work on the food problems, and he told Mounier that he accepted the constitutional decrees.

In Paris, meanwhile, other groups of people were also setting off for Versailles. The members of the National Guard determined to head there. Their commander, Lafayette, and his staff harangued the Guard members in vain to give up this enterprise, but they insisted on making the march. Apparently deciding that the guards would be less dangerous under his command and that they might help maintain order in Versailles, Lafayette asked the city authorities to authorize the march to give a semblance of preserving legality and discipline, and at about 5 p.m. they headed out, some twenty thousand strong, including many civilians and two representatives of the Paris government. Not knowing whether they would encounter resistance along the way, Lafayette was relieved to reach Versailles close to midnight and find it relatively quiet. The National Guards of Paris and Versailles took up guard duty around the château, while the King's Bodyguard maintained the protection of the interior courtyards. The representatives of the Paris government who met with the king now informed him that he was expected to move to Paris. He made no reply to this demand.

The next morning, October 6, when the crowd, which had remained overnight at Versailles, assembled once again before the château, some of them found an unguarded entrance and swarmed into the building. The King's Bodyguard, with orders not to shoot, managed to hold them off long enough for Marie Antoinette to escape as the crowd invaded her room. Two bodyguards were killed, their heads placed on pikes and paraded back to Paris. Lafayette persuaded the National Guard to protect other guards who were being threatened with lynching. But even though the troops managed to get control of the interior of the palace, the crowd still filled an inner courtyard, demanding that the king come to Paris. Louis appeared on a balcony accompanied by the queen, his children, and Lafayette. When he promised to go to Paris, the crowd cried, "*Vive le roi!*" (Long live the king!). The bodyguards replaced their white ribbons with the tricolor cockade, and they too were cheered. But after the king's party had moved back inside, the crowd continued to murmur, now calling for the queen, who was disliked for being a foreigner and an opponent of the Revolution. Bravely, she walked onto the balcony with Lafayette and faced the hostile crowd. Unable to make himself heard above the din, Lafayette bowed down and kissed the queen's hand, a gesture that turned the shouted threats into cheers.

The demands that they go to Paris immediately continued unabated, however, and so preparations were made for the king and his family to travel to Paris, accompanied by a crowd that had grown to a large number (Lafayette estimated it at sixty thousand people) and by wagons full of flour from the store houses of Versailles. The crowd rejoiced that they were bringing back "the baker, the baker's wife, and the baker's boy." It took the procession six hours to make the twelve-mile trip to Paris. After speeches of welcome at the Hôtel de Ville, the royal family took up residence at the Tuileries Palace. Shortly afterward, the Constituent Assembly, declaring that they were inseparable from the king, also decided to move to Paris.

The events of October 5 and 6 are known as the October Days and are often celebrated as another example of the people of Paris interfering to protect the Revolution from destruction. Radicals saw the event as a triumph. The radical journalist Camille Desmoulins wrote that with both the king and the National Assembly in Paris "the channels of circulation are being cleared. The market is overflowing with sacks of grain, the national treasury is filling up, the corn-mills are turning, the traitors are fleeing, the priests are down trodden, the aristocrats are expiring, . . . the patriots have triumphed. . . . Paris will be the queen of cities."[3] Paris would now be able to watch over the king and the Assembly to make sure that progress continued to be made toward a radical revolution. The king had been forced to accept the Declaration of the Rights of Man and the first decisions on the constitution. Until that point, many historians argue, the Revolution might yet have been undermined by conservatives who opposed it. But after that, their chances of stopping the revolutionary changes were much less likely.

Despite Camille Desmoulins' assessment, the October Days were not a complete triumph for the left. It is true that a few conservatives resigned from the Constituent Assembly, eleven in October and thirty-seven more before the end of the year, thus giving the left somewhat more power in that body. However, moderates, shocked at the violence, were now more likely to support the right. Mounier resigned and went home, where he tried to call the provincial estates of Dauphiné to counter the democratic impulses that now seemed to dominate the National Assembly. The National Assembly responded by outlawing provincial assemblies based on the three orders. Having been threatened with violence for his political views, Mounier went into exile in Savoy in May 1790.

If we look at the political situation in Paris after the October Days, it is not as obvious that the left had won. The radicals in Paris, who had pushed for the march on Versailles to bring the king back, were also trying to undermine the municipal government. Bailly and Lafayette stood for order and cooperated with moderates. The National Guard worked constantly to put down disorder. The first target of the crowds on October 5, after all, had been the Hôtel de Ville. But Lafayette had managed to get control of the situation, at least to the extent of preventing one of the demands: that the king be deposed and a regency created. Lafayette and many others were convinced that the Duc d'Orléans had financed the operations and egged on the radicals' demands because he wanted to be regent. After the October Days, Lafayette pressured the Duc d'Orléans to leave the country, and, given a diplomatic mission to save face, Orléans left for London. Attempts were made to arrest Marat, whose incendiary newspaper *L'Ami du peuple* had been fomenting discontent against aristocrats and the city government. He managed to hide from the authorities for a while, but then sought refuge in England for a few months in the spring of 1790. Famine abated, radicals took cover, and for the next two years relative calm reigned in Paris.

The real winners in Paris appeared to be the forces of order, at least in the short term. But moving the king and the Assembly to Paris proved to be a fateful decision. In the long run, it made a successful constitutional government less likely. Although the members of the Assembly were debating, discussing, and compromising, and the king still had a great deal of potential influence, they now were subjected increasingly to the pressures of the crowds of Paris. Possibilities for meaningful debate and compromise were lessened considerably. The Assembly would be powerless to resist the crowds when they once again entered the political scene.

REORGANIZING THE NATION

The Constituent Assembly's move to Paris in late October delayed work on the Constitution. The delegates met in temporary quarters until the Manège, an indoor riding stable near the Tuileries Palace, could be converted for their use, and began meeting there on November 9. Its rectangular form was not ideally suited for a deliberative assembly, and rendered rational discussion even more difficult than at Versailles because deputies had to shout to be heard. The seats in galleries above the deputies allowed only about three hundred spectators to attend, many fewer than at Versailles, but still enough to make their presence felt. The deputies continued to sit according to political opinion on the left and the right.

The Assembly next took up the question of who would be given the vote. They established two classes of citizenship. Active citizens, those with a certain amount of property, would have the vote. Passive citizens would have natural and civil rights, but not political rights. In order to be an active citizen, an adult male, at least twenty-five years old, had to pay direct taxes in an amount equivalent to the wages that a laborer was paid for three days of work. Although the amount was not large, it disqualified two million out of six million adult Frenchmen. Nonetheless, four million active citizens constituted a very large electorate in the eighteenth century, a much greater percentage of the population than in Great Britain and much greater than the electorate in France after the Revolution of 1830, when only around 200,000 had the vote.

Especially after the violence in October, a majority of the Constituent Assembly decided that, in order to protect property, voters should have a stake in the country. Furthermore, they feared that those without independent means would not be able to stand up to the privileged. Giving poor people the franchise would merely amplify the votes of the rich, who could influence or control their vote. This position on voting was not unusual in the eighteenth century. Property qualifications for voting existed in both Great Britain and the United States. One deputy explained, "Whatever respect one might wish to show for the rights of humanity in general, there is no denying the existence of a class of men who, by virtue of their education and the type of work to which their poverty has condemned them, is . . . incapable at the moment of participating fully in public affairs."[4] Almost universally accepted at first, the distinction between types of citizens eventually (as radical political opinions increased) came to be seen as contradicting Article 6 of the Declaration of the Rights of Man, which stated that "All citizens have the right to participate personally or through their representatives" in the formation of the law. It could be argued that representatives were still making the law and that the property qualification applied only to the way in which representatives were chosen. Still, this issue highlighted one of the disadvantages of stating principles in advance of deciding on institutions. Much more controversial was a provision that, in order to qualify to be a representative, a man had to prove greater wealth: direct taxes equivalent to fifty days' wages. Dupont de Nemours justified the higher qualification by saying, "Only the property-holder has a real stake in society, so they alone should be eligible for office. Those who lack property are not yet full members of society."[5] This provision proved so unpopular that it was dropped before the constitution went into effect, but the distinction between active and passive was retained.

The legislation provided for an indirect electoral system similar to the one employed in the elections to the Estates General. Primary assemblies of all voters chose delegates to an electoral assembly, which then chose the number of representatives allotted to them. Elections were to take place in new administrative units called departments. After August 4, when the privileges of provinces had been swept away, no reason existed for maintaining the old provinces. The revolutionaries, imbued with an optimistic faith in their ability to remake the country, saw a wonderful opportunity for eliminating the provinces along with, as Sieyès expressed it, "their esprit de corps, their privileges, their pretensions, their jealousies."[6] The new departments would create a national system based on equality and uniformity by eliminating the frustrating overlapping jurisdictions that had so complicated government in the Ancien Régime. The first proposal to create departments was presented by Thouret, on behalf of the Constitutional Committee on September 29. The final legislation, passed on November 11, 1789, stipulated that old boundaries should be respected where possible and that local economic and geographical circumstances should be taken into consideration in consultation with deputies. Generally they attempted to divide large provinces into smaller departments. They wanted to create a department small enough so that people could travel to the administrative capital and return home in a day. The designation of these departmental seats gave rise to innumerable conflicts between towns, all wanting to enjoy the prosperity that housing the government institutions would bring.

The final decree, passed on February 26, 1790, created eighty-three departments, each named for a prominent geographical feature. Each department was divided into districts, and districts were divided into cantons, which were made up of municipalities (or townships). When additional territory was added to France during the Revolution, new departments were created. Legislation provided for the election of all municipal, district, and departmental officials. Every town now had similar institutions headed by a mayor, though the number of municipal officers varied from three to twenty-one, depending on the size of the town, thus doing away with the old corporate structures and privileges of the past. Every department was to be governed by a departmental council.

ENGLAND

AUSTRIAN
NETHERLANDS

English Channel

PAS-
DE-CALAIS

NORD

SOMME

SEINE-
INFÉRIEURE

AISNE ARDENNES

OISE

MANCHE CALVADOS EURE

MEUSE MOSELLE

MARNE

SEINE
ET- SEINE-
ET-

MEURTHE BAS-
RHIN

FINISTÈRE
CÔTES-DU-NORD

ORNE

Paris

ILLE-ET- MAYENNE
VILAINE

MORBIHAN

SARTHE

EURE-ET-
LOIR

MARNE

AUBE

HAUTE-
MARNE

VOSGES

HAUT-
RHIN

LOIRET

LOIRE-
INFÉRIEURE

MAINE-
ET-
LOIRE

INDRE

LOIR-
ET-
CHER

YONNE

HAUTE-
SAÔNE

CÔTE-D'OR

DOUBS

SWITZ.

VENDÉE

DEUX-
SÈVRES VIENNE

ET-
LOIRE

CHER

NIÈVRE

INDRE

SAÔNE-
ET-LOIRE

JURA

ALLIER

AIN

ATLANTIC
OCEAN

CHARENTE-
INFÉRIEURE CHARENTE

HAUTE-
VIENNE

CREUSE

PUY-DE-
DÔME

RHÔNE-
ET-LOIRE

SAVOY

CORRÈZE

ISÈRE

DORDOGNE

CANTAL

HAUTE-
LOIRE

GIRONDE

ARDÈCHE DRÔME

HAUTES-
ALPES

LOT-ET-
GARONNE

LOT

AVEYRON

LOZÈRE

BASSES-
ALPES NICE

LANDES

GERS

HAUTE-
GARONNE

TARN

GARD

HÉRAULT

VAR

BASSES-
PYRÉNÉES

ARIÈGE

AUDE

COMTAT
VENAISSIN BOUCHES-
DU-RHÔNE

HAUTES-
PYRÉNÉES

PYRÉNÉES-
ORIENTALES

*Mediterranean
Sea*

SPAIN

| France in 1790 |
| -------- Department boundaries |
| SOMME Department name |

0   100   200 mi

CORSICA

The Constituent Assembly had applied the principle of uniformity in order to encourage national unity. But another principle, liberty, which called for local control and frequent elections, actually led to decentralization and threatened unity. In theory, the local administrators were supposed to put into effect the laws passed by the National Assembly as the embodiment of the national will. But the willingness of the many officials elected in far-flung parts of the country to follow the dictates from Paris varied, and in fact they enjoyed considerable freedom of action. The conflict between central and local authorities would continue throughout the Revolution, with the central authorities increasingly striving to exert more and more control over local institutions.

In the same spirit of uniformity, the judicial system was also organized around the new administrative units and the principle of election. The system of venality for judges was abolished. Trial by jury, as indicated in the Declaration of the Rights of Man, was provided for all criminal cases. On November 3, 1789, the Assembly, in part fearful that the parlements would challenge their exclusive claim to represent the nation, decreed that the parlements were "incompatible with the new order of things." But the courts continued to function while the Assembly worked on reorganization. It was not until the end of March 1790 that the Assembly took up the future of the judiciary. They decided that in order to create equality before the law and do away with privileges, the old tribunals had to be destroyed. Wishing to provide quick and inexpensive justice at the local level and do away with the litigiousness of the Ancien Régime, they borrowed from English and Dutch law to create the office of justice of the peace. Civil cases could be appealed to district courts. But before the appeal, the parties had to submit to arbitration by a bureau of peace and conciliation. A national appeals court, the Court of Cassation, was established as a court of last resort. To make sure the judiciary was independent and not subject to executive manipulation, they decreed that judges were to be elected for six-year terms and could be reelected. Because justice was to be free, they were given high salaries so that they would not have to charge fees. The Assembly, disliking the obfuscation and complexity of the law under the Ancien Régime, wanted every citizen to be able to plead his own case in a court of law. Law, they declared idealistically, was to be easily accessible and comprehensible. They went so far as to abolish the Order of Barristers (September 2, 1790). The legal profession was no longer needed. From now on any citizen could speak on behalf of himself or another before the courts.

Tackling such wide-ranging transformations took time. The early hopes in the summer of 1789 that the constitution would be completed in a few months gave way to the realization that the Constituent Assembly would be around for a while. As they approached the first anniversary of their existence in the summer of 1790, they could congratulate themselves on what they had accomplished. The Constituent Assembly had become the most important government institution. It acted as both a constitutional convention and a regular legislature, passing laws as the need arose. When the press of business made it impossible to keep a clear distinction between the two types of laws, they appointed a committee to differentiate between those decisions that were basic constitutional provisions and those that were regular legislation. This confusion could cause opposition to legislation to be seen as opposition to the fundamental ideas of the Revolution as a whole. It was difficult to engage in the normal give-and-take of political debate when the constitution was not yet completed and accepted.

The royal government with its councils and ministers still existed, but increasingly the ministers could not get anything accomplished without the endorsement of the Assembly. So the Assembly also came to share in the executive function by creating a series of committees. Especially important in the beginning was the Constitutional Committee, which prepared drafts of the constitutional provisions. After August 4, 1789, they appointed an Ecclesiastical Committee, a Judicial Committee (to liquidate venality of office), and a Feudal Committee. But as it took on more responsibilities, the Assembly created a number of committees—agriculture and commerce, military affairs, colonies, diplomatic relations—about twenty-five committees in all during its first year.

Despite the Assembly's involvement in the executive function, they persisted in the notion that there should be a strict separation of powers (as stipulated in the Declaration of the Rights of Man). On November 7, 1789, they therefore decreed that no member of the Assembly could serve as a minister of the king. This decree was partly aimed at Mirabeau, who made no secret of his ambitions and who was suspected of being in league with the Duc d'Orléans. It also reflected their substantial fear of executive power, which had not abated since prerevolutionary alarms over ministerial despotism and had even increased during the summer of 1789. This decree meant that cabinet government like that of Great Britain could not develop in France. In the British Parliamentary system, the monarch asks the party with the majority in the Parliament to form a government and supply his ministers (in essence, the executive). In France, the Assembly decided that a king's ministers could not be chosen from among their own members. In its separation of powers, the new French system, in theory at least, was more like the American government than the British. In practice that meant that the ministers had little base of support and less standing than the members of the Assembly, who would come to usurp the executive function.

Although the members of the Assembly frowned on the notion of political parties, considering them divisive and self-interested, factions nonetheless developed in that body. In the fall of 1789, conservatives had organized effectively to dominate the elections to the leadership positions and to turn some constitutional decisions in a conservative direction. Even after the resignation of some prominent Monarchiens, the moderate royalists (now calling themselves the "Impartials") still hoped to influence the course of the Revolution by creating a broad coalition of moderates. They met in the evening to organize, printed brochures, and sought to correspond with like-minded people throughout the country. On the extreme right sat a group of intransigent deputies, including many members of the clergy. They first met in a former convent of the Grands Augustins and were therefore known as the Augustinian Club.

In response to the organization of the Monarchiens, the more radical deputies began to meet to organize their strategy in December 1789. Including several deputies from the old Breton Club, their numbers grew rapidly and they were able to exert increasing influence on the course of debates. They, too, met in the evenings when the Assembly was not in session. Officially named the Society of the Friends of the Constitution, their nickname derived from their meeting place in a former Dominican monastery. Dominicans in France were known as Jacobins, so they became known as the Jacobin Club. They established a formal structure with committees to promote radical reform and with discussions to decide what their strategy would be in the next day's session. Their promotion of democratic and anti-clerical legislation became especially effective in the spring of 1790.

THE KING AND THE MILITARY

During the summer of 1789, Louis XVI had been unable to stop the Revolution. His hesitations at going along with the Assembly's work during the summer and fall of 1789 had raised suspicions about his willingness to serve as a constitutional monarch. But with the king in Paris after the October Days, revolutionaries believed that they might prevent his being influenced by conservative courtiers and that they could persuade him that their changes were for the good of the country. Their hopes appeared to be realized when Louis appeared at the Assembly on February 4, 1790, and endorsed the territorial reorganization and other work they had done, vowing that the dauphin (his young son and heir) would be taught to respect the constitution. At the same time, he urged that strong executive authority be preserved. Although his visit was greeted with rapturous exclamations and marked a period of popularity for the king, his suggestions were not followed, and the Assembly soon lapsed into its accustomed factional feuding.

In August 1789, the Assembly, faced with widespread violence, had acted to preserve law and order. The decree they passed on August 10, 1789, to provide forces of order also carefully ensured that the king would not control those forces. Fearful that Louis XVI might use the army to shut down the Assembly, they decreed that the army (both officers and soldiers) was to swear an oath "to remain faithful to the nation, to the King, and to the law." The army could be employed to put down disorders, but only when requisitioned by civil or municipal authorities. In other words, the king was not allowed to use the army internally, which further weakened the power of the royal government. He remained "the supreme head of the army and navy," as the constitution would later express it, but his control over those forces was carefully circumscribed. The constitution specifically stated that he had "the task of watching over the external security of the kingdom." Internal security was in the hands of the civil authorities.[7]

Civil authorities also had at their disposal the National Guards. The decree of August 10, 1789, recognized the existence of National Guard units that had been created throughout the country during the summer and gave the municipal authorities the power to use them to keep the peace. The first regulations for the National Guard of Paris stipulated that members had to have a permanent address and they had to supply their own uniforms. They wanted the members of the National Guard to be relatively well off because only men with a stake in society could be expected to protect it and not fall victim to the corruption of money. Unlike the regular army, the members of the National Guard elected their officers.

The idea of the "citizen soldier" inspired establishment of the National Guards. In the Ancien Régime, war was considered the particular province of the nobility and of professional military men. The average subject of a European king did not feel strong patriotic identification with the wars that the king fought. Traditionally, soldiers were recruited from among the downtrodden who were otherwise unproductive in society. The armed forces might also include soldiers from other countries who were paid to fight. These "mercenaries" were professional military men. For example, the king of France had a long-standing agreement with Switzerland to hire Swiss soldiers. In the eighteenth century, these assumptions about the way to organize armies were being questioned. Perhaps, some argued, soldiers would fight harder if they were fighting for their own country in a cause that they cared about. Relying on "citizen soldiers" might also lead to smaller regular armies and fewer wars. If kings controlled large professional military establishments directly they might be tempted to use them to start wars of aggression. It was hoped that a defensive force of citizens who were not professionals but who would be more motivated to fight for their country could protect the nation from attack and also eliminate needless wars. The National Guard was to be a citizens' militia to provide internal security and to help protect the nation in an emergency. The American Revolution seemed to provide a boost to this theory. According to a widely held (though somewhat mythical) view, American farmers had been able to defeat the mightiest power in the world because they were fighting for their country and their cause. Appropriately, Lafayette, who had become famous for fighting with the Americans in their revolution, had been appointed head of the Paris National Guard.

After the October Days, the Constituent Assembly wanted to strengthen the hand of municipal authorities in dealing with insurrection. On October 21, 1789, they passed a law establishing rules for declaring martial law. The authorities were to communicate the declaration to the unruly crowd by flying a red flag and ordering them to disperse. If after three summonses to do so, the crowd had not disbanded, the National Guard could use force to put down the revolt, and those who refused to obey would be punished.

Over the winter of 1789–1790, National Guard forces began to come together in regional meetings to discuss ways to cooperate and to promote the Revolution. This movement, known as "federation," culminated in the summer of 1790 with a national federation bringing together delegates from National Guards of each department to a grand festival in Paris on the first anniversary of the fall of the Bastille. Volunteers transformed the Champ de Mars into a suitable setting for the ceremonies, witnessed by an audience of hundreds of thousands.

Madame de Staël, Jacques Necker's daughter, described the scene:

> In front of the military academy and opposite the river that borders the Champ de Mars, tiers had been constructed with a tent to give shelter to the king, the queen, and the entire court. Eighty-three lances, stuck into the ground from which hung the banners of each department, formed a great circle of which the amphitheatre where the royal family were to sit was a part. At the other end was an altar ready for the mass that M. de Talleyrand, then Bishop of Autun, celebrated on this occasion. M. de La Fayette then came up to the same altar to swear loyalty to nation, law, and king; the oath and the man who pronounced it excited a great feeling of confidence. The spectators were ecstatic; to them, king and liberty now seemed completely united.[8]

Similar ceremonies took place in cities and towns throughout the country. The Fête de la Fédération (Festival of Federation) proclaimed a new type

Figure 4.1.   Fête de la Fédération, July 14, 1790. The pavilion for the king and the National Assembly is on the right. In the middle of the field is the altar at which Lafayette pronounced the oath in the name of the assembled guardsmen. The participants marched in through the triumphal arch at the far end of the field. Private collection.

of nationalism. The king once again enjoyed great popularity because he had so conspicuously joined in endorsing national unity and the constitution. The clergy, too, took part in these celebrations that marked the high point of national consensus over the new institutions.

The development of the National Guard was one of the ways the Revolution was transforming the basic institutions of the country. But the regular army also needed to be reformed. Modern armies are products of the societies that employ them and share the prevailing values of their society. The army of the Ancien Régime, dominated by the nobility and devoted to the king, obviously needed to be brought into line with the new institutions. The Assembly created a military committee on October 1, 1789, to work on its reorganization. But while plans were being made, the condition of the army deteriorated alarmingly. Desertions, always a problem in Ancien Régime armies, had multiplied in 1789. The army, like the rest of the population, was sharply divided on political questions. Though soldiers could usually be depended upon to obey their officers when ordered to put down disturbances among the civilian population, they were less willing to do so when the violent confrontations were political in nature. When soldiers learned the new ideas of equality and liberty, they resented the old hierarchy and discipline. Yet, even in democratic societies, armies generally expect soldiers to obey without question and to maintain strict order. How could these two impulses be reconciled?

The problems were made worse by the growing distrust soldiers had for their officers. French noble officers were notoriously distant from their men. Over the winter of 1789–1790, many officers continued their traditional practice of taking a six-month leave. When they returned to the army in the spring of 1790, they discovered that revolutionary political ideas had changed many of the soldiers. Through contact with civilians and with National Guard troops, some soldiers had become committed to the Revolution and suspected that their noble officers did not share their commitment. The army tried to deal with the problems by discharging troublemakers, but by the summer of 1790 misunderstandings frequently turned to outright mutiny. Insubordination of one kind or another occurred in more than a third of the Royal Army in the spring and summer of 1790. A frequent cause of complaint was that soldiers believed too much was being withheld from their pay to cover the costs of food and clothing and demanded an accounting. A dispute over this subject was the basis of the most serious incident, the Nancy rebellion of August 1790.

The garrison in the eastern city of Nancy consisted of three regiments, an elite French infantry regiment, a cavalry regiment, and a foreign regiment of Swiss soldiers. The conservative municipal authorities were frequently at odds with the National Guard of Nancy, and the soldiers had also begun to debate political questions, meet at the Jacobin club, and question the loyalty of their officers to the Revolution. Still, peace might have been maintained had those sent to negotiate the dispute over the soldiers' pay not needlessly and ineptly antagonized the soldiers. The National Assembly had issued a decree on August 6, 1790, outlining the means of settling such disputes. Many deputies, fearful that the soldiers could no longer be trusted to obey their officers, determined to put an end to mutinies by making an example of Nancy. On August 16, they authorized General Bouillé to put down the rebellion by force if the men did not return to their posts. Most obeyed, but a minority held out. On August 31, Bouillé, thinking he was entering a town that had surrendered, instead encountered resistance and took the town by force, killing around fifty soldiers and civilians, while suffering seventy-two deaths among his forces. The three regiments were moved out of Nancy, and the mutineers, especially those in the Swiss regiment of Châteauvieux, were severely punished, with twenty-two soldiers hanged. Although the Assembly officially pronounced approval of Bouillé's actions, radicals protested the severity of the punishment and demanded investigation of the "Nancy affair."

Noble officers in the army still performed their duties, but they were becoming increasingly worried about the developments in the Revolution. They felt their honor had been attacked when titles of nobility were done away with by the National Assembly in June 1790. They opposed the democratic direction taken in the army. Still, relative calm existed through the winter of 1790–1791. Large numbers of officers would not leave their posts and emigrate until the summer of 1791 after the Flight to Varennes. And that event cannot be fully understood until the momentous changes in the church are considered.

THE CIVIL CONSTITUTION OF THE CLERGY

Talleyrand called the Civil Constitution of the Clergy "perhaps the biggest political blunder of the Assembly," and indeed it probably was. This measure reorganizing the Catholic Church, which proved so disastrous to the church and to the future of a harmonious society, developed out of the Assembly's aims to create new institutions and from their conviction that they had the right to do so because they represented the will of the nation. The Revolution had not begun as an attack on the church. The *cahiers* had included demands for such reforms as better pay for priests, more priests resident in their parishes, and elimination of fees for services. These changes were meant to strengthen the role of the church in society, not do away with it. Many recognized the need to reform abuses in the church. It was scandalous that the influential nobles who dominated the upper hierarchy of the church sometimes were not sincere Catholics. When Loménie de Brienne was suggested as Archbishop of Paris, Louis XVI protested: "But surely the archbishop of Paris should at least believe in God."[9]

Radical change in the church became absolutely necessary after the night of August 4. Having abolished the tithe and priestly fees and having done away as well with seigneurial rights (another source of income for the church), the Constituent Assembly had promised that the nation would support the church in the future. But if the nation was to provide for the church, then the church no longer needed the rich landholdings, which had been an important source of income in the past. Those lands could then be used to solve the financial problems that had caused the convening of the Estates General in the first place and which had still not been satisfactorily settled.

Shortly after the October Days, Talleyrand, the Bishop of Autun, suggested that something be done with church property. Talleyrand was himself a good example of an Ancien Régime nobleman who became a clergyman out of careerism rather than religious conviction. His name has become synonymous with opportunism and diplomatic skill. Elected by the First Estate, he became an early supporter of the Revolution, but managed always to land on his feet as different regimes came and went. Except for the period of the Convention (when he was in exile), he served all subsequent governments, revolutionary and reactionary alike, until his death in 1838, a remarkable testimony to his political abilities. On November 2, 1789, the Assembly acted on his suggestion by voting (510–346) that the property of the church "be placed at the disposal of the nation." The church and conservatives resolutely opposed giving up the lands, so the wording that passed was deliberately vague. Most assumed that only some of the church's land (such as the property of monastic orders) would be taken to help shore up the country's finances.

In December, when Necker informed the Assembly that they had to come up with money to pay creditors on January 1, the Constituent Assembly began to consider confiscating and selling church lands. On December 19, they passed a law authorizing the sale of church and state lands worth 400 million livres and creating a special treasury to manage the sales. To pay their creditors, they created "assignats," which were promissory notes that the holder could redeem for church lands or for money that had been raised by the sale of those lands. Similar to bonds, assignats had a face value and paid interest (5 percent per year). When lands were sold, the assignats used to buy them were supposed to be burned. But the process did not work out as planned. There were inevitable delays in the sale of land, and so public confidence in the value of the assignats was low. In order to encourage people to accept these pieces of paper, in April 1790 they were declared legal tender and the interest was lowered to 3 percent. By September 1790, interest was dropped altogether. In other words, a paper currency had been created that was inflationary. Although they were supposedly backed up by the former lands of the church, the assignats nonetheless dropped in value as time went on. By August 1792, they were worth only about 60 percent of face value; by the end of 1794, 20 percent; and by 1796, they were worth almost nothing.

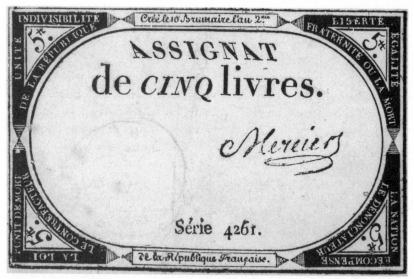

Figure 4.2.   Assignat of five livres. Originally authorized by the Constituent Assembly, the paper currency shown here was actually issued under the republic. Notice the revolutionary slogan *"Liberté, Égalité, Fraternité ou la Mort"* (Liberty, Equality, Fraternity, or Death) in the upper-right-hand corner. By the time this assignat was issued in November 1793 (in the Revolutionary calendar: 10 Brumaire, Year II), inflation had robbed it of much of its value. Private collection.

Having deprived the church of its ability to support itself, the Assembly now had to reorganize the church and provide for it. The radical revolutionaries did not question their right to reform the church. They saw themselves as the heirs of the powers of the king, who had exercised great control over the Gallican Church in the Ancien Régime and had prevented interference from Rome. Naturally, the conservatives and especially the delegates of the First Estate protested the Assembly's plans. But views on the place of religion in society were evolving rapidly. Before the Revolution, calls for reform of the church had come from many directions, including the church itself. But nobody anticipated the extent of change that would be put into place. In August 1789, debate on the Declaration of the Rights of Man had centered on whether the Catholic Church would be declared the religion of the state. By the following December, the Assembly debated a law to give religious and political freedom to both Protestants and Jews. Although they ultimately postponed a decision on Jews, they voted to give equality to Protestants. This measure passed by a large majority on December 24, 1789, indicating how rapidly opinion had changed. The small group of Sephardic Jews of southern France were granted equal rights at the end of January 1790, but the more numerous Yiddish-speaking Ashkenazi Jews of Alsace, who were organized into separate communities and maintained their traditional customs, had to wait until September 1791 before they were granted equal political rights.

Although advocates of the church might protest the sale of church lands, that measure could be justified on the grounds of pressing necessity and the need of the church to sacrifice for the good of the country. Other parts of the policy toward the church were harder to explain and revealed the deep-seated anti-Catholicism of many deputies. On February 13, 1790, the Assembly declared that monastic vows would no longer be recognized. The gates of monasteries and convents were thrown open, and monks and nuns were told they could leave. Religious orders in charge of educational and charitable institutions were exempted for the moment because their work was essential to the nation, but all contemplative orders were suppressed. Because the state had assumed the obligation of paying for the church, all priests and monks were now state employees. The Assembly therefore applied the principle of whether their work was "useful" to society to justify the expenditure of public money.

Most monks abandoned the religious life, in part because orders were going to be merged for reasons of economy. Each religious order was quite different, so this provision encouraged them to leave rather than face an unfamiliar way of life. Nuns tended to stay in their convents, in part because fewer options existed for an unmarried woman outside the convent. Although unhappy with this measure, many moderates accepted it because monastic orders were generally not held in high esteem and because it was assumed that they would be losing their property anyway and would not be able to survive. Many people still believed that it was only monastic lands that would be taken to pay the nation's debts. But rumors of impending bankruptcy in the spring of 1790 persuaded many deputies to accept the idea of the sale of all church lands. After an especially bitter debate, the opposition boycotted the proceedings, making possible the passage of a measure to sell all church lands. The advocates of the church responded by issuing a petition protesting the Assembly's right to legislate in religious matters and circulated it throughout the country.

At the end of May the Assembly began to deliberate on legislation to reorganize the church, the Civil Constitution of the Clergy. The clergy continued to protest that the Assembly had no authority to make these reforms and that any changes had to be carried out by the Church itself. Losing that fight, the right did not participate in the debates on the legislation, which was approved on July 12, 1790. The new law brought about a substantial transformation of the Catholic Church in France. Benefices without cure of souls were abolished. Over the years the faithful had left endowments to support chapels and priests who did not serve a congregation. The legislation abolished all of those in favor of parish priests who oversaw the spiritual lives of their communities. Compensation was revised. Pay for bishops was about a quarter of what it had been before, while priests' pay almost doubled. Previously, dioceses (each headed by a bishop or archbishop) had varied greatly in size and population. The Civil Constitution of the Clergy decreed that dioceses were to coincide with departments. This meant a reduction from 139 to 83 dioceses, depriving many bishops of their positions. In the Ancien Régime, bishops had been able to accumulate more than one position, thus multiplying their income. The Civil Constitution forbade this practice and required bishops to be resident in their diocese.

The most controversial part of the Civil Constitution of the Clergy was the requirement that all priests were to be chosen by the active citizens in their district and the bishops by the electors of the department. Election was an altogether new principle, which many opposed on religious grounds. The electors were not necessarily equivalent to the faithful. Indeed, in a few districts, Protestants would constitute a majority of the electors. Women and the poor would be excluded from voting. The authors of the legislation ignored these protests, arguing that previous methods of selection were hardly better. In the past, lay people sometimes had the right to name a priest. The king had named the bishops, and the king generally chose nobles who had the backing of influential families or factions at court, but who might not be the best qualified. The legislation specifically removed even the formality of the pope's role in the nomination of bishops. He was to be merely informed of the choice of bishops.

The church for the most part disapproved of this legislation, but might have been willing to compromise if the church had been consulted and had given its approval, either through a national council or through the consent of the pope. The Assembly refused to call a church council, so the French church hoped that the pope would declare his views one way or the other. The king reluctantly approved the measure, although he had grave misgivings. Practical necessity required the new system to be put into place so that priests could be paid. However, disputes quickly broke out over the application of the law, and the result would be a religious schism in the country that seriously undermined the chances for the success of the Revolution.

CONCLUSION

The actions taken by the Constituent Assembly in its first year of existence transformed the nation. No part of it was untouched. The familiar old provinces were gone, replaced by new departments. The livelihoods of people in cities and towns were affected by whether they were chosen as the site for the new political and judicial institutions. Citizens joined the National Guards and became used to the notion that they should play a role in their own security. French people went from living in a society in which very few elections took place to one in which they were constantly called upon to exercise the vote. The monetary system had been transformed. And most disturbing for many, the basis of their religious life had been altered substantially. They had learned to judge people by whether they were supporters of these changes or opponents of them. The new institutions had been intended to create unity and harmony, but they had instead divided the nation into revolutionaries and counter-revolutionaries. The slogan of the Revolution was "Liberty, Equality, Fraternity." Although the changes had brought about more liberty and equality, the sense of fraternity (or national solidarity) so evident in the summer of 1789 was in decline.

The Constituent Assembly would not complete the constitution for another year, but by the summer of 1790, its major provisions were established. Its chances for success might have been better had it gone into operation in 1790. By 1791, the divisions in the country were greater than ever.

5

POLARIZATION AND
THE FLIGHT TO VARENNES

For a Parisian, the year 1790 appeared to be a time of relative calm in the violence and disruption of the revolutionary years, despite continuing hunger and unemployment. However, in other parts of the country, Frenchmen experienced a great deal of unrest. Riots over food still broke out in many areas. Disputes over administrative and judicial boundaries caused discontent. Local autonomy was threatened by new tax laws, sales of church lands, and the reorganization of the church, all mandated and enforced by the National Assembly. Many of these institutional changes were implemented at the end of 1790 and beginning of 1791, coinciding with a religious conflict that would leave the country deeply divided.

THE CLERICAL OATH

The Civil Constitution of the Clergy immediately gave rise to disputes over which priest was authorized to serve a particular parish and receive the pay of the nation. The Civil Constitution had stated that in order to be paid, all newly elected priests and bishops had to take an oath pledging "to watch with care over the faithful . . . entrusted to him, to be faithful to the nation, to the law, and to the King, and to maintain with all his power the Constitution decreed by the National Assembly and accepted by the King."[1] On July 24, the Assembly had widened this requirement to say that all priests, not merely newly elected ones, had to swear the oath in order to receive payment. But many priests were slow to comply, waiting to hear whether the pope approved the Civil Constitution of the Clergy.

The more radical members of the Constituent Assembly suspected that those who questioned the Civil Constitution of the Clergy were not motivated by genuine religious scruples but were in fact counter-revolutionaries who were using religion as an excuse to destroy all the new institutions. Many members of the Constituent Assembly were anti-clerical and lacked a great interest in religion, so they underestimated the depth of feeling on this subject in the country. The voices of the conservatives were not being heard in the Assembly as regularly because after the passage of the Civil Constitution, the clerical members of the Assembly no longer attended sessions faithfully. The Jacobins in the fall of 1790 were able to dominate elections to leadership positions in the Assembly and to set the agenda for legislation.

Impatient at the lack of progress in church reorganization and at the contentiousness of local disputes, the Assembly, on November 27, 1790, decided to enforce the law by requiring all office-holding priests to swear the prescribed oath within a week or be removed from office. The king delayed acting on the legislation until December 26, 1790. He finally approved it under pressure from the Assembly. This law made the religious conflicts worse and split the church into two parts. Those priests who took the oath were known as "constitutional" priests. Those who did not were called "refractory" or "non-juring" priests. Of the clergy in the Assembly, about a third took the oath, and only two of them were bishops (Talleyrand and Gobel). In the entire country only seven bishops took the oath and about half of the lower clergy. But the split was not even throughout the country. Different regions took different stands. The legislation forced communities to take a position on an important issue that they might have preferred to gloss over.

Oaths were important to French people in the eighteenth century and were not taken lightly. The king began his reign by taking an oath at Rheims during his coronation. The revolutionaries likewise had demonstrated the importance of oaths at the time of the Tennis Court Oath and at the Fête de la Fédération. Even more than the reorganization of the administrative and judicial structures, the Clerical Oath dramatically confronted all parishes with the reality of the changes brought about by the Revolution. Priests and congregations tended to act together, either supporting or rejecting the Civil Constitution. In some cases the priest might lead his parish to adopt his point of view, but in most communities the priest reflected the views of the region, responding to the needs and concerns of the congregation.

Historian Timothy Tackett mapped the wide variations from one region to another. The center of the country around Paris and south to the Loire River, whose populations identified closely with the Revolution, supported the oath. Regions on the periphery of the country and those in which French was not the dominant language were less likely to support the imposition of the Civil Constitution. Areas with many priests and with a strong sense of Catholic identity were more likely to resist. In some areas where Catholics saw themselves as embattled with and on the defensive against large numbers of nearby Protestants (Alsace and parts of southern France, for example), the oath was rejected because it was perceived as an anti-Catholic measure that would benefit Protestants.

In the southeast, with a long tradition of protests against poor conditions and inadequate pay for clergy, congregations and priests tended to be in favor of the Civil Constitution because it meant an improvement in the local churches. The region of strongest refusal of the oath was in the west and northwest including Brittany, Normandy, Anjou, Maine, and the Vendée (a department south of the Loire along the Atlantic coast that would become the center of counter-revolutionary activity). In these areas a sharp distinction existed between the anti-clerical elites of the towns who tended to support the Revolution and the pious population of the countryside who held their priests in high esteem. As this summary shows, no single explanation for their choices will describe the situation in the whole country. Because the dilemma of the oath posed a religious question, its effect was even greater than most ordinary political questions. A matter of eternal salvation led to conflicts for which compromise would not be easily found.

Priests were placed in a difficult position. If a priest did not take the oath, he would be removed from the pulpit, sacrificing his career and leaving his congregation perhaps without the services of a priest. The sacrifice might prove useless in the end if the pope eventually approved the law. On the other hand, if the pope condemned the law, the priest would have offended against the Catholic Church by taking the oath. Many who took the oath added the stipulation "as much as the Catholic religion permits." Pope Pius VI had warned the king in private not to accept the Civil Constitution. But by the time the letter reached him, the king had already reluctantly given his support to the measure. The king waited in vain for the pope to pronounce on the Clerical Oath, but was finally pressured to approve it at the end of December, though he doubted that the pope would go along. It was not until April 1791 that Pius VI ordered the clergy not to take the oath and directed those who had already done so to retract their oath or face excommunication. In May, he published his official condemnation in the Papal Brief entitled *Caritas quae*. Many priests who had reluctantly sworn the oath now retracted it.

The Civil Constitution of the Clergy and its enforcement had created a split in the Catholic Church and seriously undermined support for the Revolution. At first, many members of the National Assembly had believed that the clerical opponents of the legislation were really conservatives opposed to the Revolution and that religious considerations were merely convenient excuses. But by the spring of 1791, they could recognize that opposition to the measure was widespread. Most parish priests had begun as supporters of the Revolution, but this issue turned many into counter-revolutionaries. Many devout Catholics who opposed the Civil Constitution genuinely believed that the legislation was a plot to destroy the church.

In May 1791, in an attempt to defuse the religious controversy and under the principle of freedom of worship, the Assembly decreed that non-juring priests would be allowed to rent church buildings for celebrating mass. This measure hardly stilled the controversies, however, because citizens loyal to constitutional priests protested against it. They believed that the non-jurors were dangerously unpatriotic and were stirring up counter-revolutionary sentiment in collaboration with disaffected nobles and émigrés. Revolutionaries demanded that the subversive non-juring priests be barred from saying mass. If they refused to follow the law, then they did not deserve the protection of the nation. Religious pluralism was acceptable to neither side. Riots and disorders over the use and control of church buildings were widespread.

THE FLIGHT TO VARENNES

The split in the church had a significant effect on Louis XVI, bringing the ambiguities of the king's position into the open. After the October Days, Louis and Marie Antoinette had tried to continue their accustomed courtly routine in the less elegant and less animated surroundings of the Tuileries Palace. The king and his family had been cheered at the Fête de la Fédération, where he publicly associated himself with the nationalist program of the Constituent Assembly. However, doubts persisted about his genuine devotion to the Revolution, and even more suspicion fell on Marie Antoinette. Had the king accepted the new constitutional provisions only because of force, or did he really mean to abide by them? Indeed, shortly after the October Days, Louis had written to the king of Spain that everything he had done since the fall of the Bastille had been done under duress and that he was still committed to the plan he had set forth at the Royal Session. Louis embarked on a dual policy of outward support for the new institutions while searching in secret for ways to undermine them. Many moderates, although they suspected the king's intentions, probably thought that he would eventually be brought around to their point of view and that the constitution would succeed.

Although the king was officially declared the head of the executive, his freedom to act was curtailed by the Assembly and also by National Guard troops that protected the palace. Revolutionaries recognized that the king's association with the new institutions conferred legitimacy on their side. Counter-revolutionaries believed that Louis (had he been free to do so) would have declared his support for their side. From his exile, the Comte d'Artois tried to persuade other monarchs to rescue his brother by asserting that his public declarations were coerced and could not be trusted. This argument, naturally, hurt the king's position in the eyes of revolutionaries, and they suspected that his brother surely knew what the king really believed. Rumors persisted that counter-revolutionaries intended to rescue the king, take him to a distant city, and use his prestige to dismantle the Revolution.

A plan to move the king from Paris had in fact been worked out with an unlikely confederate, the comte de Mirabeau. A nobleman and the son of a physiocrat, Mirabeau had been elected to the Estates General by the Third Estate of Aix-en-Provence. His fortune and great abilities had been squandered by a messy personal life and dissipated living. He had begun to make a name for himself as a writer, and the Revolution provided him the opportunity to become famous as a stirring orator. At the beginning of the Revolution, he seemed to be associated with the Duc d'Orléans, but after the October Days, Mirabeau offered his services to the king, warning him of the dangerous position the monarchy was in. Mirabeau believed that the reputation he had developed as a spokesman of the Third Estate and the popularity he enjoyed among the Parisian people could be used to prop up the monarchy. Mirabeau's defenders argue that his actions were not really contradictory. Despite his demagogic oratory, they argue, his policies were generally rather moderate and, while a supporter of the Revolution, he always wanted the monarchy to have a large role in the new institutions (he favored the absolute veto, for example). His reputation for immorality and ambition, however, made it difficult for Mirabeau to find allies among other moderates in the Constituent Assembly. He felt frustrated that his lack of money made it impossible for him to live up to his station, especially considering his widely recognized abilities.

The king at first rejected Mirabeau's offers of help, but in May 1790, a deal between Mirabeau and the royal family was made. Mirabeau was to help them secretly in any way that he could and they agreed to help pay his debts and give him a pension. Mirabeau reported on events in the Assembly and offered the king advice. He developed a plan for their escape from Paris. Cautioning against calling on the nobility to save him, he thought the king's best chance would be to head north into Normandy and from there issue a proclamation endorsing the Revolution and the idea of a constitution for the nation. Mirabeau died in April 1791, before his plan could be carried out. Indeed, it was unlikely that Louis XVI and Marie Antoinette would have trusted Mirabeau enough to put themselves in his hands. But the idea of escape was still bruited about in royal circles, made even more pressing by the king's religious scruples and by the approaching completion of the constitution.

In April 1791, Louis XVI wished to travel to Saint-Cloud, one of the royal family's country houses, for Easter. If he remained in Paris, he would have to take communion from a constitutional priest. He hoped that in the seclusion of Saint-Cloud, he could take communion from a refractory priest. These intentions were well understood in Paris, and when he tried to leave, his carriage was surrounded by a large crowd that prevented his departure. Lafayette ordered the National Guard to open a way for the king's carriage, but they refused to obey, and the family was forced to walk back into the palace. Although the king had made previous visits to Saint-Cloud, this time suspicion was raised because of the king's well-known preference for receiving communion from a refractory priest. To radicals in Paris, this was tantamount to a rejection of the Revolution and a flouting of the law. Furthermore, rumors circulated that the visit to Saint-Cloud was merely a pretext for permanent flight from Paris or part of a plot by the "aristocratic" party to kidnap the king. Louis protested this denial of his freedom to the National Assembly, but made no further efforts to leave the city. Instead, he now turned to plans for a genuine escape.

Serious plans had been made since October 1790 to move the king to the protection of the army in a location near the border where he could receive the reinforcement of foreign troops. The people planning this maneuver hoped that Frenchmen in the provinces would rise in support of the king. Louis, notoriously indecisive, did not give his approval for the plan until after the Saint-Cloud incident. Delays continued, however, as the planners worked to get the courts of Spain and Austria behind the scheme. If Austrian troops were stationed across the frontier, they could come to their aid if necessary. After the Saint-Cloud incident, Marie Antoinette expressed their determination in a letter to Mercy-Argenteau, the former minister of Austria to France, now living in the Austrian Netherlands:

The event which has just occurred makes us even more resolute in our plans. The chief menace comes from the [national] guard that surrounds us. Even our lives are not safe. We have to give the impression of agreeing to everything until the moment we can act, and for the rest our state of captivity proves that nothing we are doing is of our own free will.[2]

Count Axel de Fersen, a Swedish nobleman and devoted friend (probably also lover) of the queen, worked out the details in consultation with Marie Antoinette. They secured the cooperation of the Marquis de Bouillé, who commanded the army at Metz on the eastern frontier. The general was already famous as a participant in the American Revolution and as the man who put down the Nancy Rebellion. The plan called for the king to go to the fortified town of Montmédy (near the border with the Austrian Netherlands) and rally the country from there. His brother, the comte de Provence (also known as Monsieur), would travel by a different route and join them there. Bouillé and Fersen urged the royal couple to travel separately, but they refused to do so. They insisted that their two children, the king's sister, and some servants should also go with them. This required two coaches, one of them especially large and conspicuous. They obtained a passport supposedly for a Russian baroness, her children, and her servants (the king was to play the role of her steward, the queen that of the children's governess).

On the night of June 20, 1791, the royal family slipped out of the palace around midnight. Their departure from Paris was slow, and they had to stop to repair a broken harness, which put them further behind. By the late afternoon of June 21, they were confident that their escape had worked as they approached the location where the first detachment of cavalry was supposed to be waiting to escort them. But when they arrived at the crossroads, the soldiers were not there, having watched in vain for the carriage to appear. The king and his party continued their journey, but the commanders had made the fatal decision of removing the troops, assuming the king was not coming and fearing arousing the countryside by the unexplained presence of the troops.

During the journey, the king was apparently recognized at several points by individuals who kept silent. But at Sainte-Menehould, as the horses were being changed, the postmaster, a man named Drouet, recognized the king and queen and raced ahead to raise the alarm. When the carriages entered the town of Varennes at about eleven at night, they did not find the expected fresh horses, and the coachmen refused to continue without them. The officials of the town stopped the carriage. Although a few troops were not too far away and might have come to their aid, Louis refused to use them for fear that his family might be harmed. National Guardsmen from the countryside were now converging on the small town and escape was impossible. The daring attempt was at an end. Because they were stopped at Varennes, the incident is known as the Flight to Varennes, though they had intended to go to Montmédy.

POLITICAL CLUBS AND THE
GROWTH OF REPUBLICANISM

On the morning of June 21, 1791, the people of Paris learned that the king and his family were not at the Tuileries. The news spread through a city that had been transformed by the Revolution, and the news would transform it even further. After the appointment of Bailly as mayor in July 1789, the sixty electoral districts had continued to meet and be involved in politics, even though their original electoral purpose no longer existed. Over the winter of 1789–1790, a lively debate over the municipal constitution highlighted different conceptions of proper government and led to the creation of organized political groups in the city. Bailly as mayor wanted a strong mayor to rule Paris without interference, and suspected that representatives of the districts organized as a city assembly would hamper the mayor's power. Another vision of city government was based on representative democracy. The city assembly, according to this view, represented the people of the city and should make policy. The mayor would be merely an administrator to carry out that policy. A third view, advocated by the districts, was direct democracy. National government, because of population size and distance, might have to rely on representation, but cities were small enough that they could be run by direct participatory democracy. Therefore, those who held this view believed that the district assemblies needed to be constantly consulted, and power should not be in the hands of either a mayor or a municipal assembly.

Direct democracy was advocated especially by the electors of the Cordeliers district, led by Georges-Jacques Danton. A member of that district, Louis-Marie Prudhomme, published an influential newspaper, *Révolutions de Paris*. Another group (many of whom sat in the city assembly and effectively advocated the representative view of city government) decided in January 1790 to organize a Cercle Social (Social Circle) that would publish a journal in which the views of the people could be read. They set up a box (called the *bouche de fer*, or iron mouth) into which letters and articles could be deposited. Led by Fauchet, Brissot, and Bonneville, the Cercle Social opposed Bailly's administration.

When the Constituent Assembly reorganized municipal administration throughout the country in the spring of 1790, they wrote special legislation for Paris (passed on May 21, 1790) that eliminated the old electoral districts and divided the city for electoral purposes into forty-eight sections. This reorganization, moderates hoped, would disrupt the influence of radical electors who had still been meeting in the old districts. The strategy seemed to work when, in August 1790, Bailly won election for mayor, marking a victory for the conservative element in the municipal government. However, the new sections soon became centers of radical agitation, with electors meeting continually, coordinating activities with each other, and developing arguments for direct democratic government. The sections also worked closely with popular political clubs to promote radicalism. These section meetings would become the centers of power for the *sans-culottes* in Paris. This popular political movement took its name (which means literally "without breeches") from the fact that workingmen generally wore trousers and not the fancy culottes or knee breeches with silk stockings favored by aristocrats.

After Bailly's election, men in the old Cordeliers district created a political club called the Société des Amis des Droits de l'Homme (Society of the Friends of the Rights of Man), but generally known as the Cordeliers Club. Situated in the Paris publishing district, it counted many able writers and orators among its members, including Camille Desmoulins, Marat, and Danton. The Cordeliers Club was the vehicle for the rise to power of Danton, a remarkable politician, destined to compete with Robespierre as the embodiment of the Revolution in later history books. Danton had moved to Paris from a small town in Champagne and had become a minor attorney. Thirty years old at the beginning of the Revolution, he had a commanding presence, with an imposing physique and a face pockmarked by smallpox. Inspired by the Enlightenment (he owned a copy of the *Encyclopédie*), his fiery speeches lacked the literary flourishes of his contemporaries. He spoke with the directness of his peasant forebears and ably put together a kind of political machine. Unlike Robespierre, the man who would become his rival, Danton was married, had children, and enjoyed life. Indeed, he would ultimately be accused of enjoying it too much.

The Cercle Social hoped to continue their influence by imitating the Cordeliers. They created a new club called the Confédération des Amis de la Vérité (Confederation of the Friends of the Truth). They intended to bring together members of various societies who could agitate for democracy and promote Enlightenment ideas. One of their first decisions was to study the writings of Rousseau. The Cercle Social differed from other clubs in their interest in women's rights and in their willingness to work with other societies (they even sought members in foreign countries). In order to attend their meetings, one had to subscribe to their newspaper, *Bouche de Fer*.

By the spring of 1791, then, many different political groups existed, but the most influential were the Jacobins (officially the Society of the Friends of the Constitution). The membership of this club, which had begun as a meeting for radical deputies in the Constituent Assembly to coordinate their strategy for the next day's session, was originally limited to deputies. But meetings were soon opened to active citizens. They extended their reach by creating a network of patriotic clubs throughout the country. A correspondence committee maintained contact with their allies, a source of great strength for the Jacobins in Paris. Considerable variation existed among local Jacobin Clubs. Some were more like social clubs or reading clubs, but they all emphasized politics and saw themselves as guardians of and advocates for the Revolution.

As their official name indicated, they supported the constitution. They also advocated equality of political rights, and they sought to discover traitors and uncover conspiracies. The controversy over the Civil Constitution of the Clergy (which they favored) lost them some Catholic members, but it also prompted the founding of many more provincial Jacobin Clubs. Members of Jacobin Clubs were generally well off, because they were limited at first to active citizens and had to pay membership fees. When more popular societies, like the Cordeliers, began to compete with them, the Jacobin Clubs opened their doors to men of lesser means, although urban residents of various trades and professions (especially government officials) dominated. By the summer of 1791, several hundred provincial clubs were affiliated with the "mother society" in Paris. Other patriotic societies existed that were not directly affiliated with the Jacobins, and the number of societies continued to grow after the Flight to Varennes.

Because of unhappiness with the increasing radicalism of the Jacobins, in the spring of 1790, a group of moderate deputies, including such prominent revolutionaries as Sieyès, Lafayette, Bailly, Mirabeau, Talleyrand, and Le Chapelier, had broken off from the Jacobins to found the Society of 1789. As the name implied, they supported the decisions made by the Assembly in 1789, but wanted to halt further democratization. Its high admission costs and stated goal of not becoming a political party kept the Society of 1789 from developing into a widespread organization, although they tried to imitate the Jacobins by establishing ties to provincial clubs. On the right, the deputies who favored a strong monarchy (*Monarchiens* or *Im-*

Figure 5.1. Jacobin Club. The Paris Jacobin Club met in an old Dominican monastery near the National Assembly's meeting place. This engraving depicts members listening to debate in the former monastery. Incongruous religious images still decorated the room. Private collection.

partiaux) established the Society of Friends of the Monarchical Constitution in early 1790. Led by Malouet and Clermont-Tonnerre, they became objects of continual harassment in Paris. When they provided charity to the poor in Paris, their efforts were denounced as attempts to subvert the people. They were also suspected of using their wealth to fund "brigands" who were supposedly hiding in Paris and would be employed to destroy the Revolution. After several attacks against the Society, the Assembly ordered it closed in March 1791.

Fear of violence and conspiracy was widespread, heightened by these political groups, all of whom printed newspapers and published pamphlets, filled with accusations, innuendoes, and outright falsehoods. The population of Paris was the most literate in the country, and even those who were unable to read could go to cafés where newspapers would be read aloud. The authorities tried to keep informed of political movements by employing spies. Radicals in Paris assumed that aristocrats who had gone into exile were fomenting revolt, paying informers, and waiting for the opportunity to get back into power. These suspicions were often justified.

The aristocrats and noble officers in exile had hoped to gain the help of foreign governments, but they had no success in that endeavor. Despite their small number, in the spring of 1791, émigrés began to organize military units. One of the motivations of the king's flight had been Louis XVI and Marie Antoinette's fear that Artois and other nobles in exile intended to mount an invasion that would have put their lives in danger (or at least have made flight no longer possible). Even more significant for the future, counter-revolutionary movements had begun to organize within the country, brought together especially around the Catholic cause. A pitched battle had already occurred between Catholics and Protestants in Nîmes in May 1790. Counter-revolutionaries encouraged people who opposed the Civil Constitution to harass constitutional priests and to boycott their services. Refractory priests, who continued ministering to their congregations, made implementing the Civil Constitution impossible. This led to violence, as the National Guard and other officials representing the new institutions resorted to forceful (and often illegal) means to exact compliance. Women frequently dominated the demonstrations in support of refractory priests. They saw the constitutional priests as aliens to the community and as threats to its moral life. These religious struggles became worse after the Flight to Varennes.

Considering the escalation of religious confrontation throughout the country and the degree of political engagement in the capital, Paris remained surprisingly calm after Louis XVI's disappearance was discovered. In part, this can be attributed to prompt and decisive action by the authorities. Not knowing what had happened, they announced that the king had been kidnapped. The municipal government worked with the National Assembly to make sure that order was preserved. The National Assembly met around the clock and declared that their decisions carried the force of law, even without the approval of the king. Their declaration proved that it was surprisingly easy to dispense with the monarchy. Before the Flight to Varennes, Louis XVI had still been accorded the paternal devotion traditionally enjoyed by the king. He was pictured as the "good father" who cared for his children and who, though he might perhaps be somewhat weak and led astray by evil counselors, wanted nonetheless to do what was best for his people. Except for a handful of fanatics, nobody had expressed support for a republic (that is, a government without a king). But that changed immediately with his flight. Crowds defaced buildings and signs that referred to royalty. One newspaper asked, "How could one ever again have confidence in anything the king might say?"[3] Not only had he contradicted his earlier promises by flight, but confident that he would enjoy the devotion of the people outside of Paris if he could just escape from the city, the king had left behind a document in his own handwriting explaining in detail his unhappiness with the Revolution.

In his declaration, the king complained that the country had dissolved into anarchy and that he had been held in captivity. He especially protested that he had been given no role in making the constitution, contrary to the desires expressed in the *cahiers* that laws should be made "in concert with the King."[4] He reviewed in detail the provisions of the new institutions that he deplored, insisting that he had no desire to return to absolutism, but that his role now was only "a vain semblance of monarchy." The committees in the Assembly, he charged, had taken away much of his power and were themselves acting despotically. Louis warned that the Jacobin Clubs now constituted "an immense corporation" whose every proclamation was obeyed by the authorities, including the National Assembly itself. He asked, "Would you want the anarchy and despotism of the clubs to supplant the monarchical government under which the nation has prospered for fourteen hundred years?" The king pledged to create a constitution that would respect religion and to establish liberty on firm foundations.[5]

The news that Louis XVI had been caught reached Paris on the night of June 22. The next day, a large demonstration took place. A celebration of the religious festival of Corpus Christi had for some time been planned for that day. The procession now became a patriotic celebration of the capture of the king by ordinary citizens who wound their way through the city singing the revolutionary song, "*Ah, ça ira! Ça ira! Ça ira!*" (It'll all work out! It'll all be okay!). That night thousands of people converged on the National Assembly, marched into the chamber, and insisted on following the example of the National Guardsmen, who had sworn an oath of devotion to the constitution.

The Assembly began to make preparations for war, fearing that the king's flight had been coordinated with foreign powers. Although a secret envoy had delivered a letter from Marie Antoinette begging her brother, the Austrian emperor, to place troops in the Austrian Netherlands to help them if necessary, the Austrians had done nothing. The Assembly sent deputies to the border departments with full powers to take any necessary measures. They also sent three deputies to meet the returning king. Two were moderates, Antoine Barnave and César de Latour-Maubourg (a close friend of Lafayette), and a third a radical, Jérome Pétion. The three men squeezed into the already crowded conveyance. Their trip back to Paris was delayed by enormous crowds that surrounded the king's carriage along the route. When they reached Paris on June 25, 1791, the streets were lined with people who watched in stony silence as the royal convoy passed by.

The Assembly now faced an agonizing decision. What were they to do about the king? He was suspended from his functions as king and kept under watch while the Assembly hotly debated the issue. The question could not, of course, be confined to the Assembly as debate raged throughout the country. Ordinary people expressed their sense of betrayal at Louis's faithlessness. At first, fearing that the escape was a signal that the country was to be invaded, people took extraordinary steps to arm themselves, and they attacked nobles and refractory priests, who were assumed to be in on a massive conspiracy. Suspicious-seeming individuals were arrested, the mails were intercepted, and in the border regions, civil authorities took over fortresses and forced out the noble officers. The first reactions were panic and fear of conspiracy. Rumors spread that foreign troops had already invaded the country.

In Paris, the Jacobin Club took up the question of the fate of the king at a particularly stormy session on June 21. Radicals led by Robespierre accused those deputies who wanted to retain the king of being counter-revolutionaries. Moderates managed to get the Jacobin Club to endorse the idea that they would stand behind whatever the National Assembly decided, a decision that they hoped would heal the great split that had been created by the Flight to Varennes. In the discussion at the Assembly, moderates argued that the law gave the king immunity from prosecution. Robespierre, on the other hand, charged that the king could not be trusted and was therefore unfit to rule. It was obvious to the Assembly that public opinion in Paris had turned against the king. But they did not know whether the opinion in the rest of the country agreed with Paris. Furthermore, moderates declared, decisions should be based on rational attention to the law, not on temporary and passionate public opinion.

Ultimately, the National Assembly made a decision based on fear of a republic and on fear of what would happen if the king were removed from office. No acceptable alternative to Louis XVI existed if they decided to replace him with another king. His son, the dauphin, was only five years old, and if he were declared king the country would have to be ruled by a regent. With the king's two brothers in exile, the most likely regents were the Duc d'Orléans, whom they distrusted, or Marie Antoinette, who was obviously unacceptable. Deciding for a republic might cause foreign powers to declare war. Furthermore, unruly demonstrations by republicans did not instill confidence in the people's ability to govern themselves. Besides, if they opted for a republic all their work of the previous two years in writing a monarchical constitution would have to be thrown out and the process started all over again. The king made a gesture of reconciliation in a second declaration on June 27, 1791. He asserted that he had left Paris because of the outrages committed against him in April (the Saint-Cloud incident). He offered assurances that he had no intention of leaving the country and that he had come to realize on his journey that public opinion supported the constitution and that he was therefore resolved to accept the will of the people.

Convinced of the king's obvious duplicity, many radicals published calls for a republic and began to advocate insurrection. The anniversary of the fall of the Bastille on July 14 was celebrated by a festival similar to the previous year's, but with the king conspicuously absent and not mentioned. The next day, the National Assembly decided that the king would be retained. Eagerly affecting to believe General Bouillé, who sent a letter from exile taking full responsibility for the "abduction," the moderates led the National Assembly to declare that the king had been kidnapped. On July 16, the final vote on the decree and its amendments was taken. Louis XVI would once again take the throne, but only after the constitution had been completed and he had freely accepted it (whether a king who was under arrest could make such a decision freely was, of course, problematic). The constitution was amended to specify that if the king left the country or took up arms against the nation or retracted his oath to the constitution, "he shall be deemed to have abdicated the throne."[6]

The Cordeliers Club, which had unsuccessfully sent petitions to the Assembly asking them to depose the king, now took the lead (along with the Friends of the Truth) in protesting the Assembly's decision and demanding a referendum on the fate of the king. On the evening of July 15, when a crowd of demonstrators broke into the Jacobin Club to urge them to join in their protest, most of the deputies, disgusted by the extreme behavior and appalled that the decisions of the National Assembly were being questioned, left the club never to return. The radicals who remained in the Jacobin Club, including the deputies Robespierre and Pétion, though sympathetic to the Cordeliers' demand for the removal of the king and their call for a national referendum on the king and the constitution, eventually chose not to question the decision taken by the Assembly, which they considered the voice of national sovereignty. The Jacobins did not join in the Cordeliers' project of another petition to be signed on July 17 at the Champ de Mars, the site of the recent festival in commemoration of the fall of the Bastille.

The Assembly watched the rising agitation with considerable alarm, and ordered the municipal authorities to take vigorous action. On the morning of July 17, as large numbers of people gathered to sign the petition, an unfortunate incident occurred. Two men were discovered hiding under the platform. Most historians conclude that they had probably chosen that location to look up the skirts of the women who came to sign the petition. But those who found them, fearing that they were spies or aristocrats who intended to set off explosives, arrested them. Before they could deliver them to the authorities, some of the crowd seized them and hanged them from a lamppost. The Assembly sent a letter to Bailly urging the municipal authorities to take "the most vigorous and efficient measures possible to halt the disorder and find the instigators."[7] In the late afternoon, after some six thousand people had signed (or made their mark on) the petition, the city authorities declared martial law and ordered the National Guard to clear the Champ de Mars. When the troops entered the area, they were pelted with stones and apparently also were shot at, although the exact order of events is controversial. The warning to disperse as required by law was not issued. The troops, apparently feeling themselves to be under attack, fired some warning shots, then began firing on the crowds. Nobody knows for certain how many were killed, though a reasonable estimate is that around fifty died and many others were wounded. The Massacre of the Champ de Mars (as it came to be known) on July 17, 1791, polarized the population of Paris.

AFTERMATH OF THE FLIGHT TO VARENNES

The Flight to Varennes had transformed the political landscape. One result was a thriving republican movement. Even though most of the country went along with the decision of the National Assembly to retain the king, they did so out of respect for the National Assembly or because of fear of what a republic would bring about, not because of love for the king. In a message to the Assembly, the authorities in a village near Bordeaux expressed their sentiments this way: "We would rather be burdened with a king who is worthless and deceitful, than be forced to face the horrors of civil and foreign war."[8]

A second result of the flight was a polarization among the patriots. Radicals were now even more suspicious of authority and more prone to believe in conspiracy. If the king had been deceiving them all along, how many were in on the deception, they wondered. The people had put their trust in Bailly and Lafayette, but those men had allowed the king to escape and had led the troops to the atrocities of the Champ de Mars. The authorities, on the other hand, feared the increasing radicalism of the republican movement. Despite guarantees of freedom of the press, they closed down incendiary newspapers, rounded up radical writers, and arrested people who disturbed the peace by shouting criticisms of the National Assembly or who harassed the National Guards. Many of those arrested protested later that they had been kept in solitary confinement for weeks.

The leaders of the Paris government and the National Assembly felt justified in taking extraordinary measures to protect the state whose very survival seemed threatened by this emergency. Even men who had identified with the left in the Assembly now began to question whether the revolutionary movement had gone too far. If they were to succeed in creating a new order, the constitution needed to be completed and regular institutions set up. The republicans, they believed, were threatening the work that the Assembly had been doing for the past two years. They thought it was time to end the Revolution.

A third result, therefore, was a split in the Jacobin Club in Paris as a substantial majority of the deputies created another Society of the Friends of the Constitution. From the name of the old monastery in which they met, they were nicknamed the Feuillant Club. Both groups claimed to be the real Society of the Friends of the Constitution, and at first the Feuillants had the better claim to the name. Only a handful of the most radical deputies (most notably Robespierre, Pétion, and Grégoire) remained at the

Jacobin Club, and their membership was only a fraction of the Feuillant membership. Both societies sent circulars to provincial clubs inviting them to join in association. At first the provincial societies were unsure what to do, but the superior propaganda of Robespierre and Pétion and the fact that most radical newspapers in Paris remained loyal to the Jacobins turned the tide. By fall of 1791, the Jacobins were recovering their numbers and affiliates. More radical than before because the moderate deputies had left, the Jacobins were poised to grow even more influential in the future.

Fourth, the Flight to Varennes influenced the shape of the constitution. It was almost complete when the king left. Indeed, that was one of the reasons for the timing. If the king could hope to have any influence on the constitution he had to act before it was finalized. The Feuillants, who dominated the Constitutional Committee and the Committee on Revisions, now pushed through a few changes in the constitution to make it more palatable to the king. The Civil Constitution of the Clergy was removed from the constitution, designated as ordinary legislation, and therefore made subject to revision in a regular legislative assembly. Many Feuillants hoped to do more, to create a two-house legislature and give more power to the king. But neither those on the left nor on the far right were willing to make such changes.

Three prominent deputies, nicknamed the "Triumvirate" (Adrien Duport, Antoine Barnave, and Alexandre Lameth), had looked forward to the completion of the constitution and realized that it would be necessary to work with the king. After the death of Mirabeau, they had tried to negotiate secretly with the king. Their negotiations became more serious after the Flight to Varennes. Barnave, one of the deputies sent to accompany the royal family back to Paris, had been struck by the woeful predicament of Marie Antoinette. During that journey he had pledged to help her, and from then on he maintained a correspondence with her, sending advice on ways to make the constitutional system a success. These three deputies, formerly bitter rivals of Lafayette, now worked with him and other moderate revolutionaries in the Assembly to finish the constitution. Other deputies suspected their maneuvers were ambitious schemes for power. Many deputies, even those who shared the political goals of the "Triumvirate," continued to interpret desire for office or attempts to coordinate political activities as throwbacks to the intrigues and "despotism" of the Ancien Régime.

Finally, the Flight to Varennes had important repercussions on the international front. The powers of Europe could no longer pretend to believe that the king was free and in control of the French state. But in the state system of the eighteenth century with its continual rivalries and competitions, the weakness of the French government merely meant to the other powers that they did not have to worry about France and could pursue their aggressive intentions without hindrance from that quarter. The emperor of Austria, Leopold II, was Marie Antoinette's brother, but he had no interest in launching a crusade to save the power of the king of France unless he was joined by other countries, and that was unlikely. Austria and Prussia were both worried about Catherine the Great of Russia, whose aggressive policies had resulted in the first partition of Poland in 1772, in which each of those powers had gotten a piece of Polish territory. Catherine was urging Leopold II and Frederick William II of Prussia to go to the rescue of the French monarchy. They could easily see that she wanted to keep them busy in France so that she could take over more territory for Russia in Eastern Europe. Naturally, they did not want to allow that to happen.

It is important not to assume that the revolutionaries' fears were true. They tended to believe that a conservative Europe was going to invade the country to stamp out the French Revolution before it could spread throughout all of Europe. But the other powers did not yet see the French Revolution as a danger to their own power. They faced many other dangers at the time that seemed much more serious, and they were content at first to watch France sink into chaos and thus impotence. They distrusted each other and were not cooperating in an ideological crusade. In foreign policy, ideology is rarely the most important concern. State interest and security are much more important.

Nonetheless, the émigrés were agitating for the powers to do something. Leopold, wanting to make a gesture in support of his sister to uphold family honor, persuaded the king of Prussia to join him in issuing a statement called the Declaration of Pillnitz of August 27, 1791. They pledged that the two monarchs would undertake joint action to restore order in France *if* other powers joined them. Leopold knew that this cooperation was highly unlikely, but he hoped that the declaration would help Louis and Marie Antoinette in their struggle with the revolutionaries. Marie Antoinette immediately realized that they had been abandoned. However, the émigrés were heartened by the declaration, and the revolutionaries interpreted it as a genuine threat. The moderate revolutionaries recognized that the best way to prevent a European crusade against France was to keep the king on the throne. So they made changes in the constitution and persuaded the king to accept it. In no condition to fight a war, the French army continued to be disorganized, with mutinous troops and an officer corps decimated by emigration. Emigration of noble officers became even more frequent after the Flight to Varennes.

LEGISLATIVE ASSEMBLY

On September 13, 1791, the king formally accepted the new constitution and on September 30 the National Constituent Assembly, which had pledged to write a constitution, ended its work. The new National Assembly, elected according to the constitution for a two-year term, was known as the Legislative Assembly. In a rather puzzling gesture of seeming self-sacrifice, the Constituent Assembly had voted on May 16, 1791, that none of the current deputies would be eligible for reelection to the new legislature. Robespierre introduced this measure because he wanted to prevent the moderate leaders of the Constituent Assembly from continuing to exercise power. He assumed correctly that without those well-known candidates, more radical members would be chosen. He found support in his ideological opposites on the extreme right, who hoped to undermine the new institutions from the very beginning in the hopes that they would fail and a strong monarchy could again emerge from the wreckage. Moderates had difficulty opposing the measure (often called the "self-denying ordinance") because to do so would make them look ambitious and greedy for power. Indeed, the deputies in the middle who voted for this measure apparently were motivated by concern that, even if drawn from within their own ranks, leaders might be susceptible to the temptations of power and become despotic. They were persuaded by Robespierre's arguments that four years in office would expose them "to royal seductions, to the seduction of their own power, and to all the temptations of pride and cupidity."[9] In his view, efforts to organize the assembly amounted to little more than "intrigue." They would be better off without their experienced leaders.

This dramatic gesture deprived the new Legislative Assembly of those who had gained experience in government and who were devoted to the constitution that they had worked so hard to write. It also deprived the new assembly of people who understood the religious issues, especially the views of those opposing the Civil Constitution of the Clergy. Very few priests were elected in 1791, and all of those were constitutional priests. Noblemen were much less numerous in the Legislative Assembly. Most deputies were men of property with reputations that had been earned since the beginning of the Revolution. They tended to be local or departmental officials. One consequence was that deputies of some standing in the old assembly who wanted to continue to have an effect on decision-making now could devote more time to radical politics in the clubs. For example, Robespierre, no longer in the Assembly, came to dominate the meetings of the Jacobin Club.

Also in the spring of 1791, in another measure against "ambition," the Assembly had reaffirmed the decision made in November 1789 that no member of the Assembly could serve as a minister of the king. They further decreed that departing deputies had to wait four years before they could serve as ministers. So the men who had made the Revolution and written the constitution had no part to play in working for its success when it was finally put into effect. The king, deprived of the support of members of the Constituent Assembly who could not be his ministers and who would no longer be even members of the Assembly, now entered into a policy of outward support for the constitution, while he continued a secret diplomacy through agents at foreign courts in hopes of finding some way to reestablish the power of the monarchy. This double-faced policy did not augur well for the future of the new government.

CONCLUSION

Any person who tried to work with the king was accused by radical revolutionaries of being an intriguer or unpatriotic or counter-revolutionary. The result was a gradual drift to the left, as those on the right of the political spectrum lost influence or disappeared from the scene. More and more people were assumed to be associated with the royalist émigrés or their allies within France. The political position of men, like Mounier, who at the beginning of the Estates General had seemed quite revolutionary, came to seem moderate or even counter-revolutionary as more extreme positions developed on the left. The point can be illustrated by focusing on a few of the major leaders. With the disappearance of Mounier and Mirabeau, those who had once been considered quite radical found themselves on the right of the political spectrum. By 1791, Lafayette, for example, now found Lameth and Duport on his left, and on their left were Robespierre and Pétion, with the Cordeliers and Marat still further left. So even though Lafayette had not substantially changed his political position, more ardent revolutionaries now saw him as a counter-revolutionary, especially after the Massacre of the Champ de Mars. The Flight to Varennes had accelerated this trend. Jacobins believed one of their main purposes was to watch for intriguers and to discover treason and to "unmask" it. Any sign of lack of devotion to the revolutionary cause was construed as treason.

The difficulty all leaders faced was making the new institutions stable. The constitution was generally respected in the country, and many were willing to forgive the king. But they were unable to forget what had happened and remained suspicious of his intentions. The Legislative Assembly, which was intended to be the beginning of a permanent new regime, lasted less than a year.

6

THE FAILURE OF
CONSTITUTIONAL GOVERNMENT

The Constituent Assembly considered itself the embodiment of the national will with the authority to write the founding document for the country. The constitution was put into effect with the election of the Legislative Assembly, which opened on October 1, 1791. The Revolution was presumably over, as the king declared when he accepted the constitution and as the Constituent Assembly likewise declared when it granted a general amnesty to all those under arrest for various public disturbances. France now established a regular government following the provisions of the constitution, with the king and his ministers as the executive branch to carry into effect the laws written by the Assembly as the legislative branch. But conflicts did not end. Disputes arose over exactly how the new institutions were supposed to operate and who was to exercise ultimate authority.

THE NEW GOVERNMENT UNDER THE CONSTITUTION

The king had been deprived of a great deal of the power he had enjoyed under the Ancien Régime (the right to make law, for example). Although under the Constitution of 1791 the monarchy was weaker even than the British monarchy, the king still had considerable authority had he chosen to exercise it. Louis XVI's attitude to the new institutions was ambiguous at best. He apparently intended to follow the letter of the law as set out in the constitution in order to show the country that the system was unworkable. He believed that if he did, "public opinion will change; and since without this change new convulsions will be inevitable, I will have more chance of achieving a better state of things by my acceptance than by my refusal."[1] He rarely took the initiative and hoped the country would be persuaded that he was right when they saw the new institutions fail. The problem with this strategy was that many came to blame the king himself for the failure, rather than the institutions. The new Assembly was intensely suspicious of the king, especially since the Flight to Varennes, and believed its primary responsibility was, not so much to make laws, as to watch over the royal executive.

It is instructive to compare the Legislative Assembly's organization to that of the new Congress of the United States, also first formed under a new constitution in 1788. In the United States, Congress at first did not establish permanent committees, but instead relied on ad hoc committees that would be disbanded as soon as the work was done. This procedure gave the president and his advisers the initiative in setting the agenda and drafting legislation. In the French Legislative Assembly, on the other hand, permanent committees were immediately created because the deputies believed their major obligation was to keep an eye on the executive branch. Their suspicion of the executive was obvious in the remarks of one deputy, who announced that the purpose of the diplomatic committee was to "oversee the operations of the minister of foreign affairs and to know our political state vis-à-vis the other powers who see with sorrow the destruction of despotism and the dawn of liberty rise over the universe. . . ."[2] In contrast to the United States where the executive power was in the hands of an elected and respected national hero, the French executive was an untrustworthy king, and the Legislative Assembly resolved right away to combat the executive power.

According to the constitution, the Legislative Assembly could not remove the king, nor could they dismiss the king's ministers (just as the American Congress cannot dismiss a member of the president's cabinet). However, the constitution did allow the Assembly to bring charges against the king's ministers for gross dereliction of duty. In November, the Assembly ordered its committee on legislation to prepare a decree on the means of enforcing ministerial responsibility, thus showing that they were already thinking of removing ministers. In a genuine parliamentary system, when the king chooses his ministers from among the members of the legislature, the legislature can remove them from office by passing a vote of no confidence. Because the French constitution was based on the concept of a strict separation of powers, the only way the Legislative Assembly could remove ministers was to accuse them of impeachable crimes. They very quickly began to use this power for political ends. At the end of November they created a committee specifically charged with hunting out incidents of treason against the nation.

The Assembly was not merely suspicious of the power of the executive. They feared as well the development of leadership within their own body. The more radical deputies wanted to avoid the kind of leadership group that had existed in the Constituent Assembly, dominated by moderates who sat on several committees at the same time. That leadership had been successfully destroyed when the "self-denying ordinance" forbade their election to the new body. In the Legislative Assembly, they hoped to prevent individuals from gaining too much experience and power by stipulating that each deputy could sit on only one committee and by providing for new committee members every six months.

The members of the Legislative Assembly were younger than those of the Constituent Assembly. Fewer former nobles and only a few priests (all of them constitutional priests) sat in the new Assembly. Although we can conclude that, overall, the deputies were more to the left than those of the Constituent, the political views of individual deputies are hard to determine because political party affiliations of a modern kind did not exist. It is difficult to judge their views on the basis of voting because, except for seven occasions, the votes of individual deputies were not recorded.

At the beginning, of the 750 deputies in the Legislative Assembly approximately equal numbers were members of the Jacobin Club and the Feuillant Club.[3] But most deputies were not associated with either political club, and it would be inaccurate to see all that happened within the Assembly as a struggle between these two groups. The most prominent Jacobin in the Legislative Assembly was Jacques-Pierre Brissot, while Robespierre (no longer in the Assembly) held sway at the meetings of the Jacobin Club. The Jacobins, who considered the Feuillants to be dangerous compromisers with the royal government, were now convinced that a grand conspiracy threatened France, bringing together the royal government, the émigrés, former nobles, non-juring priests, and foreign powers that supported them.

Counter-revolutionary forces did not, in fact, all agree. Emigrés wanted their positions in France back, and many of them (including the king's brother Artois) considered the king a fool for cooperating with the revolutionaries. Some believed that the king might have to be sacrificed for the sake of restoring a strong monarchy and nobility. Louis XVI did not rely on the émigrés because he realized that their agitation was hurting his position inside the country and would cause civil war, which he desperately wanted to avoid. He had sent a trusted envoy, the Baron de Breteuil, to negotiate for him with foreign powers. Louis and Marie Antoinette (who often wrote letters in the king's name when he was depressed or unable to take firm positions) backed the idea of an "armed congress" that had first been proposed by the Austrian chancellor Kaunitz in July 1791. The European powers, backed by armies, would meet at a location near France (perhaps Aix-la-Chapelle) and demand that France live up to its international obligations. Marie Antoinette believed that the king could then play the role of mediator between the foreign menace and the people of France, thus increasing his authority and rallying the people behind him. Although this meeting was never held, it was much discussed among the powers, and news of these discussions increased fears in France of foreign intervention and heightened suspicions of the king.

BRISSOT AND THE GIRONDINS

The deputy who had the greatest impact on France's foreign policy decisions was Jacques-Pierre Brissot, the son of a chef and caterer from Chartres. Like others in the eighteenth century who aspired to nobility, Brissot added an ending to his name to make it sound noble. He called himself Brissot de Warville. Other pronounced revolutionaries had done the same thing. Roland called himself Roland de la Platière, Pétion added "de Villeneuve," and Danton engaged in creative spelling, "d'Anton." Brissot studied law, then became a journalist and a writer. After a failed publishing venture in London, he returned to France in 1784, only to be imprisoned in the Bastille for two months for writing satirical pamphlets against the government. He made a living by writing pamphlets to promote the interests of the banker Etienne Clavière and the Duc d'Orléans. At the same time he became involved in reform groups, especially the Gallo-American Society, which encouraged exchanges between France and America.

Inspired by Enlightenment ideas, Rousseau's egalitarian notions, and the British anti-slavery movement, Brissot founded the Society of the Friends of the Blacks in 1788. Essentially a French branch of an English anti-slavery committee, this society was more radical, advocating suppression of the slave trade and ultimately the abolition of slavery. Although the group was not large, it counted among its members such prominent revolutionaries as Lafayette, Pétion, Condorcet, Sieyès, and Grégoire. The institution of slavery did not exist in metropolitan France, but slave labor was employed on the sugar plantations in the French colonies in the Caribbean, the source of great wealth for the country. Brissot founded his influential newspaper *Le Patriote Français* in the summer of 1789 and continued to publish it even after he had been elected to the Legislative Assembly.

Convinced of the king's duplicity, Brissot sought ways to bring the king's treachery out into the open. Brissot and his associates are known as the Brissotins or the Girondins, a name given to them because several important orators in the Legislative Assembly who were allied with Brissot (including Gensonné, Guadet, and Vergniaud) came from the area of Bordeaux in the department of the Gironde. These deputies were important because, despite being a minority in the Assembly, their exceptional oratorical skills enabled them to dominate the proceedings. The Girondins did not constitute a modern political party, with set membership, well-coordinated activities, and a large body of citizens out in the country who identified with them. They cooperated in the Assembly but were always, as one historian wrote, "a small and loose-knit group or coalition of individuals" who maintained "their personal independence."[4] During the period of the Legislative Assembly they participated in the debates in the Jacobin Club. Later they would lead the opposition to Robespierre, whose associates would be called the Mountain, the best organized group of all.

Indeed, none of these groups can really be called a political party. People in the 1790s were in general opposed to political parties. Inspired by the ideas of the Enlightenment, they believed that by applying reason one could arrive at the truth. If only one truth exists, then two parties with different views could not both embody the truth at the same time. Anybody who persisted in opposition to the true good of the commonwealth was assumed to be motivated by selfish reasons. The influence of Rousseau's notion of the general will is important here. The general will was what was best for the nation as a whole—what was best for the collectivity. Individual wills, on the other hand, were by definition particular and therefore different from the will of the nation. The very word "party" reflected the idea that it promoted only the interests of a part of the commonwealth, not the whole.

But during the French Revolution, aiming for unanimity would result in a search for traitors. Because the constitution was so new and had dangerous opponents, supporters of the Revolution were especially apprehensive that those who disagreed with them might actually be cooperating with the enemies of the nation and the Revolution. All sides in the conflict (including the right) denied they were political parties. They proclaimed that they were acting for the good of the nation and that their opponents were a "faction" that did not have the best interests of the country at heart. Such attitudes were not held exclusively by French people. In the United States in the 1790s, the federalists and republicans likewise denied they were political parties while engaging in fierce debates with each other and acting very much like political parties.

THE COMING OF WAR

The king recognized that the agitation of the émigrés was undermining his assertion that he had willingly accepted the constitution. On October 14, 1791, he issued a proclamation calling on the émigrés to return from exile, and he wrote to his brothers with the same message. Brissot did not trust the sincerity of this declaration. In response he called for military force to disperse the émigrés. In retrospect, the émigrés appear to be a small, disorganized band of discontented exiles who could hardly aspire to overthrow the government of France. But the members of the Assembly generally regarded them as a serious danger. The bitter debate in the Assembly over what should be done about the émigré threat resulted in the decree of November 9, 1791, which stated that all Frenchmen assembled beyond the border were "suspect of conspiracy against the *Patrie* [the Fatherland]."[5] If they did not return by January 1, they would be declared guilty and be subject to the punishment of death. The princes and public officials who had left the country were to lose their positions and incomes immediately. Any army officer emigrating would be treated as a deserter. The decree seemed to violate the Declaration of the Rights of Man by not allowing people to travel freely, and the king vetoed it.

Because of their experience as departmental and local officials, the deputies were well aware of the religious troubles agitating many parts of the country. They placed the blame on the non-juring priests, who were said to be stirring up their followers to resist the provisions of the Civil Constitution of the Clergy. The Legislative Assembly decided to put an end to these troubles by requiring non-juring priests to take a civic oath within a week of the issuance of the decree. If they did not, they would be forced to leave their places of residence and be declared suspect of revolt against the nation. In his speech in support of this measure, Maxim Isnard (a Girondin) declared that a single priest could do more harm than "all your other enemies."[6] Not surprisingly, the king vetoed this measure as well.

As Isnard's remark shows, the two measures were related. The deputies believed that they faced a conspiracy of enemies within the country allied with enemies outside the country. They were confronted with large demonstrations in the Vendée protesting the religious laws and by armed émigrés just over the border. Internal and external considerations were also brought together by the issue of Avignon. The Comtat Venaissin and the city of Avignon comprised a small area in the south of France completely surrounded by French territory that had been property of the popes for hundreds of years. As the Revolution gathered steam, some inhabitants of this papal territory asked to be united to France. Although the Constituent Assembly had hesitated to take it over because they wanted the pope's co-operation in religious reforms, after the pope condemned the Civil Constitution, they formally annexed Avignon and the Comtat Venaissin in September 1791. In October, when violence broke out there between those who favored and those who opposed annexation, the response of the Assembly was the decree on refractory clergy. To the revolutionaries, the lesson was clear: The Catholic Church was standing in the way of democracy and progress. To foreign rulers, the annexation of Avignon spelled a different message: The French Revolution was beginning to have an impact on international law and to threaten the territory of other states.

The two vetoed decrees are indications of the growth of fears of conspiracy. To the deputies both émigrés and refractory priests seemed suspicious, even if they were not actually engaged in counter-revolutionary activity. And if refractory priests could not be trusted, maybe anybody who advocated Catholicism was suspicious. Suspicions of treason became even more pronounced when war started in the spring of 1792. The man who led the Assembly to declare war was Jacques-Pierre Brissot.

Motivated by ambition, fear, and trust in the soundness of French institutions, Brissot advocated "a crusade of universal freedom."[7] He urged the Assembly to close down the camp of the émigrés at Coblenz (in the territory of the elector of Trier) and to fight any foreign power that tried to protect them. He optimistically believed that the French would prevail if they struck first, instead of waiting for their enemies to attack. The Girondins believed that war could be won easily by French soldiers imbued with ideas of liberty and dedicated to the cause. They predicted that Austrian armies, made up of paid soldiers, would collapse, and areas subject to Austrian rule would rise up to throw off their oppressors. They looked with special interest at the neighboring Austrian Netherlands (often called Belgium, the name the area would adopt officially after independence in the nineteenth century). These hopeful expectations were promoted by Belgian refugees in Paris who assured the Girondins that their countrymen were eager to expel the Austrians. Brissot endorsed open warfare, believing that it would be less dangerous than the current situation where nobody knew who could be trusted.

Brissot particularly hoped that war would force the king to show his true colors. In December 1791, Brissot declared that "the chief executive officer will be forced to rule in accordance with the constitution. If he does his duty, we will support him whole-heartedly; but if he betrays us, the people will be ready."[8] The Assembly greeted these pro-war speeches, with

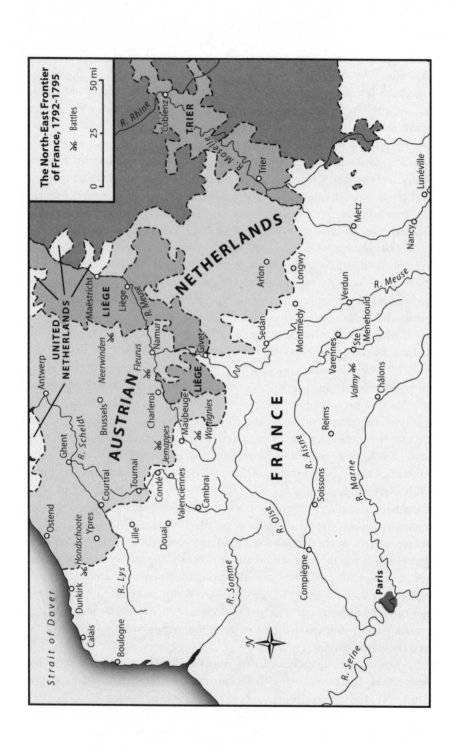

The North-East Frontier
of France, 1792-1795

Battles

0   25   50 mi

Strait of Dover

R. Rhine

Coblenz

TRIER

Trier

R. Moselle

Lunéville

Nancy

Metz

NETHERLANDS

Arlon

Longwy

Verdun

R. Meuse

UNITED
NETHERLANDS

Maëstricht

LIÈGE

Liège

R. Meuse

Namur

Sedan

Montmédy

Ste
Menehould

Antwerp

Neerwinden

Givet

LIÈGE

Varennes

Valmy

Châlons

AUSTRIAN

Brussels

Fleurus

Maubeuge

Wattignies

Reims

R. Marne

Ghent

R. Scheldt

Charleroi

Jemappes

Condé

R. Aisne

FRANCE

Ostend

Courtrai

Tournai

Valenciennes

Cambrai

Soissons

Hondschoote

Ypres

Lille

Douai

R. Oise

Compiègne

Dunkirk

R. Lys

R. Somme

Calais

Boulogne

N

R. Seine

Paris

their calls for upholding the honor of the French nation, with wild applause.

In the Jacobin Club, although the majority favored war, the war policy encountered the determined opposition of Robespierre. He became especially suspicious when the king's government seemed to advocate war. Robespierre was haunted by the fear of conspiracies and of hypocrites who merely seemed to be patriots. As early as the elections to the Estates General he had written a pamphlet in which (as the title proclaimed) he would "unmask" the enemies of the nation. He now believed that the real danger to the Revolution lay at home, not abroad. He declared that "the real Coblenz is in France."[9] Rejecting the suggestion that people in foreign countries would greet the French as liberators because they would help them throw off their rulers and allow them to adopt the new French institutions, Robespierre warned, "No one loves armed missionaries; and the first counsel that nature and prudence give is to repulse them as enemies."[10] He feared that war would shift power to the king and the generals, none of whom could be trusted: "You propose to give supreme power to those who most want your ruin."[11] In the heated debates at the Jacobin Club, Robespierre insisted that "war in the hands of the executive power is only a means to subvert the Constitution, only the climax of a profound conspiracy hatched to destroy liberty."[12] He was correct in warning that some of their enemies also wanted war. Marie Antoinette wrote to Fersen: "The imbeciles! They don't even see that this serves our purpose."[13] The attitude of the king was less sanguine. He did not trust that the émigrés or the foreign powers had his best interests at heart. If they fought a war, they would do so for their own interests. And war would cause the devastation of France, which he had tried so much to avoid by giving in to the revolutionary demands.

Also favoring war was a group of military men and moderate deputies aligned with Lafayette and with the Feuillants who wanted the constitutional monarchy to succeed. In the summer of 1789, the king had been deprived of command of the army inside the country. According to the constitution, he could have a small guard, but only in wartime could the king command the army. So a limited war to disperse the émigrés and punish those who harbored them would be a way for the king and the central government to gain more power. War, they confidently expected, would rally the country to the king and reduce its internal divisions.

In December 1791, the comte de Narbonne (who was reputed to be the illegitimate son of Louis XV and who was Mme de Staël's lover) was named minister of war and began cooperating with the Assembly in order to carry out this war policy. On December 14, Louis XVI appeared before the Assembly to announce that he had told the elector of Trier to oust the émigrés from his territory by January 15 or he would be considered an enemy of France. The king's appearance was greeted with prolonged applause. The elector, who wanted to avoid war, ordered the émigrés to disband. The French revolutionaries either did not believe the news that the émigrés had been dispersed or thought they were being tricked. Their enemies, they suspected, were merely buying time until they were prepared to attack France.

The principality of Trier constituted part of the Holy Roman Empire, and the Holy Roman Emperor was also the ruler of Austria, Leopold II. Leopold was becoming alarmed at the bellicose pronouncements coming out of the French Assembly and determined to take action. He believed that the Declaration of Pillnitz (issued in the summer of 1791) had exerted a restraining influence on the revolutionaries, and the king had been consequently put back on the throne. Hoping to repeat this beneficial action and strengthen the moderates in France, at the end of December Leopold announced that if the French army invaded the territory of the elector of Trier, the Austrian army in the Netherlands would come to the elector's aid. And he further threatened that all the European powers would join with the Austrians to maintain public order. This statement was a grave mistake, because it merely confirmed the Girondins' contention that a grand conspiracy existed that threatened France, and it made it impossible for moderates to negotiate a compromise solution with Austria. The debate in January over these matters resulted in frenzied expressions of patriotic devotion, with deputies crying out, "We shall live in freedom or we shall die! The Constitution or death!"[14] On January 24, 1792, the Assembly instructed Louis XVI to demand from Leopold that he would not interfere in French internal affairs or threaten French security. If Leopold did not respond satisfactorily by March 1, they declared, a state of war would exist between the two countries.

Leopold could not focus exclusively on the French Revolution. Much more threatening to Austria was the possibility of war in the east, where Russia's Catherine the Great had set her sights on more Polish territory. Leopold therefore sought closer ties with Frederick William II of Prussia, suggesting an international congress to deal with these issues, and hoping to bring Russia and other powers into this coalition as well. He saw a conference as a way of preventing war, and of defusing the demands coming from all sides that he intervene in France, which he did not want to do. In early February an alliance was signed between Prussia and Austria, and the two powers stationed armies along the borders of France to prevent an invasion of the Netherlands and the small principalities along the Rhine. By that time, however, the chance of avoiding war was almost gone. The French revolutionaries had misinterpreted Leopold's motives and believed that the foreign powers were ganging up on them. The foreign powers, on the other hand, did not understand that their traditional diplomacy of negotiation and compensation looked quite different from a revolutionary point of view. The revolutionaries especially resented any suggestion that foreign powers would meddle in their internal affairs, seeing such intervention as a threat to national sovereignty. Leopold died suddenly on March 1 and was succeeded by his young and inexperienced son, Francis II. But even had Leopold survived, it is unlikely that he could have prevented war.

The Girondins' campaign to bring about war encountered an obstacle. The constitution stated that a declaration of war was to be made "by a decree of the legislative body, rendered upon the formal and requisite proposal of the king, and sanctioned by him."[15] The assumption of those who wrote the constitution had been that kings entered into war for their own aggrandizement and that an assembly would need to restrain them. They believed that the people of a nation would be less eager for war than a king. The constitution expressed this idea directly: "The French nation renounces the undertaking of any war with a view of making conquests, and it will never use its forces against the liberty of any people."[16] But they now faced the opposite situation: The Assembly wanted to declare war (a war of self-defense, rather than conquest, they would argue), but the king and some of his ministers were trying to avoid it. The way out of the dilemma was found when the ministry was changed.

The peace party in the ministry seemed to have prevailed when the king dismissed Narbonne, the minister of war, who was promoting war as a way to increase the king's power. The Assembly then responded by bringing charges of treason against the foreign minister De Lessart for not being aggressive enough in his dealings with the Austrians. With the Assembly threatening further charges of treason, the king apparently decided fatalistically to appoint as his ministers Girondins who would have the support of the Assembly and who would share responsibility for the war. General Dumouriez, who had close ties to the Girondins, became the new foreign minister, De Grave was named minister of war, and Roland became minister of the interior. This Girondin ministry (or, as it is often called, the "Patriot ministry") successfully steered a declaration of war against Austria (France's traditional enemy) through the Assembly on April 20, 1792. The king came in person to deliver "with a certain faltering of the voice" the request for a declaration of war.[17] Fewer than ten deputies voted against this popular war.

Dumouriez was the driving force in the new ministry, serving as foreign minister as well as dominating the ministry of war. His policies suffered from two miscalculations. He hoped that Prussia would not remain loyal to Austria and might even be induced to side with France. Further, he believed that the Belgians, who had revolted unsuccessfully against Austria in 1790, would join the French in fighting the Austrians if the French troops invaded the Austrian Netherlands. The invasion of Belgium, begun on April 28, 1792, was a disaster. Dumouriez ordered the attack against the advice of the senior general, Rochambeau (who had been the French commander in the American Revolution). Rochambeau favored a defensive strategy, fearing that the soldiers were not sufficiently trained, that revolutionary propaganda had undermined discipline, and that the army lacked experienced and trustworthy officers. The soldiers understandably had little confidence in their noble officers, because they had seen so many of them emigrate. Not only did the French army advancing into Belgium turn and run, it also murdered its general (a man named Dillon), believing that he had betrayed them and led them into an ambush.

When the news of the retreat reached Paris, the Girondins immediately blamed the defeat on treachery, not incompetence. They invoked the specter of an "Austrian Committee" including Marie Antoinette and others who were undermining the French cause from within. In this time of danger, the only thing that saved France was that the Austrians and the Prussians were slow to take advantage of their opportunity because they were distracted by Russia. Catherine's armies moved into Poland in May 1792, not coincidentally at the very time that French armies invaded Belgium. The crisis in the east led to the second partition of Poland, in which Russia and Prussia took more Polish territory. Austria agreed to this partition in the vain hope that Prussia would support what Austria really wanted, an exchange of the Austrian Netherlands for Bavaria, which was closer to Vienna and easier to protect and govern. In 1795, the rest of Poland was divided between Austria, Prussia, and Russia, and Poland as a separate nation disappeared from the map.

Both sides in the war had assumed a quick victory. The Austrians and Prussians believed that France was too demoralized and disorganized to mount a successful campaign and that it would be easy to defeat the incompetent revolutionaries. The French assumed that the Old Regime armies of its opponents, dependent on mercenary soldiers, could be easily defeated by the armies of the French nation, consisting of citizen soldiers fighting for a just cause. Thus began a period of war that would last twenty-three years and eventually spread to all parts of the European continent.

War accelerated the radicalization of the French Revolution. The hunt for traitors and the unmasking of villains, already a theme in Jacobin and Girondin rhetoric, became more insistent. Drastic changes could now be justified as measures necessitated by war.

WOMEN AND THE REVOLUTION

One of the key figures in the Girondin government of 1792 was the minister of the interior, Jean-Marie Roland de la Platière. Equally important in the history of the Girondins was his wife. Born Manon Phlipon, she was the daughter of a master engraver. She received a classical education, came to admire the republican government of the Greeks and the Romans, and was inspired by the noble deeds of ancient heroes. Her reading of Rousseau converted her to a type of natural religion, a sentimental deism. She was a talented musician and writer, but she rejected careers in those fields because of the difficulties a woman would have encountered in them during the Ancien Régime. Manon's prospects for marriage were not good because her father had lost his small fortune and would not be able to provide her with a suitable dowry. She eventually married Roland, a man considerably older than she, who served as an inspector of manufactures in the royal government. Manon helped him in his publication of a three-volume *Dictionary of Manufactures*. They went to live in Amiens, she gave birth to a daughter, and her interest in politics appeared to lessen. When a male acquaintance tried to engage her in a debate on the superiority of the sexes, Madame Roland responded with a denial of the superiority of women:

> I believe . . . in the superiority of your sex in every respect. In the first place, you have strength, and everything that goes with it results from it: courage, perseverance, wide horizons and great talents. It is up to you to make the laws in politics as it is to make the discoveries in science. Govern the world, change the surface of the globe, be proud, terrible, clever, and learned. You are all that without our help, and through all that you are bound to be our master. But without us you would not be virtuous, loved, or happy. Keep therefore all your glory and authority. As for us, we have and wish no other supremacy than that over your morals, no other rule than that over your hearts. . . . It often angers me to see women disputing privileges which ill befit them. . . . No matter what their facility may be in some respects, they should never show their learning or talents in public.[18]

And, indeed, Madame Roland always tried to be self-effacing in public. She recounts in her memoirs that when her husband's political associates met with him in their home, she sat quietly to one side, pretending to be absorbed in letter-writing, though she listened intently while they discussed affairs. Behind the scenes she cooperated in promoting radical politics and in writing reports and speeches for her husband. And when he became a minister she worked alongside him, got her friends appointed to office, and tried to influence events. But she did not abandon traditional gender roles.

If someone of Madame Roland's talents, ambition, and radical politics did not embrace equality for women, it is not surprising to discover that the voices promoting equal rights for women during the Revolution were weak. The Revolution did not prove to be terribly revolutionary for women. When it took up the issue of voting rights, the Constituent Assembly excluded the poor and servants from the franchise after some debate. The exclusion of women was not even debated. The widely held assumption, even among women, was that women should devote themselves to home and family and that men would exercise the political rights for the family. Sieyès expressed the prevailing view this way: "Women, at least in current circumstances, children, foreigners and those who make no fiscal contribution to the state should not directly influence public affairs. All may enjoy the benefits of living in a particular society, yet only those who pay taxes are real stakeholders in the great social enterprise. They alone are truly active citizens, full members of the association."[19]

Rousseau's ideas, widely embraced by revolutionaries, offered no real challenge to the traditional exclusion of women from the public sphere. In a famous polemic against aristocratic culture that focused on the elite's enjoyment of the theater, Rousseau criticized the theater for artificiality and actors for selling themselves for money. He especially excoriated the actress as a "public woman," essentially a prostitute, because "any woman who shows herself off disgraces herself."[20] This criticism of women in public was extended as well to any women in public life, including the rich and prominent women who sponsored salons. If women were prominent, men would be relatively weak. Rousseau believed that the power of women in monarchical government as influential mistresses or consorts signaled the Ancien Régime's political degeneracy. He criticized absolute monarchy for destroying the natural gender roles in two ways. Because it was rule by individuals rather than by law, it allowed women to exercise power through influence behind the scenes. Furthermore, absolute monarchy emasculated men by reducing them all to the status of dependents of the king. Rousseau envisioned a republican order in which all men were equal, independent, and capable of preserving freedom. He admired the system in Greek republics in which men and women had separate spheres.

In the new institutions in France, representative bodies open only to men were the centers of power replacing the royal court, organized along the lines of a family and thus giving prominent roles to women. To those observing the Ancien Régime, the "public women" were especially notorious. Madame de Pompadour and Madame du Barry, the two most prominent mistresses of Louis XV, had in fact started their careers as public women, that is, as prostitutes or as courtesans who made their way in society by the affairs that they had.

There would appear to be little similarity between them and Marie Antoinette, who was a Habsburg princess. But anti-monarchical pamphleteers accused her of wanting power just as Louis XV's mistresses did. Marie Antoinette was the subject of a great deal of pornographic literature during the 1790s. Pamphlets pictured her supposedly insatiable sexual appetites as the ultimate symbol of the corruption of the Ancien Régime. In 1791, a book entitled *The Crimes of the Queens of France* linked her with Catherine de Médicis and Marie de Médicis, other queens of France who were foreigners. The queen's foreign birth, especially her Austrian birth, became a heavy liability as nationalism grew and the country went to war against Austria. She also suffered criticism simply because she was a woman in a position to influence events.

Women by their very nature, many revolutionaries believed, could not be trusted with public responsibilities. The historian Sarah Maza explained this point of view: "Feminine nature, characterized by deceit, seduction, and the selfish pursuit of private interest, was construed as the extreme antithesis of the abstract principles of reason made law that were to govern the public sphere. Femininity . . . became radically incompatible with the new definition of the polity."[21] The new style of government was supposed to be open, based on law and reason, and supported by the virtue of men who could defend their rights. The term "virtue," as used by the revolutionaries, was derived from the Latin term for man (*vir*) and might almost be defined as "manliness." Women were supposed to be interested in the personal, the private, the family, not in the wider issues of the commonwealth.

The revolutionary ideal really had no place for women, and yet women played prominent roles in the Revolution itself. They had followed political events with interest. They had taken part in demonstrations and had been the leaders of the October Days. The Revolution had made a big difference in women's lives. They had observed the debates in the Assemblies and had joined a few political clubs. Etta Palm, for example, had been a member of the Cercle Social, where she agitated for improving the status of women. Palm founded a female section of the Confederation of the Friends of the Truth, which immediately took up the issue of primogeniture and advocated equal inheritance for male and female children. Although their efforts were supported by a few men (notably Brissot and Condorcet), the feminist movement in the French Revolution received scant support from male revolutionaries.

In 1791, Olympe de Gouges wrote a feminist declaration modeled on the Declaration of the Rights of Man. The first article of her Declaration of the Rights of Woman and Citizen stated: "Woman is born free and lives equal to man in her rights. Social distinctions may be founded only upon common utility." She asserted that because women were subject to the laws and to the death penalty just as men were, they should have the right to speak freely about those laws and to take part in forming them. Like those who wrote the Declaration of the Rights of Man, she based her arguments on an Enlightenment view of nature. She urged women to arise and "recognize your rights. The powerful empire of nature is no longer surrounded by prejudice, fanaticism, superstition, and lies. The flame of truth has dissipated all the clouds of folly and usurpation."[22] Although traditional patriarchal views of society did not offer support to feminist arguments, there were limits as well to the effectiveness of the Enlightenment argument from nature. Opponents could retort that the legal distinctions among men had been created by society and should therefore be removed, but that the differences between men and women were "natural" and could not be removed. Although the French revolutionaries perceived of rights as having universal validity, women obviously did not share in those rights. Olympe de Gouge favored a constitutional monarchy and addressed the preamble of her appeal for the rights of women to Marie Antoinette. Her political moderation spelled trouble when more radical revolutionaries came to power, and she was sent to the guillotine in 1793. As we shall see, the more radical government of the Jacobins was no more interested in giving political rights to women than were the moderates.

The most widespread and important political statement made by women during the Revolution came from opposition to the Revolution: many women fought for the Catholic Church and sought to protect priests who were persecuted. Despite the increasingly anti-religious policies of the central government, women in towns and villages throughout the country resisted the dismantling of churches and the disruptions of religious observances. Their resistance often forced local officials to back down and give up trying to enforce the laws on religion. There were more women than men in religious orders at the end of the eighteenth century (80,000 religious, of which 55,000 were women). They carried out essential functions in society by teaching and by taking care of orphans, the old, and the sick. When religious orders were done away with in 1790, the orders that provided these essential services were at first exempted. Eventually the revolutionaries concluded that the state should provide these services rather than private charity, especially religious charity. But the French state, saddled with the costs of war and a disrupted economy, lacked the money for this work. The needs of poor families were frequently made worse by the Revolution. Women had often contributed to the family economy by working in textile and luxury trades, which were undermined by emigration and the revolutionary attack on luxury. The inability of the state to provide for the needs of poor people became acute during the Terror, when the government was most intent on attacking the church, and these policies help to explain the growth of counter-revolutionary sentiment in the country.

COLONIAL AND ECONOMIC POLICIES

The revolutionaries were, for the most part, advocates of free enterprise. Opponents of the corporatist structure of the Ancien Régime, they dismantled the guilds and did away with barriers to free trade. In the fall of 1790, internal customs duties were abolished and free trade in grain was instituted. In the attempt to ensure uniformity and to promote industry, a national system of weights and measures was created to take the place of the bewildering variety of measurements that had been used under the Ancien Régime. A commission of the Academy of Science was appointed in May 1790, which developed a new system (adopted in 1795): the metric system with its now familiar liters, meters, and grams.

In the spring of 1791, responding to labor unrest in Paris, the Constituent Assembly decided to codify their commitment to free enterprise. The resulting "Le Chapelier Law," passed on June 14, 1791, reaffirmed the abolition of corporations and guilds and forbade workers' coalitions, thus stifling the development of any kind of union activity. The decision, coming as it did in the midst of increasingly radical politics in Paris, also had a political consideration. Groups of workers demonstrating against the closing of charity workshops had been supported by the Cordeliers Club.

By the summer of 1791, the Revolution had seriously disrupted the economic life of the country, especially its colonial trade. In the late eighteenth century, the most vibrant part of the French economy was the trade

Figure 6.1. Sugar plantation. This engraving from the *Encyclopédie* shows an idealized version of a sugar plantation, with the master's house looming over the sugar cane fields and the slave quarters. The cane was crushed to extract the juice in the mill, pictured on the right. Courtesy of Special Collections Library, Penn State University.

in sugar and other commodities from colonies in the West Indies. Martinique, Guadeloupe, and especially Saint-Domingue (the French portion of the island of Hispaniola, later to be called Haiti) prospered in the production of sugar and tobacco on plantations run by slave labor. Profits went especially to the port cities of the west coast of France, whose residents engaged in trade and shipping and who invested in the plantations. Sugar plantations were expensive in both slaves and in equipment to process the cane into sugar, and thus required the investment of large merchant houses.

As we saw with the rights of women, the universalist pronouncements of the Declaration of the Rights of Man and Citizen were not automatically extended to anybody except white males. Just as in the United States, where revolution did not lead to the elimination of slavery (except in the northern states where it was economically insignificant), the obstacles to emancipation were both theoretical and practical. Although the Declaration said all men were born equal, it also declared in more than one place the sanctity of property. Doing away with slavery would, of course, deprive somebody of his property. More practically, many wealthy people depended on slavery for their livelihood, including investors from the city of Bordeaux, many of whom were strong supporters of the Revolution (the area from which the Girondins took their name). Constrained by political considerations, Brissot, the founder of the Society of the Friends of the Blacks, despite his genuine interest in doing away with the slave trade and slavery, did not push for slave emancipation immediately.

The issue that arose at first in the National Assembly concerned the status of free people of color. Saint-Domingue, the largest and most important of the French Caribbean colonies, had a population that was overwhelmingly black. In 1789, the colony counted 465,000 slaves, 31,000 whites, and 28,000 free-coloreds. The category of free-coloreds included freed slaves as well as free people of mixed ancestry. Many of the free-coloreds were themselves quite wealthy, owning slaves and plantations of their own. They cooperated with white plantation owners in supporting the institution of slavery and in participating in the colonial military forces that maintained order. The Code Noir (Black Code) of 1685, which provided regulations for all aspects of the treatment of slaves, also stated that freed slaves enjoyed the same status as white people. Over the course of the eighteenth century, however, both officials in France and plantation owners in the colonies began to fear that the presence of a large population of free people of color would undermine slavery. They steadily eroded the rights of free-coloreds by closing off certain trades to them, forbidding them to use the same last name as white people, and making a distinction between those with some European ancestry and free blacks without.

News of the Revolution in France was greeted by the plantation owners in Saint-Domingue with considerable trepidation. They feared that talk of rights and liberty would lead to emancipation of slaves. They at first demanded representation in the National Assembly and were allotted six seats. When elections for local assemblies were held in Saint-Domingue in February 1790, voting was restricted to white colonists who met the property qualifications for active citizens. Free-coloreds who met the property qualifications demanded that they be given the rights of citizens. To further complicate matters, poor whites in Saint-Domingue objected to their exclusion from political life and incited riots and founded political clubs.

The free-coloreds sent representatives to France to lobby for their inclusion in the political process. There they encountered the opposition of the Club Massiac, a small group that promoted the interests of the white planters (so named because it met in a building called the Hôtel de Massiac). In March 1790, the Assembly created a Colonial Committee, which decided that the colonies would not be subject to the same laws as France but would instead be under "particular laws" to be drawn up by their own colonial assemblies. However, they did not declare that free-coloreds would be given the right to participate in choosing those bodies. Despairing of getting the Constituent Assembly to back the petitions of the free-coloreds, one of them, Vincent Ogé, returned to Saint-Domingue in October 1790 and began an armed uprising against the local assembly. His troops were defeated, and he was executed.

Demands by free-coloreds for inclusion continued to be presented to the Constituent Assembly where their cause was supported by Brissot, the Abbé Grégoire, and others, who assured their fellow deputies that the free-coloreds had no intention of threatening the institution of slavery. Finally, on May 15, 1791, the Assembly declared that, regardless of color, persons born of two free parents would have the same rights of citizenship as whites. The white plantation owners refused to accept the decree and began to talk of seceding from France or of asking Great Britain to take over the island.

Taking advantage of the divisions among the free people in Saint-Domingue and convinced of the truth of rumors that the king wanted to give them freedom but was prevented from doing so by the plantation owners, slaves in the north of Saint-Domingue rebelled in August 1791. Under interrogation later, some slaves asserted that they had conspired to revolt because "they wanted to enjoy the liberty they are entitled to by the Rights of Man."[23] By late September, at least twenty thousand slaves had joined the uprising, and they had attacked more than two hundred sugar plantations and twelve hundred coffee plantations, and killed more than a thousand whites. A majority of slaves in Saint-Domingue were African natives, an indication of the harsh conditions under which they labored. The mortality rate on the plantations was so high that continual imports of new slaves were required. Some of the African-born had experience as soldiers in the civil wars raging in the region of the Congo, and their military experience helps to account for the success of the rebellion.

The authorities in France were slow to respond to the violence in Haiti, despite the serious consequences to the economy as sugar production came almost to a halt. The struggles between the whites and the free-coloreds continued, with the two sides now reflecting the political divisions caused by the French Revolution. Free-coloreds supported the Assembly and called for obedience to its decrees, while the whites rejected the radical policies of the Revolution and accused the anti-slavery Brissotins of fomenting slave insurrection. The free-coloreds recruited slaves to help fight by promising them freedom. The whites then were forced to do the same thing or risk defeat.

In September 1791, the Constituent Assembly rescinded the decree of May giving some rights to free-coloreds. But by the spring of 1792, the Legislative Assembly was forced to change direction again. As the Brissotins in France were preparing to declare war against Austria, they decided that the only real support they had in Saint-Domingue came from the free-coloreds and that only by including them in the political system could the slave uprising be put down. The Brissotins now saw the white plantation owners as part of the international conspiracy to destroy the Revolution. On April 4, 1792, the Legislative Assembly therefore unequivocally declared that the free-coloreds would enjoy the same political rights as whites. In July, special commissioners embarked for the Caribbean with an army to help put down the violence. By the time they reached Saint-Domingue after the long ocean passage, the political situation in France had changed dramatically, making consistent attention to Saint-Domingue impossible and allowing the slave rebellion to become even better established and more widespread.

THE REVOLUTION OF AUGUST 10, 1792

The war in Europe was not going well for the French in the summer of 1792. When the commonly held belief that the French army would quickly be able to rout the country's enemies proved not to be true, patriotic citizens began looking for conspiracies and plots to explain the misfortune. The disorganization of the army was blamed on the officers, former nobles who resented the Revolution and whose numbers were declining as more and more abandoned their posts and left the country. Rochambeau resigned in May 1792. Marshal Luckner, the Prussian general who had been in the service of France since 1763 and now commanded one of the armies on the frontier, did enjoy the confidence of the radicals in Paris. However, the reputation of the other general commanding on the eastern front, Lafayette, had never recovered from the Massacre of the Champ de Mars. He was widely assumed to be in league with counter-revolutionaries and to be harboring the ambition to make himself military dictator of France. Even less to be trusted were the king and the queen, suspected of wanting the foreign armies to succeed and to rescue them from the Revolution. The fears of conspiracy became even more pronounced in the summer of 1792 as it became clear that the armies of Austria and Prussia were poised to invade French territory.

The Jacobin Club was especially devoted to rooting out counter-revolution. Since the split in its membership in 1791, the club had reestablished connections with clubs throughout the country and its membership had grown dramatically. The conception of its purpose changed from a group that supported and emboldened the Constituent Assembly to a group that questioned all authority, including the authority of the Legislative Assembly. Their evening meetings were opened to observers as well as members. While still officially called the Friends of the Constitution, the speeches made in the Jacobin Club in 1792 revealed that they did not really admire the constitution written in 1791. Instead they saw themselves as protectors of the principles of constitutional government now under threat by various conspirators. The debates in the Jacobin Club were often more important during this period for highlighting conflicting views than were the debates in the Legislative Assembly. More and more, the Jacobins saw themselves rather than the Assembly as the true incarnation of the will of the people, reflected through their network of around a thousand affiliated societies. But there were challengers to that role. Other political clubs (such as the Cordeliers) still existed to compete with the Jacobins. And the city's sectional assemblies, which brought together active citizens to discuss affairs, were insisting that their views be heard.

By the summer of 1792, the *sans-culottes*, who thought of themselves as the ordinary hard-working, honest, and patriotic people of Paris who had saved the Revolution more than once by their direct action, expected to be consulted. The French word *peuple* has more than one meaning. It can be used to mean a crowd. It can also mean the people who constitute a nation, as in *le peuple français* or the French people. But it is often used to refer to the lowest classes as distinguished from the upper classes in society. The *sans-culottes* of Paris saw themselves as the true "people" of France, in all the meanings of the word. The Jacobin Club stood up for them, but the *sans-culottes* expressed their views more directly in the popular societies that had grown up in the sections of Paris. Many radicals believed that the direct democracy of the section meetings expressed the will of the nation more accurately than the corruptible Legislative Assembly.

The French had suffered initial reverses in the invasion of Belgium, but the armies, now under the command of Marshal Luckner, once again entered the Austrian Netherlands in June 1792. In Paris, radicals continued to bemoan the lack of progress and blamed former noble officers and the "Austrian Committee." Suspicion naturally fell on the king as well and became more pronounced when he exercised his veto power. In late May 1792 the Legislative Assembly passed a decree calling for the deportation of refractory priests who were denounced by twenty active citizens. The Assembly next disbanded the king's guard, accusing it of harboring dangerous enemies of the country. The king went along with the disbanding of his guard, despite the fact that the guard was guaranteed to him in the constitution and its demise left him to be defended only by the National Guard. But he distrusted another measure calling for establishing a camp near the capital made of twenty thousand National Guardsmen from throughout the country. The justification for gathering these guardsmen (called *fédérés*) was that they would take the place of soldiers who were on their way to the front, and they could be trained before they in turn headed off for the war. The threat this camp represented to the king was obvious, and when Louis XVI seemed ready to veto this measure (along with the one on priests), Roland decided to act in order to distance the Girondin ministers from the veto. He wrote a letter to the king on June 10, 1792, lecturing him on his patriotic obligations. In a thinly veiled threat he prophesied violence if the king did not promptly approve the legislation. The insulting tone of this letter, actually written by Madame Roland, suggesting that the king was in league with the opponents of the constitution, made it impossible for Louis XVI to continue to work with the Girondin ministers. When the king dismissed them, Roland forwarded his letter to the Legislative Assembly on June 13 where it was read aloud to great applause, thus reviving Roland's stature as an uncompromising republican and beginning a new assault on the king.

After the Girondins' fall from power, in an atmosphere of increasing crisis, a ministry of Feuillants was charged with conducting the war and protecting the king. Lafayette, from his post with his army on the frontier, wrote a letter to the Legislative Assembly warning of the grave dangers the country faced and proposing dismantling the Jacobin Clubs as threats to the authority of the Assembly itself. This letter was read to the Assembly on June 18. On June 19, Louis XVI vetoed the decrees on refractory priests and on the camp of *fédérés*. On June 20, the anniversary of the Tennis Court Oath, a crowd of perhaps eight thousand Parisians (including National Guardsmen, ordinary citizens armed with pikes and other weapons, women, and children) converged on the Legislative Assembly, marched through the hall, and then made their way to the Tuileries Palace. This demonstration, originally planned to put pressure on the king to reinstate the Girondin ministers, had been forbidden by the departmental authorities and by the Assembly. It now took on added intensity because of the king's vetoes. The crowds stormed into the palace and forced the king to listen to them as they denounced the veto and demanded the recall of the patriot ministers. Louis sat in the recess of a window for four hours as the crowds marched by. To humor them, he donned the red cap of liberty and drank to the health of the nation. But he refused to back down on the question of the vetoes. The mayor of Paris, Pétion (a Girondin elected in November 1791), who sympathized with the demands of the demonstrators and who did not want to lose popularity, finally arrived and urged the crowds to disperse.

Indignant protests against the humiliation that the king had suffered during the invasion of the Tuileries were heard throughout the country. Petitions poured into the Assembly demanding that the demonstrators be punished. Pétion was relieved of his duties, and the tide seemed to be turning away from the radicals. But the moderates would not prevail. Pétion was soon reinstated. The popular societies and sections of Paris now began to demand the ouster of the king and the establishment of a republican form of government. Hoping to take advantage of the sympathy toward the king, Lafayette arrived in Paris on June 28 to try to rally support to save the king and the constitution. He addressed the Legislative Assembly, urging them to close down the Jacobin Clubs and to help him save the constitution and the king. He hoped that the National Guard might still follow his lead. But a review of the National Guard that the king was scheduled to hold was canceled at the urging of Marie Antoinette, who wanted nothing to do with Lafayette. Only about thirty guardsmen answered Lafayette's appeal. Succeeding in rallying neither the Assembly nor the National Guard, Lafayette returned disheartened to his army at the front. He offered to help Louis and Marie Antoinette escape from Paris to the safety of his army, but they refused his help.

Figure 6.2.   Invasion of the Tuileries, June 20, 1792. Parisians stormed into the palace and forced Louis XVI to wear the Phrygian cap of liberty (held above his head and worn by the man on the left) and to drink the health of the nation. Although many people throughout the country protested this treatment of the king, the radicals in Paris would depose Louis XVI less than two months later. Courtesy of the Division of Rare and Manuscript Collections, Cornell University Library.

Panic over the impending foreign invasion led the Assembly to declare on July 11 that the country was in a state of emergency (*la patrie en danger*). This decree allowed extraordinary measures to be taken to defend the country. The section assemblies now met in permanent session, and volunteers streamed into Paris. The Festival of Federation on July 14, 1792, brought National Guardsmen from throughout France to Paris. The delegation from the notoriously radical city of Marseilles arrived in Paris on July 30 after the festival had already taken place. As they marched in they sang a patriotic anthem that had originally been written by Rouget de Lisle to celebrate the army of the Rhine. The song, which would eventually become the national anthem of France, was given the name of their hometown, "La Marseillaise." Although the king participated in the festival on July 14, signs that an uprising against him was being planned were everywhere.

The suspicion that the king was working with the foreign invaders received apparent corroboration when the commander of the allied enemy forces, the Prussian Duke of Brunswick, issued what was called the Brunswick Manifesto, which reached Paris on July 28. He stated that the aim of Austria and Prussia was "to put an end to the anarchy in the interior of France, to stop attacks against the throne and altar," and to reestablish the king's legitimate power. He further declared that if the royal family suffered the "least violence or outrage," they would "exact an exemplary and ever-memorable vengeance, by delivering the city of Paris over to a military execution and to complete ruin."[24] Far from helping to protect the royal family, this intemperate declaration merely convinced many Parisians that the king was a traitor whose presence at the head of the government and the army at a time of war and invasion could no longer be tolerated.

In the middle of July, the French armies under Lafayette and Luckner that had been operating on the frontier of the Austrian Netherlands moved into the area of the Meuse and the Moselle rivers where the impending invasion was expected to take place. Dumouriez (now serving as a general in the armies) denounced these movements for dangerously denuding the frontier of defensive troops and wrote to Paris to protest an order from Luckner that he join his army. The people of Paris feared that they were being left defenseless by these troop movements. Accusing Lafayette of treason and of intending to carry out a coup d'état, Jacobins instituted proceedings in the Assembly to impeach Lafayette.

On August 6, a large rally at the Champ de Mars called on the king to abdicate. The sections sent a petition to the Assembly demanding that the Assembly depose the king or they would do so themselves. On August 8, the Assembly voted not to impeach Lafayette. Now it seemed clear to the revolutionaries that the Assembly, which would neither dethrone the monarch nor impeach Lafayette, could not be trusted to protect the country. The expected insurrection, therefore, was aimed at both the king and the Assembly. On the morning of August 10, 1792, the tocsin sounded calling the revolutionaries to action. Crowds invaded the Hôtel de Ville, suspended the municipal government, and created a new revolutionary city government called the Commune. It assumed command of the Parisian National Guard. The uprising, including ordinary Parisian *sans-culottes* and numerous National Guardsmen, who had been arriving in Paris to train before heading for the front, now turned on the Tuileries Palace. Louis XVI, once again demonstrating that he was unwilling to take up arms against his own people, had decided to seek safety among the members of the Legislative Assembly and was not at the Tuileries when the attack began. The National Guard units that defended the palace joined the uprising, but the Swiss Guard, whose orders had apparently not been countermanded, continued to hold the palace against the attackers, who greatly outnumbered them. Belatedly the king sent orders for them to cease firing. But the attackers did not stop. The result was the bloodiest day so far in the Revolution. Almost four hundred of the attackers lost their lives (including three women), and six hundred of the Swiss Guards.

Meanwhile the king and his family were squeezed into the small room reserved for the stenographer who took the minutes of the Assembly. Still scrupulously maintaining the constitutional separation between the legislative and the executive, the Assembly had not allowed the king to sit with them as they debated his fate. The outcome was predictable. The Assembly, now acting under the pressure of the Commune and the crowds that surrounded their meeting hall, voted to suspend the king until his fate could be decided by a Convention, which would be elected to create new institutions for France. The constitutional monarchy had come to an end.

CONCLUSION

The uprising of August 10, 1792, is sometimes called the Second French Revolution. The Revolution had begun in 1789 with the overthrow of an absolutist monarch and the creation of a constitutional monarchy. August 10 destroyed the constitutional monarchy and replaced it with a republic. Louis XVI had lost the confidence of so many French people that they did not trust him to serve as king, especially when the country went to war. It is impossible to overstate the significance of the declaration of war. With war raging, the suspicions of counter-revolutionary plots became intense, and people worried that traitors in league with the enemy were everywhere. The fall of the king brought about a republic, but not stability. Divisions within the country grew worse and would soon lead to outright civil war.

7

THE CONVENTION

Soon after the overthrow of the king on August 10, 1792, France would become a republic. The Legislative Assembly, bound still by the Constitution of 1791, had suspended the king. But the more important decisions on the fate of the king and on a constitution to replace the Constitution of 1791 (which had been written for a constitutional monarchy that no longer existed) were entrusted to a newly elected Convention—a body conceived in imitation of the American constitutional conventions. Unlike a legislature, which is elected according to the provisions of a constitution, a convention is theoretically endowed with the full sovereignty of the people to establish the founding document of the nation. The Convention could therefore exercise enormous power, unhindered by the strictures of a written constitution. Any attempts to question or limit the decisions of the Convention had to contend with the particular status of the Convention as the repository of the people's will.

However, unlike the American revolutionaries, the members of the Convention did not immediately write a constitution, write *only* a constitution, and then retire. When the Convention first assembled, foreign armies were on French soil, and they continued to threaten the security of the nation. In addition to the foreign threat, the French Convention faced the challenges of civil war, economic disruptions, and factional strife. The Convention was forced to take on all aspects of government and exercised extraordinary powers. The period of the Convention was the most radical period of the French Revolution, culminating in the Terror.

THE SEPTEMBER MASSACRES AND VALMY

Fear of the king's collusion with the approaching foreign armies had precipitated the August 10 uprising. Officials in some parts of France protested
this essentially Parisian event. Lafayette hoped to take advantage of this opposition sentiment by putting together a coalition of departments that
would pledge to maintain the Constitution of 1791. When his army refused
to back his scheme and when he was declared an outlaw by the Assembly,
he fled the country. Attempting to cross the Austrian lines on his way to
England, the Austrians, who saw in him only a dangerous revolutionary, arrested him, and he was kept in prison for the next five years.

The insurrection of August 10 succeeded because most officials in the
departments and towns, who still felt a great deal of respect for the Assembly, obeyed its pronouncements. Their main source of knowledge about
events in Paris was the official communications of the Assembly, which presented the overthrow of the king as entirely its own initiative—a measure
to save the country from the treason of the king. They maintained that their
action fell within the legal boundaries laid out by the Constitution, which
gave them authority to suspend the king. The Assembly did not mention
the pressure of the radical Paris Commune. Furthermore, the crisis came at
a time of great uncertainty, when France was about to be invaded, and the
country rallied round the Assembly to protect the nation. The Assembly
immediately replaced the royal ministers with men it could trust. They organized a Provisional Executive Council and reinstated the Girondin ministers, including Roland as minister of the interior and Clavière as minister
of finance. The ministry of justice was given to Danton, doubtless as a way
for the council to stay on good terms with the revolutionary Commune.
The fiery revolutionary showed his pragmatism by his willingness to work
alongside Girondins and his opportunism by giving jobs in the ministry to
many of his friends from the Cordeliers Club.

On August 19, the Prussian and Austrian armies crossed into French
territory and began marching toward Paris. On August 26, news reached
Paris that the important border fortress of Longwy had fallen. Large numbers of people, suspected of being in sympathy with the enemy, were arrested in Paris. The National Guardsmen who had come to the city for the
Federation festival needed to leave to reinforce the army. The fear soon
spread through Paris that, once these *fédérés* left the city, a conspiracy of
counter-revolutionaries would liberate the royalist prisoners from captivity
and the now-defenseless city would fall into their hands. On September 2,
Parisians learned that the fortress of Verdun had fallen, leaving the way
open for the enemy to march to Paris.

Panic now precipitated one of the most frightful events of the Revolution, the September Massacres. Prisoners being escorted to the Abbaye prison were seized by crowds and executed. The violence spread to other prisons that night. At one of them, the Hôtel de la Force, executions of the prisoners by the crowds continued for several days. Only two prisons in Paris were spared. When the violence ended on September 6, between 1,100 and 1,400 prisoners had been slaughtered, about half the inmates of the nine prisons involved. No officials tried to put a stop to the crowds, who sometimes carried out a sort of trial before the summary executions. About a quarter of the victims were priests, nobles, or other political prisoners, but the great majority of the dead were ordinary criminals who had been locked up for prostitution, theft, or other crimes. After it was over, nobody claimed credit for having inspired or led the executions, and it is difficult to determine a concerted plan. Historians often interpret the September Massacres as an incident of mass hysteria, but the effect it had on the elections in Paris (which returned a notably radical delegation) might have been the real motive of the perpetrators.

The September Massacres certainly discouraged anybody who wanted to protest the revolution of August 10, and the elections to the Convention (held in September) confirmed that radicals were now in control in Paris. Eligibility to vote was widened by lowering the minimum age to twenty-one and by dropping the income qualification. The distinction between active and passive citizens no longer existed. It was not quite universal manhood suffrage, however, because domestic servants and men without income were excluded. The two-step election process attracted probably fewer than one in five of the eligible men in the country. Royalists often neglected to show up, the poor showed little interest, and it was harvest time. Out of the 749 delegates chosen to the Convention, only 23 were former nobles and 46 were clergy. The largest category consisted of lawyers (250). Considerable continuity existed with the previous Assembly. Two hundred of the delegates had served in the Legislative Assembly, but only eighty-three had been in the Constituent Assembly. Reflecting the revolutionary changes that had taken place, youth predominated, with two-thirds of the delegates below forty-five years old.

The formal institution of the Convention was scheduled for September 20. But two other important events also took place on that day. Before handing over power to the Convention, the Legislative Assembly passed legislation furthering the principle enunciated in the Constitution of 1791 that the "law considers marriage only as a civil contract."[1] They transferred registration of births, marriages, and deaths from the church to the state, legalized divorce, and gave women equal status within the marriage, thus applying the principles of liberty and equality to the area of family law. These measures further weakened the power of the church and helped to create a decidedly secular government by attacking the sanctity of marriage, one of the fundamental principles of the Roman Catholic faith.

The most dramatic event of September 20 occurred when the French army under Dumouriez's command stopped the advance of the Prussians at the battle of Valmy. Valmy was immediately pictured as the brilliant victory of free people, who, inspired by revolutionary fervor after throwing off their own king, were able to defeat the professional armies of monarchical Europe and save the Revolution. Nationalist interpretations of French history continue to picture Valmy this way. However, the battle was not as glorious as it is remembered in myth. The decisive factor on the battlefield was the French artillery, which was still controlled by the trained soldiers of the old regime, rather than the new recruits. The Prussians and Austrians, assuming that it would be easy to defeat the disorganized revolutionaries in France, just as they had easily put down the revolts in Belgium and Holland, had not committed large numbers of troops to the enterprise. But when they saw that they would be forced to fight, that the effort would be extensive, and that they would perhaps be defeated, they gave up the attempt. Although the Prussians' march to Paris had been halted, their army had not been routed. The Prussians decided to retreat because they did not want to get bogged down in France without support or supplies.

THE CONVENTION

The Convention held its first public session on September 21, 1792, and on the following day the delegates proclaimed that henceforth they would date the new era starting from that moment. They were now in "the first year of the Republic." A few days later, they proclaimed the existence of the "French Republic one and indivisible." The triumphant unitary principle behind that phrase was belied by the myriad divisions that actually existed in the country, divisions that split even the Convention itself. Furthermore, the power of the Convention was challenged by the new revolutionary city government in Paris, the Commune, made up of representatives from the sections into which the city was divided. The sans-culottes in their sectional meetings justified their intrusions into national decision-making by their belief in direct democracy, rather than in representative government. They were suspicious of the elected delegates to the Convention, many of whom distrusted them in turn. The Conventionnels (members of the Convention) always worked under the threat of further uprisings in Paris.

The three main groups in the Convention usually go by the names Girondins (or Brissotins), the Mountain (or Montagnards), and the Plain (or Marsh). Although not equivalent to modern political parties, the Girondins and the Mountain consisted of individuals with similar points of view and with recognized leaders and orators who advanced the political programs of the group. The majority of people in the Convention, who fell into neither of these groups, were called the Plain or the Marsh, and they voted with one side or the other as issues developed and as circumstances changed. A major difference between the Girondins and the Mountain was their relationship to Paris. The Mountain (so-called because they took the upper seats on the left side) depended on the support of Paris and submitted to the demands of the *sans-culottes*. The Girondins drew their support from the departments.

Prominent Girondins such as Vergniaud and Gensonné were delegates from the department of the Gironde. Brissot and Pétion also sat in the Convention. They all congregated at the home of the Rolands. The Girondins were convinced that the horrible violence of the September Massacres had been aimed at them as well as the royalists. They feared that the pressure of the Paris crowds would not allow the Convention to act independently. They proposed an armed guard for the Convention made up of people from the departments; they suggested that the Convention be moved out of Paris to another city; and they criticized the radicals Paris had elected.

Maximilien Robespierre had masterminded the election of the Paris delegation and he was the first elected. Other famous Jacobins chosen were his brother Augustin Robespierre, Camille Desmoulins (a journalist who had been Robespierre's friend since school days), Danton, Billaud-Varenne (Robespierre's associate on the revolutionary Commune), and (most shockingly from the Girondin point of view) Marat. They responded to Girondin criticism by expelling Brissot and his associates from the Jacobin Club in October. From that point on, the term Jacobins meant the Mountain, since the Girondins were no longer associated with the Jacobin Clubs. The Jacobins accused the Girondins of being in league with the king. The discovery in November of documents that the king had secreted away in an iron box concealed in the walls of the palace (the famous *armoire de fer*) revealed the king's correspondence with Mirabeau and Lafayette. Although nothing in the box implicated the Girondins, the Jacobins believed that Roland had destroyed the documents that incriminated them.

THE FATE OF THE KING

The Convention had to decide what was to be done with the king, and on that issue the Girondins and the Mountain disagreed profoundly. The king had been handed over to the Commune, who imprisoned him and his family in a medieval prison called the Temple. At first the family members were housed together, but at the end of September they were separated, Louis and their son in one tower, Marie Antoinette, their daughter, and the king's sister in another. They were permitted an hour's walk together each day. While the king passed his time in this decrepit prison by reading history books, the Convention debated his fate.

Even in prison, the king constituted a potent symbol that could be used by counter-revolutionaries. Yet legal issues complicated the question of his fate. Under the Ancien Régime, kings were the source of the law and therefore theoretically incapable of committing a crime. Nor could they be accused of treason because they embodied the state. The framers of the Constitution of 1791 had continued part of this tradition by stating that Louis XVI was inviolable, that is, he could not be accused of a crime. He could be removed as king for taking up arms against the nation, for refusing to defend it, or for abandoning the kingdom. But the only penalty specified was removal from office. After abdication he became a regular citizen and could then be tried for crimes committed after his abdication. The question was how could the king be tried for crimes committed while he ruled under a Constitution that declared him inviolable.

Since the Constitution of 1791 had been overthrown on August 10, the Convention decided that its provisions no longer applied. They argued that the people might have temporarily given him immunity from prosecution under the old constitution, but that the principle of the sovereignty of the people gave them the power to deprive him of inviolability and to put him on trial for being an oppressor. A further issue involved the legal principle that the same body could not be both accuser and judge. If the Convention conducted the trial of the king they were themselves accusing of treason, that principle would be violated. Nevertheless, the Girondins insisted upon a trial because they wanted to set a precedent for the rule of law: legal procedures would be maintained, even in the case of traitors during dangerous and extraordinary circumstances.

Jacobins saw things differently, arguing that a trial was not necessary. One young Jacobin, Saint-Just, made his mark speaking on the question. Only twenty-five years old at his election to the Convention from the

Aisne, Saint-Just (after an unruly childhood) acquired a law degree, but instead of practicing law passed his time writing a novel that was a mixture of anti-monarchical diatribe and pornography. Saint-Just would find purpose and discipline in the Revolution and become Robespierre's devoted disciple and associate. In his first speech in the Convention, Saint-Just argued that kings were by definition not a part of the French people and therefore could not be placed on an equality with them in a court of law. Basing his argument on the Old Regime view of kingship, that the king could not commit an ordinary crime, Saint-Just concluded that the only way to deal with kings (that is, tyrants who ruled without the consent of the people) was to remove them by insurrection. As enemies of the nation, kings should be treated as aliens were in time of war.

Some Jacobins argued that a trial was not only unnecessary, it was positively dangerous. Robespierre expressed the logic clearly: ". . . Louis cannot be judged; he has already been condemned, else the Republic is not cleared of guilt. To propose a trial for Louis XVI of any sort whatever is to step backward toward royal and constitutional despotism. Such a proposal is counter-revolutionary since it would bring the revolution itself before the court."[2] In other words, if Louis was innocent, then the August 10 revolutionaries were guilty. Robespierre believed that the Girondins' concern for legal niceties was proof that they lacked devotion to true republican principles. The only way to found the republic was to declare war against all vestiges of monarchy. Robespierre concluded: "Louis must die because the nation must live."[3] The threatening crowds that milled around the Convention reinforced the political pragmatism of such a view.

Although some Girondins wanted to spare the king, they recognized that such a move would be difficult. They settled for a trial in which the charges against the king could be aired to persuade royal sympathizers that removing him had been justified. Furthermore, not wanting the Convention to take sole responsibility and insisting on the idea of the sovereignty of the people, the Girondins favored an appeal to the people to decide on punishment if he were found guilty. They hoped that the ordinary people in the provinces would spare the king's life and thus deal a blow to the Mountain and its radical supporters in Paris. But if the country voted to spare him, the result might very well be civil war. Some members of the Convention suggested that the king be sent into exile in the United States.

The Convention decided that the king would be tried and that he could be assisted by counsel. At his initial interrogation the king had showed his usual courage in responding to accusations, protesting especially against the charge that he had caused bloodshed in the country. His defenders, Malesherbes (a former minister, now seventy-one years old), Tronchet, and De Sèze, presented their case on December 26, 1792, stressing again the king's love for his people and his unwillingness to cause bloodshed. Few, including the king himself, doubted he would be found guilty, so the extensive debate that followed focused on whether the people should decide his punishment.

On January 15 the vote on whether "Louis Capet" (as they insisted on calling him despite his objections that this had never been his name) was guilty of conspiracy against the state resulted in an almost unanimous decision of guilt. The next question—whether the people would be asked to ratify their judgment—was turned down by a substantial majority (424–283). They then turned to the question of what the penalty should be. Each Conventionnel rose to declare his decision, often explaining his vote at some length. The results:

361 for death without conditions
26 for death, but with the possibility of reprieve
46 for death, but only under certain conditions (for example, after peace had come)
286 for imprisonment, detention, banishment
2 for imprisonment in irons[4]

The vote seemed dramatically close with 361 for death without conditions and 360 on the other side. Commentators often point out that if only one person had changed his vote, the king would have been spared. But an analysis of the vote shows that it was not as close as it first appears. Those who voted for death only after peace or some other event obviously hoped that circumstances would have changed by then and the king would be spared. That is not the case of the other twenty-six who voted for death with the stipulation that if the majority voted for death they would then consider a reprieve. Their votes helped to make up the majority for death. The totals then are 387 for death and 334 against out of the 721 who voted. One last vote on whether the king should be reprieved was voted down (380–310) on January 20. The next day, January 21, a carriage (he was relieved it was not a tumbril) took Louis under heavy guard to the Place de la Révolution (formerly Place Louis XV) near the Tuileries, where he was guillotined. In an attempt to wipe out the stigma of the guillotine, the square is now called the Place de la Concorde.

Figure 7.1. Execution of Louis XVI, January 21, 1793. The mechanism of the guillotine is evident in this picture. The plank is lowered and the body placed on it face down. The head is then inserted into the bracket and the blade falls from above. Dr. Guillotin, the promoter of the guillotine, had hoped to make execution quicker than by hanging and therefore more humane. Instead, his invention became the symbol of inhumanity during the Revolution. Courtesy of the Division of Rare and Manuscript Collections, Cornell University Library.

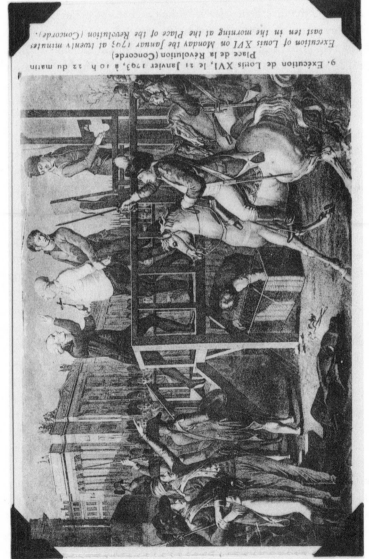

9. Exécution de Louis XVI, le 21 Janvier 1793, à 10 h. 22 du matin
Place de la Révolution (Concorde)

Execution of Louis XVI on Monday the Januar 1793 at twenty minutes
past ten in the morning at the Place of the Revolution (Concorde).

RESPONSES TO THE REVOLUTION

The execution of Louis XVI had removed him as a rallying point for royalists, but it had not destroyed all royalist sentiment in the country. On the contrary, his death provided a further moral argument to people already turning against the revolutionary program. The changes brought about by the Revolution had affected different regions and groups differently. Parisians did not always see things in the same way as the inhabitants of the provinces, and the divergence between the two became greater as time went on. Furthermore, the great variations within the country meant a wide range of responses to the changes taking place. It is impossible to describe the impact on "peasants," for example, because no such thing as a typical peasant existed. This short introduction to the French Revolution, of course, can hardly do justice to the variety of circumstances, so it should be borne in mind that the discussion here is general and does not include all experiences.

At first, peasants were more radical than the legislation coming out of Paris. In the fall of 1789, acting on the assumption that the night of August 4 had abolished all aspects of the seigneurial system, many peasants refused to pay harvest dues to the lords. In the spring of 1790, peasant violence against the continuing exactions of the seigneurial regime was renewed in many parts of the country. In March 1790, the Feudal Committee of the Constituent Assembly (created to translate the abolition into specific legislation) issued a report that conservatively stressed the property rights inherent in many feudal obligations. Their report included as many obligations as possible under the list of those that had not been abolished outright, but for which the lords would have to be compensated. Peasants expected more generous terms and were angered to learn that legislation in May 1790 stipulated that the price of redemption would be set at twenty times the yearly payment if it were in cash, or twenty-five times the yearly payment if it were in kind, and that they must continue to pay until the total had been reimbursed. Peasants generally did not have the means to accumulate such vast sums. The legislation was actually a compromise intended to make the landowners in the Assembly (and landowners in general) willing to accept the notion of redemption. Still, the result in the countryside was resistance to paying the dues and escalating violence against the lords and the symbols of lordship. The Constituent Assembly tried to calm the discontent by doing away with hereditary nobility in June 1790, while making no change in the amount the peasants were to pay in dues or redemption of dues. The abolition of nobility, meant to placate the peasants, in turn provoked many conservative nobles (whose sense of honor and tradition had been wounded) to move from lukewarmly acquiescing to the Revolution to opposing it outright.

A poor harvest and inflationary pressures brought on another wave of rebellion in the countryside in the spring of 1792. Now faced with war, invasion, and fears about the reliability of the army, the Assembly wanted to calm rural violence. In June it decreed many payments abolished unless the owners could prove that they had legal title to them. This constituted a great advance for the peasant, who was no longer required to furnish the proof that he did not have to pay. Instead the lords had to furnish proof that the dues were owed. After the Revolution of August 10, a more sweeping measure did away with all annual payments unless the owners could produce proof that the obligation derived from their (or their ancestors) having ceded land to the peasant. Peasants now felt free to cease payments altogether. A complete abolition of the seigneurial system without compensation was finally decreed by the Convention on July 17, 1793.

By the spring of 1793, seigneurial conflicts were abating, but religious issues continued to agitate the countryside and so did conflicts over control of land. Although the tithe had been abolished on the night of August 4, in practice only those farmers who owned their own land benefited from the abolition. Because landowners were allowed to add the former tithe payment to the rents their tenants and sharecroppers paid, renters had not benefited by the abolition of the tithe. In regions where sharecropping predominated, the peasants continued to agitate against the status quo. Great variety of land tenure and types of payment existed throughout the country. Sometimes peasants' unhappiness led them to the side of counter-revolution, in other cases they might demand more extreme revolutionary measures. In the short run, the disruptions of the Revolution and the high taxes exacted to pay for the revolutionary wars kept agricultural productivity down and delayed economic recovery. But in general and in the long run, peasants benefited by the abolition of the seigneurial regime, even if the better off peasants gained more benefits than did landless laborers. Other sources of conflict (in addition to seigneurialism) that agitated the countryside included the sale of church lands and the fate of common lands. Both of these issues revealed the conflict between urban and rural communities.

City dwellers were more likely to support the Revolution and benefit from it than were residents of rural areas. Every town of any size had at least one political society. Jacobin Clubs were especially numerous. By 1792, around 1,500 local Jacobin Clubs had ties with the "mother society" in

Paris. Urban dwellers looked down on rural residents as country bumpkins, whose lack of learning and sophistication prevented them from appreciating the progress offered by the Revolution. They published newspapers and reports with a mission to educate the farmers. The peasants took offense at the patronizing air of townspeople and resented their lack of understanding of the needs and interests of the rural economy. One important example is the legislation providing for the sale of common lands. The politicians in Paris, imbued with ideas of economic liberalism and convinced that it would be to the advantage of peasants to be able to enjoy private ownership of land, decreed on June 10, 1793, that common lands could be divided up if one-third of the villagers agreed. In some prosperous areas this division proved advantageous to the interests of the peasants. But in areas where poorer peasants depended on the common lands for grazing their livestock, this measure sometimes led to conflicts. The sale of the lands confiscated from the church (known as national lands or *biens nationaux*) did not always benefit farmers because they were sold in large lots, which cost more than many peasants could afford. The more well-off farmers might buy them to increase their holdings. Most of the sales went to such rural landowners, but many town dwellers also bought lands. Bourgeois investors saw the purchases as both economically advantageous and as part of their patriotic duty to support the Revolution. The farmers' resentment of the intrusion of bourgeois landowners into the countryside proved especially significant in the Vendée area in the west of France. There a peasant rebellion broke out in the spring of 1793.

The interference of revolutionary authorities in village affairs proved troublesome when they tried to enforce the Revolution's policy toward the Catholic Church. Towns tended to be more anti-clerical than the country, and Paris was the most anti-clerical of all. When non-juring priests were forbidden to minister, many villages in strongly Catholic areas conspired to hide the priests and keep their successors out of the churches. In some cases, the National Guard was called in to force a village to accept its designated constitutional priest. The villagers naturally resented the imposition of urban values on their communities, and they began to believe that Paris was the center of immorality and evil. The Paris crowds seemed bloodthirsty and irreligious. In the south where memories of the Wars of Religion still existed, Catholics believed the religious legislation was meant to bring about the triumph of Protestantism. Parisians, on the other hand, interpreted all resistance to the religious laws as signs of counter-revolution and obscurantism, not as indications of genuine religious concern.

Laws dealing with the family illustrate the divisions within the country. Divorce (made legal by a law of September 20, 1792) was much more common in urban areas and employed more frequently by women than by men. If divorce by mutual consent is excluded from consideration, in Rouen and Dijon (for example), 71 percent of divorces between 1792 and 1803 were sought by women. Studies of Rouen, Toulouse, Metz, and Lyon indicate that divorce was more common in those cities than in the rural areas nearby. In Rouen, the rate of divorce was five times greater in the city than in the surrounding countryside. Ideological and religious differences are doubtless important in explaining the variation between city and country, but also important are economic issues. Most French people made a living by farming, and the family was the work unit. Rural women who divorced their husbands could do so only if they had resources of their own or if they were willing to move to a city to seek employment that was not available to them in the country. Men were somewhat more likely than women to initiate divorce in rural areas.

Other sources of conflict in the provinces were departmental reorganization, abolition of the parlements, and ecclesiastical reform. Different towns vied to be the head of the new department or to be the location of the new court. Towns whose rivalry began over which one would gain the new institutions might afterward end up on opposite sides of political issues as well. These local political squabbles for the control of municipal government—both between towns and within towns and cities—proved to be important in 1793, when resentment against Paris escalated into outright revolt in some places.

CRISIS OF 1793

In January 1793, Jean Bon Saint-André (a former Protestant pastor, who was a Montagnard deputy) declared on the floor of the Convention, "Remain united, and we are invincible."[5] But the trial of the king had shown that deep divisions existed within the Convention itself, and the country was also divided over the direction the Revolution was taking. Many people in France were shocked at the execution of the king. Equally important was the reaction from abroad. Foreign governments now began to fear that the radical nature of the French Revolution could seriously threaten the stability of their own institutions and began to pay more attention to the war against France.

After the French victory at Valmy in September 1792, the French armies had scored further successes in the Low Countries. On November 6, 1792, at the battle of Jemappes, Dumouriez (the hero of the battle of Valmy) triumphed over the Austrians to gain control of Brussels and the

Austrian Netherlands. But with the annexation of the Austrian Netherlands, the French were now in a position to threaten Holland. Great Britain
could not allow French expansion into Holland because with France in
control of the northern coastline (just across the English Channel) the
British could be denied access to the continent. The French conquest of
Holland would also give them control of the Dutch navy. The combined
Dutch and French navies would create a formidable threat to British predominance at sea. Great Britain began putting together an alliance to fight
France, seeking the support of Spain, Russia, Sardinia, and Portugal.

French expansion threatened the status of foreign countries, not just
because of invasion, but because the French Convention declared that their
armies were on a crusade to spread republican institutions to the continent.
On November 19, 1792, the Convention decreed that France would help
"all peoples who wish to recover their liberty." On December 15, 1792,
they followed that threat to monarchical power by ordering French armies
to suppress feudal institutions in conquered territory, to declare the sovereignty of the people, and to take over public property. Any individual remaining loyal to the former prince or "privileged castes" would be considered an enemy. These two so-called Propagandist Decrees made it clear that
the French republican government was conducting war on an entirely new
basis and intended not merely to defeat the enemy governments but to create other republics in Europe.

Of course, they could do so only if they were winning the war. On
February 1, 1793, the French declared war on Great Britain and Holland
and soon found themselves facing a broad coalition of powers. In the
spring, the French armies suffered reverses in Holland and Belgium. Despairing of the situation after the French defeat at Neerwinden on March
18, and having lost faith in the government in Paris, the head of the army,
General Dumouriez, declared himself a constitutional monarchist and tried
to turn his army against the Convention. When the soldiers would not follow him, he defected to the Austrians on April 5, 1793, and eventually
ended up in the pay of the British. Faced with these reverses, the Jacobins
in Paris charged that anybody who counseled moderation was playing into
the hands of the nation's enemies. Dumouriez's treason seemed proof of
their repeated assertion that the country was riddled with people who could
not be trusted, traitors who hid behind the mask of patriotism. Because
Dumouriez had been allied with the Girondins, his defection made the
Girondins look suspect as well.

The Convention desperately needed more troops. France faced a
strong coalition with an army disrupted by the emigration of noble officers

and by indiscipline among the soldiers. By the end of 1791, more than 60 percent of the noble officers had emigrated. A call for volunteers in 1791 had brought many committed revolutionaries into the National Guard who were available for active duty when the war started in 1792. When a similar call went out in 1792, Frenchmen, now faced with active warfare, did not respond in as great a number. The volunteers of 1792 were committed revolutionaries whose zeal for the cause emboldened them to fight hard and to be willing to sacrifice for the nation. But their revolutionary enthusiasm led them to resist military discipline and to distrust the leadership of former noble officers. Integrating these new recruits into the army would take time. The army, like the rest of society, had been transformed by the Revolution. Soldiers joined Jacobin Clubs, read propaganda sent to them, and were on the lookout for traitors. Controlling the army and maintaining its allegiance were obviously crucial for the success of the government and the survival of the republic.

When the war widened in 1793, troops were urgently needed but recruiting became more difficult. On February 24, the Convention ordered the raising of a further 300,000 troops. Each department had a quota, which was divided up among the municipalities of the department. Individuals were invited to "consecrate themselves to the defence of the *Patrie*."[6] But, if the number volunteering did not meet the quota, the municipality could designate (by election or drawing of lots) the remainder from men between the ages of eighteen and forty who were bachelors or widowers without children. To avoid the draft, young men married or provided a substitute. The expedient of providing a substitute was available only to the well-to-do because the draftee had to pay for the clothing and arms of the substitute.

Although some departments (notably in the east and in the area around Paris) willingly complied with the levy, the military draft proved very unpopular in many parts of the country, causing riots and attacks on the officials sent to enforce it. Especially unpopular was the exemption of departmental and municipal officials from the draft. It appeared that the principal promoters and beneficiaries of the Revolution were not being asked to fight for it. The discontent over the levy became most serious in the west, where it soon escalated into rebellion against the central authorities. Although the authorities managed to get control in the area north of the Loire River, the region to the south of the Loire along the Atlantic coast (an area known as the Vendée) became the center of a full-fledged counter-revolutionary insurrection. The struggle in the Vendée, sparked by conscription, was fueled by many other discontents as well. To the people of the west, the Revolution had brought on economic hardship, attacks on their religion, domination by city people who promoted the Revolution and bought up *biens nationaux*, and the execution of the king. The peasants formed an army (the Catholic and Royal Army), fighting under a white banner proclaiming their devotion to God and king. The "Whites," soon joined by other counter-revolutionaries, hoped in vain to coordinate their campaigns with a projected invasion by émigrés and the British. The authorities sent "patriot" armies (the "Blues") to put down the rebellion with great ferocity. Each side massacred the other. The suppression of the Vendée has become a byword for brutality and bloodthirstiness (it has even been termed a "genocide").

Beset by crop shortages, dislocations because of requisitions for the war, rising prices, and low returns on taxes, France suffered a crisis in the economy and in government finances in the spring of 1793. By January 1793, the assignats were worth only 51 percent of face value. Food shortages and high prices in Paris fueled radical political movements. Representatives from the sections, assuming that high prices were caused by peasant hoarders unwilling to put their grain on the market until prices rose, presented a petition to the Convention on February 13 demanding that grain prices be controlled. The Convention, dominated by men devoted to free-trade principles, still intended to maintain the free-trade provisions promulgated in the Le Chapelier Law of 1791. Both Montagnards and Brissotins agreed on laissez-faire principles. But the people of Paris increasingly demanded price controls on food (the Maximum). One group of *sans-culottes* who protested prices were led by a former priest named Jacques Roux and became known as *enragés* (madmen). They helped spearhead attacks against markets at the end of February, and they demanded that food be requisitioned in the countryside and that hoarders be punished by death. The National Guard was able to restore order, but the violence frightened the Convention and exacerbated political divisions within it.

MARAT AND THE PURGING OF THE CONVENTION

The Convention responded to the escalating problems in the country by taking steps to centralize power. Radicals now began to see all expressions of local attachment as dangerous and potentially counter-revolutionary. Their goal became what had been proclaimed earlier: a "republic, one and indivisible." The institutions they created in the spring of 1793 would become the basis of the Terror in the fall.

They had already established in October 1792 a committee of the Convention to deal with police measures, investigate spies and traitors, and deal with matters of security: the Committee of General Security. In January 1793, its membership was set at twelve members to be elected from among the members of the Convention. In the spring of 1793, the Convention took further steps to ensure the security of the republic from its enemies. On March 10, 1793, they created a special court, the Revolutionary Tribunal, to try the enemies of the republic. Also in the spring, the Convention began the practice of sending its members out into the provinces as "representatives on mission." These representatives, who took with them the unlimited powers vested in the Convention, were sent to the armies and into the provinces to maintain loyalty, put down rebellion, deal with emergencies, and make sure that the armies were supplied with what they needed. The Convention decreed that committees of surveillance be created in every commune to ferret out foreigners who were enemies of the nation. These committees soon became local vigilantes who watched over and interrogated any suspect person in the neighborhood. Those found worthy would be given *certificats de civisme* (certificates of good citizenship). Those deemed guilty would be handed over to the police.

On April 6, 1793, the Convention tried to solve the problem of the weakness of the executive power by creating the Committee of Public Safety. Still attached to the principle of separation of powers, however, they originally meant the Committee of Public Safety to be a committee of the Convention charged with overseeing the Executive Council. Elected by the Convention, the Executive Council was very weak, in part because members of the Convention were not eligible for election. The Committee of Public Safety would eventually take over all the functions of the ineffective Executive Council and became the most important power in France during the Terror, although the Executive Council lingered on uselessly until April 1794. The membership of the Committee of Public Safety was to be elected every month by the Convention from among its own members. During the first few months of its existence, the Committee of Public Safety was dominated by Danton. This period saw the escalation of the struggle between the Jacobins and the Girondins.

Exemplifying the conspiratorial views of the times, the radicals of the Paris Commune believed the Girondins were worse than lukewarm revolutionaries; they were traitors in collusion with the counter-revolutionaries. The Girondins, reflecting the view of the provinces from which they derived their support, believed the Parisians were bloodthirsty radicals with dangerous egalitarian ideas. The Girondins rejected the Commune's belief in direct participatory democracy and their assumption of the right to intervene in government matters whenever they felt like it. The Jacobins, who knew that it was essential to maintain the support of the Parisian radicals, generally supported the demands of the Commune, even if the demands did not always conform to their professed principles.

In the spring of 1793, the struggle between the Jacobins and the Girondins focused on the flamboyant journalist, Jean-Paul Marat. Before the Revolution, Marat had been a doctor and a writer, and he had fancied himself an important scientist. In September 1789, he launched the newspaper that brought him fame: *L'Ami du peuple* (The Friend of the People). Although his political ideas had not been radical before the Revolution, he now proclaimed his devotion to the sovereignty of the people. His newspaper was little more than an extended editorial page filled with intemperate calls for violence against traitors and for an elected dictator to serve for a limited time to save the Revolution. Several times Marat was forced into exile or hiding to avoid arrest. He opposed the declaration of war in 1792 because he thought it would give too much power to the king. His attack on the National Assembly for endorsing the war forced him into hiding again, but he emerged in time for the Revolution of August 10 to issue an address entitled *"L'Ami du Peuple aux Français patriotes"* (The Friend of the People to Patriotic Frenchmen):

> No quarter! You are irrevocably lost if you do not hasten to beat down the rotten members of the municipality and the department, all unpatriotic justices of the peace, and the most gangrened members of the national assembly. . . . No one more than I abhors the spilling of blood; but to prevent floods of it from flowing, I urge you to pour out a few drops.[7]

His reputation as a bloodthirsty writer who called for the executions of counter-revolutionaries made many suspect that he was behind the September Massacres.

Elected to the Convention, Marat immediately came into conflict with Brissot and the other Girondins, who deplored and feared the presence of this sanguinary figure. Marat worried that the Convention was too weak and that the leniency of the Girondins toward the king was a sure indication of their treachery. The defection of Dumouriez (who had been associated with the Girondins) in April furnished what he saw as further proof. The Girondins, who believed Marat was responsible for the disturbances in February and for incidents in March when crowds attacked shops where Girondin newspapers were printed and wrecked their presses, now made a tactical mistake. They decided to try to get rid of him by bringing him up before the recently established Revolutionary Tribunal on charges of inciting murder, attacking the Convention, and seeking to destroy the sovereignty of the people. Although the members of the Convention (like those of many legislative bodies) were originally exempted from arrest for political activities, this regulation had been changed on April 1 in the wake of Dumouriez's defection, to allow the arrest of his presumed confederate Philippe Egalité (the name by which the Duc d'Orléans, now a member of the Convention, was known). Marat was the next member (but certainly not the last) to fall victim to the Convention's power to arrest those of its own members who were thought to be in league with the nation's enemies.

The vote by which Marat was brought to trial began at 10 a.m. on April 13 and dragged on until 7 the next morning, as all the delegates gave speeches explaining their votes. As expected, the Girondins voted for accusation and the Jacobins opposed it. But what is striking about the vote is that Girondins carried the day, not because they had the majority of the Convention behind them, but because so many Jacobins were absent as representatives on mission in the provinces. Also striking is the large number of abstentions, even among Girondins, who were uncomfortable with the attack on a fellow member of the Convention and who protested the unseemly haste of the procedure, which did not give Marat a chance to defend himself. Their trepidation was justified, as the Girondins would soon find the same procedures used against themselves.

Marat was not arrested until April 23 and appeared before the Revolutionary Tribunal on the following day, surrounded by large, cheering crowds and deputations from the sections of Paris. The outcome was never seriously in doubt, as the court, perhaps intimidated by his supporters, bent over backward to give him the benefit of the doubt. Marat's speech in his own defense was wildly cheered by the galleries. In announcing the unanimous verdict of acquittal, the chairman of the jury declared that he could not "impute criminal and counter-revolutionary intentions to the intrepid defender of the rights of the people."[8] Marat was then carried triumphantly from the courtroom on the shoulders of his supporters, who marched to the Convention and paraded around the aisles. That night there was further celebration at the Jacobin Club.

Many sections in Paris meanwhile had fought back against the attack on their hero by drawing up a list of twenty-two Girondin deputies (including Brissot, the deputies from the Gironde, and Pétion) and demanding their expulsion from the Convention. The sections also called for economic measures, especially controls on the price of bread and grain. The

Figure 7.2.   Triumph of Marat. In this obviously unsympathetic depiction of *sans-culottes*, the people of Paris are shown parading Marat in triumph after his acquittal before the Revolutionary Tribunal on April 24, 1793. The power of the people of Paris to influence political decisions reached its height in 1793. Later, after his assassination, Marat was celebrated as a republican martyr. Private collection.

Girondins argued that these demands showed the petitioners were economic illiterates. Increasingly fearful of the boisterous Parisian crowds that attended the meetings of the Convention, the Girondins proposed that the Convention be moved to some safer place, perhaps Versailles or Bourges. The radicals won the economic argument after eight thousand demonstrators invaded the Convention and pressured the assembly to set maximum prices for grain and bread. Passed on May 4, the law is known as the first Law of the Maximum.

Although they had at first been reluctant to support the demands of the sections that the Girondins be expelled, the Jacobin leaders were becoming apprehensive about their ability to maintain their majority in the Convention. The absence of many of their fellow Jacobins, who had been sent to the armies and to the rebellious provinces as representatives on mission, gave the Girondins a numerical advantage (as the vote on Marat showed). By the middle of May, plans were under way to get rid of the prominent Girondins. When the Girondins heard of them, they managed to get the Convention to create a special commission to investigate the municipal government.

On May 24, this commission, dominated by Girondins, ordered the arrest of municipal authorities, including Jacques-René Hébert. Hébert had won fame as a journalist who appealed to the lower classes in Paris by assuming the personality of a garrulous old man, Père Duchesne (the name of his newspaper). Written in colloquial and vulgar language, Hébert's paper hurled epithets indiscriminately at the upper classes and the enemies of Paris. The Girondins demanded that his paper be shut down. The Jacobins, temporarily marshaling enough votes, abolished the commission, but it was reinstated again. The stalemate in the Convention was broken by insurrection. On May 31, the tocsin rang out and crowds began to gather. However, the uprising was premature because it fell on a workday when the *sans-culottes* could not join in. The petition demanding that the Girondin leaders be arrested was referred to the Committee of Public Safety.

The real decision over the fate of the Girondins was not made in the Convention or by its committees. It was made in the streets of Paris. On June 2, the members of the Convention were once again debating the issue in the Tuileries Palace (their meetings had moved there on May 10) when word was brought in that the Palace was surrounded. This time the crowds were larger and more threatening because it was a Sunday when the *sans-culottes* were not working and because they had taken control of the city government and therefore had secured the backing of the National Guard. A large crowd (estimates vary widely from eight thousand to eighty thousand), many of them National Guardsmen, surrounded the Tuileries Palace demanding that the Girondins be expelled and that their economic problems be addressed. Bertrand Barère, speaking for the Committee of Public Safety, urged the Girondins to resign. Arguing that the Convention ought not submit to armed force, the Girondins refused to resign. To prove that they were acting freely and not under the coercion of the crowds, some of the deputies marched out of the chamber, but were unable to get through the crowd. They returned, and a new member of the Committee of Public Safety, Georges Couthon, put the best face on their situation by announcing that they could now be assured that they were acting freely: "You have marched out to the people; you have found it everywhere good, generous and incapable of threatening the security of its mandataries, but indignant against conspirators who wish to enslave it. Now therefore that you recognize that you are free in your deliberations, I move . . . a decree of accusation against the twenty-two denounced members. . . ."[9] Many Girondins, whose opposition to the political extremism of Paris had been their undoing, were now arrested. Some managed to escape into the provinces where they urged their supporters to fight back against the Jacobins.

The purging of the Convention on June 2 did not really constitute a change of power. The Jacobins already had the support of most of the Convention. But the purging removed their opponents who were thwarting more rigorous centralization. To many people in the provinces, the purge seemed illegal and unjustified. The Girondins, after all, were legally elected representatives of the nation. By kicking them out, the Jacobins had attacked the sovereignty of the nation. The event confirmed their view of Paris as lawless, anarchical, and hostile to the rights of the people whom the Revolution was supposed to stand for. The purge, although it consolidated the power of the Jacobins in the Convention, created an even more serious crisis in the country, the federalist revolt.

THE FEDERALIST REVOLT

The west of France had risen in revolt against the Convention in March 1793. By the end of May further signs of resistance to the authority of the Convention were beginning to appear, this time, surprisingly, in urban areas. Eventually the revolt would include the three largest cities in France after Paris (Marseilles, Lyon, and Bordeaux). The first indication of trouble came from Marseilles. Despite that city's reputation for stalwart republicanism (the "Marseillaise," after all, took its name from the city's enthusiastic volunteers in 1792), the economy of Marseilles had been hard hit by disruptions in sea-borne commerce, especially the blockade that Great Britain was now effectively putting on France. Though republican sentiment there was still strong, factions within the city split between the radical Jacobins and the more moderate city elites. When the anti-Jacobin faction won control of the municipal government, they protested against the centralizing tendencies of the Paris government and demanded that the city's economic problems be addressed.

Factional fighting among republicans had also occurred in Lyon, made especially bitter by economic distress. The silk industry (which employed as many as one-third of the city's population) had been in decline throughout the eighteenth century. The Revolution had made the condition of the luxury trades even worse. The artisans of Lyon organized political clubs with ties to the Jacobins in Paris. The old city elite promoted a more moderate style of politics and vied for control of the city government with the

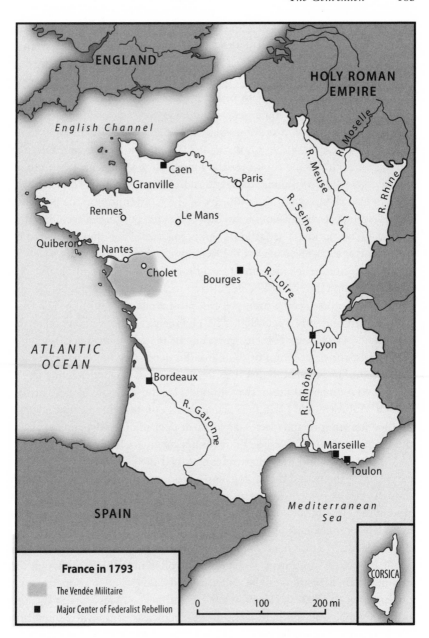

ENGLAND

HOLY ROMAN EMPIRE

English Channel

R. Moselle

Caen

Paris

R. Meuse

R. Rhine

Granville

R. Seine

Rennes

Le Mans

Quiberon

Nantes

Cholet

Bourges

R. Loire

Lyon

ATLANTIC OCEAN

Bordeaux

R. Rhône

R. Garonne

Marseille

Toulon

Mediterranean Sea

SPAIN

CORSICA

France in 1793

The Vendée Militaire

■   Major Center of Federalist Rebellion

0   100   200 mi

popular clubs. By May 1793, the population had begun to distrust the rabble-rousing proclamations of the Jacobin city government, who seemed no more capable of providing food than the moderates. Resentment against the Lyon Jacobins and their ties to radicals in Paris grew when representatives on mission arrived in the city to make sure the Jacobins kept control of the city government. When some grain warehouses were attacked, the representatives on mission used that event as an excuse and called for an army to be sent to Lyon. On May 29, the departmental authorities in Lyon called out the National Guard and took over the municipal government. In an unfortunate coincidence of timing, the factional fighting in Lyon had thus brought the city into revolt against the authority of the Convention (in the person of the representatives on mission) mere days before the purging of the Girondins from the Convention. The factional fighting in these cities thus seemed to be part of a far wider revolt against the Jacobin government in Paris.

Other cities rebelled against the authority of the Convention after the purging of the Girondins. The population of Bordeaux had doubled in the eighteenth century on the strength of its prosperous trade with the West Indies. Its economy was especially hard hit by the disruptions in commerce by sea caused by the war. The city government reacted with special indignation against the persecution of the Girondin deputies who came from their department. They believed that the Convention was no longer acting freely, having been forced to purge the Girondins by the violence of the Parisian crowds. Authorities in Caen in Normandy also protested the Parisian attack on the Convention, and Caen's department declared its independence from the Convention until that body could once again act freely.

These cities and their departments gained the support of departments neighboring them, and the protests spread to some forty-three departments, though serious revolt was confined primarily to Normandy and the areas around the cities in the south. The Jacobins in Paris combined these actually quite separate incidents of rebellion against Paris into something they called the "federalist" movement or "federalism." In fact, the federalists never formed a united movement or expressed a coherent ideology, although the outlines of their position can be understood and they tried to cooperate with one another. In 1793, the Jacobins saw federalism as a heresy against the idea of the republic one and indivisible. To the federalists, it was the centralizing Jacobins who were the heretics, and it was the extremist crowds in Paris who threatened the revolutionary ideal of the sovereignty of the people by constantly bullying the Convention and purging its members.

The Revolution had originally been quite decentralizing, giving cities and towns a great deal of autonomy and instituting elections for all manner of local officials. Under the pressures of war and rebellion, the Convention now sought to gain more control over the resources of the country and wanted to make sure the officials in the far-flung regions were loyal to the republic. Naturally, these attempts to centralize control and to make sure authorities conformed to the directives of the Convention met resistance. To the Jacobins the resistance seemed more than mere political jockeying for power. After all, the Convention in theory embodied the will of the French people. Any opposition to the Convention's decrees could be considered opposition to the will of the people. Therefore, to the Jacobins, resistance was not political opposition (anti-Jacobin); it was treason (anti-republic). They found it especially difficult to make a distinction between different kinds of opposition. They did in fact face many people who were genuine, committed, and organized enemies of the republic (émigrés and the Vendée, for example). And the opponents of the Jacobins, though disagreeing on aims, could occasionally work together. The federalist revolt began as a republican movement in opposition to the Jacobins, but it soon attracted the participation of others whose political views were royalist or anti-revolutionary. So the Jacobins worried when signs of resistance appeared, when the federalist cities sought each other's help, and when the Girondins escaping from Paris went to Normandy or the Gironde to egg on the revolt. Although the depth of commitment varied greatly, the federalist revolt continued into the fall of 1793, made even more worrisome to the Convention by the continuing crisis of the war.

THE DEATH OF MARAT

On June 3, Marat resigned from the Convention, believing that the arrest of the Girondins had brought his work to a close. He had been seriously ill since December with acute pruritus, a kind of skin disease that was now complicated by a lung ailment. He suffered such severe pain and itching that he worked in a bathtub filled with a medicinal bath, with a top over it that served as a desk and that also allowed him to receive visitors. He continued to write letters, but his health prevented more strenuous activities.

Some Girondin deputies who escaped from Paris made their way to Normandy. In Caen, a young woman named Charlotte Corday was appalled to learn of their treatment and pledged to be their avenger. Inspired by the biblical story of Judith, she set out for Paris to kill the leaders of the Jacobins, particularly Marat. She looked for him first at the Convention, then sought him out at home. The woman with whom Marat lived refused to let her in, arguing that he was too ill. Corday then wrote a letter to him: "I come from Caen. Your love for the country ought to make you anxious to know the plots that are being laid there." Without waiting for a reply, she went to Marat's house on the evening of July 13. Again, she was about to be turned away when Marat, hearing her voice, asked that she be let in. "What is going on at Caen?" he asked her. She responded, "Eighteen deputies from the Convention rule there in collusion with the Department." Marat asked for their names, which Corday provided as he wrote them down. "They will soon be guillotined," he declared. At that point, she approached the bathtub and plunged a knife into Marat's lungs. He died immediately. The last issue of his paper appeared on July 14, 1793. Charlotte Corday was guillotined on July 17.

Marat's assassination proved to have the opposite effect from that desired by Charlotte Corday. Marat had been a rather marginal figure, too radical for most revolutionaries. His stature had risen only recently in the spring in the struggle with the Girondins. But his illness had left him incapable of exerting much influence on the Convention or on municipal politics. With his assassination, however, Marat was transformed into a martyr, into a symbol of pure revolutionary virtue. His image was exploited by the Jacobins as they increased the power of the revolutionary government under the Terror. The bust of Marat was installed in the chamber where the Convention met in the Tuileries Palace. The image of the man whom many had condemned as too bloodthirsty now presided over the deliberations of the Convention as it created the institutions of the Terror.

CONCLUSION

The removal of the king and the defeat of the constitutional monarchists had not eliminated divisions within the country. Indeed, it had made those divisions even more serious. The revolutionaries' attempts to unite the country and harness its resources for the widening war pushed royalist sympathizers into active revolt. The republicans themselves fell victim to factional disputes as they debated the fate of the king and the question of who was ultimately to make decisions for the country. In their desperate but futile attempt to create unanimity where none existed, the Convention purged the Girondins from the chamber. But even though the Mountain now dominated, factions did not end, and neither did attempts to get rid of them. As the famous quotation so aptly reminds us, "The Revolution is like Saturn, it devours its own children."[10]

8

TERROR AND WAR

In the summer of 1793, republican France confronted foreign enemies bearing down on its boundaries and rebellious citizens within the nation. In order to appease the Parisian radicals who were clamoring for extreme measures, the Convention (which had been called originally to write a republican constitution for France) appointed a committee, which hastily wrote a constitution in about a week. This extremely democratic document with an expanded declaration of rights was adopted on June 24 but never put into operation. Faced with many emergencies and enemies, the Convention realized that a constitutional system with free elections would have spelled the defeat of the Jacobins. Instead, they suspended the constitution and moved to strengthen the only central authority that existed, the Committee of Public Safety.

BEGINNING OF THE TERROR

Created by the Convention in early April 1793 as one of its committees, the Committee of Public Safety faced reelection every month. At first, the commanding figure of Georges-Jacques Danton dominated the shifting membership of the group. But when his attempts to negotiate peace terms failed, he was not reelected on July 10, 1793. Robespierre, who would become famous as the spokesman of the Committee, was elected on July 27. The Convention hoped that his popularity with the *sans-culottes* would keep them loyal and subservient.

The military reverses seemed even more frightening than the *sans-culottes'* agitation, now that the French armies had retreated within France's borders. On August 14, at the request of the Committee of Public Safety,

189

two members of the Convention with military experience were added to the committee: Lazare Carnot and Prieur of the Côte d'Or. On August 23, the Convention took an important step toward transforming traditional warfare by passing the *levée en masse*. This decree, a harbinger of many mass mobilizations of the future, requisitioned the entire population for the defense of the country. The men were to be immediately mobilized for the army, industry organized for war production, and buildings taken over as needed. All citizens, of both sexes and all ages, were expected to contribute as they could:

> The young men shall go to battle; the married men shall forge arms and transport provisions; the women shall make tents and clothes, and shall serve in the hospitals; the children shall turn old linen into lint [bandages]; the old men shall repair to the public places, to stimulate the courage of the warriors and preach the unity of the Republic and hatred of kings.[1]

The Convention called for the creation of a "nation in arms," an entire country mobilized for war. Although the Convention could not carry out this goal to the same extent as governments of the twentieth century could call up their resources for "total war," the aim marked a significant departure from the way of war of the Ancien Régime. Revolution was transforming society and warfare at the same time. Huge armies now took the field. Clausewitz, the German military theorist famous for his analysis of the warfare of this era, wrote that in 1793,

> a force appeared that beggared all imagination. Suddenly war again became the business of the people—a people of thirty millions, all of whom considered themselves to be citizens. . . . The people became a participant in war; instead of governments and armies as heretofore, the full weight of the nation was thrown into the balance. The resources and efforts now available for use surpassed all conventional limits: nothing now impeded the vigour with which war could be waged.[2]

Of course, this did not happen instantly. The members of the Committee of Public Safety, who were to oversee the war effort, had first to make sure that they stayed in power.

The immediate threat to the authority of the Convention came from Parisian *sans-culottes* who pressured the Convention to take measures to alleviate the food shortages. Leading this agitation were the *enragés* (under the leadership of Jacques Roux) and Hébertists (followers of Jacques-René

Hébert). They demanded that hoarders and monopolists be punished, along with rich people who undermined the Revolution. Roux declared, "Liberty is but a vain phantom when one class of men can starve the other with impunity. Equality is but a vain phantom when the rich exercise the power of life and death over their fellows through monopolies. The Republic is but a vain phantom when the Counter-Revolution is accomplished daily through the price of provisions which three quarters of the citizens cannot pay without shedding tears."[3] To appease the people of Paris, the Convention decreed the death penalty for hoarders and took measures to assure the supply of grain. But at the same time, Robespierre responded to Jacques Roux's criticism of the leadership of the Jacobins by accusing him of being in the pay of the Austrians and of not being a true revolutionary. Arrested in early September, Roux committed suicide in prison in February 1794 rather than face the Revolutionary Tribunal.

On September 2, 1793, the news reached Paris that the naval installation at the Mediterranean port of Toulon (already in revolt against the Convention as part of the federalist revolt) had handed the installation over to the British. This depressing news brought on another of the revolutionary *journées*, September 5, the first day of the Reign of Terror. Led by the municipal authorities, a large crowd converged on the Convention demanding "war on tyrants, hoarders and aristocrats."[4] To ensure an adequate supply of food, they forced the Convention to authorize the creation of a so-called Revolutionary Army, *sans-culottes* organized in military fashion to roam the countryside searching for grain and forcing hoarders to supply it.

Although aware that flocks of people issuing from the cities to scavenge the countryside for food added up to a recipe for violence, the Convention was unable to derail this demand. Danton gave an impassioned speech praising the energy of the people and recommending that *sans-culottes* who attended their local sectional meetings and surveillance committees be given a stipend. This measure, which appeared to be aimed at supporting the participation of the people in public affairs, was probably intended to eliminate the domination of extremists in sectional affairs. If paid, ordinary citizens might attend meetings, whereas only zealots came to them now. Finally, the Convention memorably decreed that terror was to be "the order of the day." To protect itself from its enemies, the Revolution would be severe. The Convention proclaimed that henceforth terror was a deliberate government policy. But when one speaker urged that they be "brigands for the good of the people," Thuriot (then a member of the Committee of Public Safety) remonstrated with him, declaring that revolutions were made "for the triumph of virtue." France, he asserted, "thirsts only for justice,"[5] not for blood. Such language continued throughout the Terror. Everything they did (however bloodthirsty) was justified by invoking the will of the people, the desire for virtue, and the search for justice.

THE COMMITTEE OF PUBLIC SAFETY CONSOLIDATES ITS POWER

The Convention had been forced to give in to the demands of the *sans-culottes*, but it intended to get back in control. In September 1793, the Committee of Public Safety took on the shape that it would have for the next ten months and began the process of gathering the reins of power in its hands. In order to co-opt the extremists, two members of the Convention who were associated with the Hébertists were added to the Committee of Public Safety: Billaud-Varenne and Collot d'Herbois. On September 20, Thuriot resigned, leaving twelve members of the committee, who (except for one member who was arrested) would guide the affairs of France until July 1794.

These twelve men can be conveniently organized into four groups. The first group, made up of Billaud-Varenne (a former lawyer with literary aspirations) and Collot d'Herbois (a former professional actor), was the most radical. The second group consisted of five members who were best known as administrators. For his indispensable work in the reorganization of the army, Lazare Carnot, an army captain, became known as the "Organizer of Victory." Jean Bon Saint-André, a former Protestant minister, endeavored to shape up the navy. Two men with similar names were told apart by the addition to their names of the department that had elected them. Prieur of the Marne and Prieur of the Côte d'Or both spent a great deal of time outside of Paris organizing the armies and putting down the civil war. Robert Lindet, a lawyer and the oldest of the group, worked on subsistence and supply. Clustered around Robespierre in the third group were his closest allies: Couthon (also a lawyer) who came from the Auvergne and who suffered from a paralysis that left him unable to walk, and Saint-Just, the youngest of the group (only twenty-two years old when the Revolution began), who was utterly devoted to the work of the Committee of Public Safety. The final two were Barère, who drafted legislation and often served as a spokesman for the Committee in the Convention; and Hérault de Séchelles, the only former nobleman in the group, who would be the first member of the Committee of Public Safety to fall victim to the Terror.

The Committee of Public Safety did not have an acknowledged leader. The members worked as a group, gathering at night after the meetings of the Convention to conduct business. They did not always meet together because members were frequently on mission to the provinces. Only Robespierre never went on mission. His abilities to rally the crowds to the policy of the government and to give speeches to keep the Convention loyally supporting the Committee of Public Safety were valued too highly to risk having him absent from Paris. In part because of his more visible role as the spokesman for the Committee, Robespierre is sometimes described as the "leader" or "head" of the Committee of Public Safety. But he had no such official or even unofficial title. The twelve members took joint responsibility for the work of the Committee. All members present signed their decrees and decisions.

Figure 8.1. Robespierre. A champion of the people of Paris, Robespierre did not dress like a *sans-culotte*. Even in the midst of the Terror, he maintained the appearance of a middle-class lawyer. This portrait of a well-dressed Robespierre reminds us that revolutionaries came from a variety of backgrounds. Courtesy of the Division of Rare and Manuscript Collections, Cornell University Library.

Maximilien Robespierre came from Arras, north of Paris. He had trained as a lawyer and was elected to the Estates General. A bachelor, Robespierre lived austerely in the home of friends, dedicating himself to the cause of the Revolution. The people of Paris, whom he seemed at times to confuse with the people of France, recognized him as their champion. An important figure at the Jacobin Club, his reputation for honesty had earned him the nickname of the "Incorruptible." Convinced of the rightness of his cause, Robespierre was constantly on the lookout for traitors to the Revolution (who often turned out to be those who disagreed with him). He was a devoted disciple of Rousseau and believed that politics and morality were inevitably connected. Unable to serve in the Legislative Assembly because of the "self-denying" ordinance that he had championed, Robespierre had accepted a position as a judge. But he did not stay out of the public eye for long, using the forum of the Jacobin Club to denounce his enemies and to oppose the war, before his election to the Convention in the fall of 1792. His speeches before the Convention often conveyed the aims and intentions of the Committee of Public Safety.

Several measures in September 1793 increased the power of the Committee of Public Safety and gave it the tools with which to set up a dictatorship. On September 14, the Committee obtained the right to name members of the other committees of the Convention. On September 17, the Convention passed the Law of Suspects, arranging for committees of surveillance in each neighborhood to arrest "suspected persons," vaguely defined as those who had shown themselves to be "partisans of tyranny or federalism and enemies of liberty."[6] Former noblemen and émigrés and their families were automatically suspect. The Committee of General Security was to oversee the jailing and trials of those arrested.

On September 29 the Convention gave the national government control over the economy by passing the law of the General Maximum. Although still declaring their belief in the principle of free trade, they chose to ignore it during this time of emergency, when the enemies of the republic, they argued, could take advantage to deprive them of necessities. The General Maximum now extended price controls (earlier applied only to grain) to a range of goods considered essential to the republic. Prices were capped at one-third more than the price that had been current in 1790. Wages could rise to one-half higher than the level of 1790, thus giving a slight advantage to the wage earner.

The strengthening of the power of the committee did not go unchallenged. But on September 25, when questions were raised in the Convention about what the committee had done, the Committee of Public Safety responded by offering to resign as a group unless the Convention gave them a vote of confidence. Robespierre argued that criticism of the Convention could not be allowed: "Whoever seeks to debase, divide or paralyze the Convention is an enemy of our country. . . ."[7] The Committee could not carry out their weighty responsibilities if they were being denounced and did not have the confidence of the Convention, he warned. The Convention, fearful of the chaos that might ensue if the Committee of Public Safety disappeared, backed down. For the next ten months the same men were reelected every month, becoming a dictatorship whose actions were almost impossible to question.

Further measures in the fall consolidated the power of the central government. On October 10, the Convention declared, "The provisional government of France is revolutionary until the peace."[8] In other words, while it had to deal with the dangers of war and civil war, a revolutionary government would rule outside the realm of established law, and the constitution would not be put into effect. This decree also recognized the Committee of Public Safety as the government of France. Even greater centralization ensued when the Committee of Public Safety gained control of the Jacobin network of clubs and could send out orders directly to the Jacobin branches throughout the country. Especially important for the consolidation of the dictatorship was a law passed on December 4, 1793 (known as the Law of 14 Frimaire), which gave even more power to the Committee. It now controlled all representatives on mission sent by the Convention to the provinces. Furthermore, the law allowed the Committee to appoint and remove local government officials. This constituted a major change from the political philosophy of 1789 when most offices had been declared electable. Now free elections were banned in the interests of order and efficiency. Such a sharp deviation from the founding principles of the Revolution required an explanation. Couthon provided it, asserting that they were not attacking the principle of free elections:

> The right of election belongs essentially to the sovereign people. To impair it is a crime, unless extraordinary circumstances demand it for the people's welfare. Now, we find ourselves in these extraordinary circumstances. . . . Those who appeal to the rights of the people mean to pay a false homage to its sovereignty. When the revolutionary machine is still rolling, you injure the people in entrusting it with the election of public functionaries for you expose it to the naming of men who will betray it.[9]

Everybody understood that free elections would have almost certainly brought defeat for those running the government, and they could not run that risk. But their decision, of course, had to be justified in the name of protecting the people.

The consolidation of power for the Committee of Public Safety in the fall of 1793 also included getting rid of enemies who were already imprisoned. Marie Antoinette was tried for wickedness and treason and executed on October 16. In a Europe in which chivalric values still held sway, her execution seemed more barbaric than the death of the king, who, after all, had held a position of responsibility in the government. The Girondins who had been arrested after the purge of June 2 went to the guillotine on October 31, followed shortly after by the Duc d'Orléans and Bailly. Madame Roland was guillotined on November 9. When her husband (who had escaped arrest and sought refuge in Normandy) heard the news, he went into the country and committed suicide.

Another victim of the increased authority of the government was the feminist movement. Olympe de Gouges, author of the "Declaration of the Rights of Woman and Citizen," was executed in November 1793 for being a moderate royalist. As the Revolution became more radical, so did women's organizations. In May 1793, *sans-culotte* women with economic as well as feminist concerns organized themselves into a club called "Citoyennes Républicaines Révolutionnaires" (Revolutionary Republican Women). Their goal, like other political clubs, was to save the nation and the Revolution. While the men were fighting the foreign troops, they pledged to save the Revolution at home and demanded arms. They argued that they shared natural rights with men, that as mothers of all citizens, women guaranteed the survival of the state and should therefore have a prominent place in it. They believed that the considerable contributions women had made during the Revolution had earned them the rights of citizens. But the Jacobins in power opposed rights for women just as the constitutional monarchists had before them.

In the fall of 1793, the Convention accused the Citoyennes Républicaines Révolutionnaires of being under the sway of Jacques Roux and the *enragés* and closed down the club on the grounds that its exaggerated expressions of revolutionary fervor were fomenting disorders. However, the report of the committee did not confine itself to this purely political issue, but instead asserted that women should not participate in politics "because they would be obliged to sacrifice the more important cares to which nature calls them. The private functions for which women are destined by their very nature are related to the general order of society; this social order results from the differences between man and woman." They declared that it was immoral for women to debate publicly with men and to "meddle in affairs of government." They concluded:

> There is another sense in which women's associations seem dangerous. If we consider that the political education of man is at its beginning, that all its principles are not developed, and that we are still stammering the word "liberty," then how much more reasonable is it for women, whose moral education is almost nil, to be less enlightened concerning principles? Their presence in popular societies, therefore, would give an active role in government to people more exposed to error and seduction. Let us add that women are disposed by their organization to an overexcitation which would be deadly in public affairs and that interests of state would soon be sacrificed to everything which ardor in passions can generate in the way of error and disorder.[10]

All women's clubs were shut down. The reasoning in the report reveals the Convention's assumptions that women were irrational and hysterical and incapable of exercising responsible political power. But it also shows their fear that public affairs could be easily corrupted and their belief that morality had to be at the basis of a successful republic. Those ideas would take on added emphasis as the Reign of Terror continued.

DECHRISTIANIZATION AND THE CALENDAR

The French republicans genuinely believed in the transforming power of the new political system. People involved in the Revolution were enthralled at the possibilities that now opened before them. A sense of collective dedication to their task gave special meaning to their lives, engaging them in an enterprise that seemed much larger than themselves and more important than anything they had experienced before. The changes that had taken place were so remarkable that anything seemed possible.

Nothing more aptly symbolizes this optimistic embrace of the future than the changing of the calendar. The new era of happiness, they believed, required a complete break with the evils of the past. They created an entirely new calendar, abandoning completely the Christian calendar, with its saints' days and myriad reminders of Christ's story. The calendar, like the metric system on which it was based, was to be uniform and consistent with nature and the principles of science. The metric system has survived and become the standard throughout the world. The calendar proved less long-lasting.

The new era began with the proclamation of the French Republic on September 22, 1792. That date would retrospectively be labeled the beginning of Year I. Year II began on September 22, 1793. Each week (called a *décade*) had ten days and each month consisted of three *décades*. Naming these new measures of time was entrusted to a poet, Fabre d'Eglantine, now a deputy in the Convention. The days of the week were called *primidi*, *duodi*, *tridi*, and so forth up to *décadi*, the day of rest. Months were grouped into four seasons and named for aspects of nature characteristic of that part of the year. Autumn months were Vendémiaire (grape harvest), Brumaire (fog), and Frimaire (cold). Winter consisted of the months of Nivôse (snow), Pluviôse (rain), and Ventôse (wind). Spring months were Germinal (germination), Floréal (flowers), and Prairial (prairies). The year ended with summer: Messidor (crops or harvest), Thermidor (heat), and Fructidor (fruit). The five days left over (six in leap year) were called the *sans-culottides*. Despite its overtly anti-Christian inspiration, the calendar imitated the Christian custom of devoting each day to a saint. The republican calendar devoted each day to a product of the vegetable kingdom, or to an animal, or to an agricultural implement. The *sans-culottides* were to be days in which to celebrate Virtue, Genius, Labor, Recompense, and Opinion. People understandably resisted the ten-day week as it limited days of rest to one in ten rather than one in seven.

The calendar was only one part of a wholesale attack on Christianity. The constitutional church put in place by the Civil Constitution of the Clergy of 1790 still existed, but the persecution of priests steadily increased. In August 1792, after the fall of the king, all convents and monasteries were shut down and sold and priests were required to swear an oath to liberty and equality, like all other civil servants. They could no longer wear ecclesiastical dress, form processions, or make other public displays of religion. In the September Massacres, the crowds assassinated more than two hundred priests and three ex-bishops. The revolt in the Vendée, with its explicit appeals to religion, identified the church with rebellion against the nation. In order to support the war, church bells were melted down to manufacture cannons, silver vessels and other church treasures were requisitioned, and church buildings were commandeered to store supplies. Within the old churches of France, monuments had accumulated over the years with references to nobles, kings, and the feudal system. They were vandalized, and symbols of nobility and monarchy were destroyed or mutilated. The churches had already suffered numerous attacks, but in the fall of 1793 the persecution escalated in a concerted campaign known as the Dechristianization movement.

The first stirrings of this movement occurred in late September in the provinces where Joseph Fouché, a former priest and now a representative on mission, took over a church in Nevers and created his own atheistic civic religion, a "Feast of Brutus." He asserted that he intended "to substitute for superstitious and hypocritical worship . . . that of the Republic and of a natural morality."[11] Other representatives (Couthon in Auvergne, for example) began to impose their versions of religion and to forbid the exercise of the Christian religion. But the Dechristianization movement soon developed a popular element as well.

When the movement spread to Paris, the Hébertists demanded that churches be shut down, and they instituted ceremonies that were mockeries of the traditional Catholic rituals. On November 10 (20 Brumaire) a Festival of Reason was held at the Cathedral of Notre Dame; the great medieval building was henceforth to be known as the Temple of Reason. The ceremony revolved around a large mountain (a symbol of Jacobinism) and an actress playing the role of Liberty. The Convention signaled its endorsement by taking part in the ceremony and by decreeing that communes could shut down churches. Enthusiastic followers of the Revolution changed their names from those of Catholic saints to those of heroes of antiquity or modern republican heroes. Especially popular were Gracchus, Brutus, and Marat. Streets and towns received new names, losing any references to saints, nobles, or kings. Even the kings and queens in a deck of cards disappeared.

Robespierre looked askance at the Dechristianization campaign. As a sincere Deist, he disapproved of the atheism behind the movement. He also opposed it because he disapproved of the Hébertists who championed it. But mostly he opposed it because he believed it was politically dangerous. The mass of people in the country were religious. In a speech at the Jacobin Club on November 21 he declared, "Atheism is aristocratic; the idea of a great Being that watches over oppressed innocence and punishes triumphant crime is altogether popular." He spoke, he assured them, not as a philosopher, but as a representative of the people.[12] The Convention soon fell into line, reaffirming freedom of religion and prohibiting church closings. But the Dechristianization movement continued nonetheless, with priests being pressured to abandon their calling and to marry. Of the 130,000 who had been priests before the Revolution, around 20,000 left the priesthood and 6,000 of those married.

The Dechristianization movement also seemed suspect because it was tied in with the so-called Foreign Plot. In October, Fabre d'Eglantine had denounced to the Committee of Public Safety some prominent foreigners identified with radicalism who were, he alleged, using foreign money provided especially by the British Prime Minister William Pitt to bribe deputies. Similar accusations were made by another deputy, François Chabot. Robespierre naturally believed all the evils attributed to foreigners and assumed his political enemies were in their pay. In truth, the plot seems to have been an invention of Fabre and Chabot, who were using it to divert attention from their own corruption in the liquidation of the publicly owned East India Company. But from then on, Robespierre believed that radicalism and Dechristianization were supported by foreign money as a way to cause division and undermine the republic.

One of the reasons for increasing the power of the government under the Law of 14 Frimaire was the desire to centralize authority and take the initiative out of the hands of local radicals and Dechristianizers, whom the Committee of Public Safety did not trust. By the end of December, one of the members of the Committee itself, Hérault de Séchelles, had fallen under suspicion of involvement in the Foreign Plot and was forced to resign. In the middle of January, the Committee became convinced that Fabre d'Eglantine, who had originally revealed the Foreign Plot, was himself implicated in it. On January 17, Fabre, Hérault de Séchelles, Chabot, and two others were sent before the Revolutionary Tribunal.

DESTRUCTION AND CREATION OF CULTURE

The Dechristianization campaign was the culmination of the attacks on the church. Although the early revolutionaries had not set out to destroy either the church or the monarchy, when they disappeared the destruction spread out to encompass any aspect of society that was associated with these old institutions. Names were changed, monuments torn down, buildings destroyed or rededicated to other uses. Anything that reminded the new citizens of the old regime was a target of the rampaging crowds or of official policy. In the fall of 1793, the authorities commissioned workers to remove the statues of the kings (actually the kings of Judah, not of France) on the façade of the Cathedral of Notre Dame in Paris. The tombs of the kings of France at Saint-Denis were also targeted for destruction, and the embalmed remains of the kings were taken from their tombs and buried in quicklime.

Such vandalism was commanded in order to remove the symbols of the past so that a new public sensibility and political allegiance could be created. But even as they recognized the necessity of such work, many revolutionaries also wanted to preserve as much as possible the great works of art of the past. As early as 1790, a Commission of Monuments was given the task of preserving important works of art, and a special museum was created to receive them. By putting the pieces into museums, the royal and religious works of art would lose their character as devotional objects and could be appreciated for their artistic or historic qualities. After the fall of the king, the Louvre was designated as the national museum, where great works of art from the former royal collections and from religious houses were gathered together. Painting and sculpture from the estates of émigrés (either confiscated or sold by their families) added to the national collections, which were greatly supplemented later by treasures brought home to France by the Napoleonic armies.

Art, formerly enjoyed by the aristocracy, had now become the possession of the nation. But the aims of the revolutionaries were not merely to destroy (or preserve) the vestiges of the past. They intended to create a new culture to take the place of the old. Imbued with the ideas of Locke's sensationalist psychology, they wanted to use the arts and the physical environment to transform the subjects of the past into the citizens of the future. To that end, they restructured the theaters and artistic corporations of the Ancien Régime to make them conform to the new values of openness and freedom. Theaters in the Ancien Régime had operated only with special permission of the government, had been heavily censored, and had existed mostly for the amusement of the upper classes. Theaters owned the rights to the plays they presented, so that playwrights could not sell their works for another group to perform. The special privileged status of theaters was eliminated in January 1791, and by the end of that year, thirty-five new theaters had opened. Always subject to political pressure from the crowds and from the authorities, the subjects of plays came to reflect the increasing radicalism of the Revolution. Theaters were forced to change their names and their ownership as they fell under the suspicions of the Jacobins.

The anti-corporatist and anti-elitist thrust of the policy toward theaters was likewise seen in the transformation of the artistic establishment. The royal academies, which could choose their members and thus decide which works of art could be exhibited and which artists would receive commissions, had been deeply resented by those excluded. Arguing that since guilds had been abolished, guilds of artists should be done away with as well, Jacques-Louis David and the Abbé Grégoire proposed that the academies be replaced with an institution more appropriate to the times. The Commune générale des arts (decreed in the fall of 1793) was open to all artists who could furnish proof of good citizenship and proof that they made a living by their art. Works of art were more likely to be judged on the basis of patriotism than on pure artistic merit.

David, the neoclassical painter who had become a deputy to the Convention, used his art to further his political views. His works on classical historical themes before the Revolution (*The Oath of the Horatii*, for example) had helped to popularize the notions of patriotism and willingness to sacrifice for one's country. During the Revolution he identified with the Jacobins, helping to design festivals and costumes. His austere neoclassicism was employed to great effect in one of the famous paintings of the period: the assassinated Marat lying in his medicinal bath. David enjoyed even greater success later as an official painter for Napoleon. Artistic talent could be found equally on all sides of the political spectrum, as the examples of two prominent portraitists demonstrate. Elisabeth Vigée-Lebrun, a royalist famous for sympathetic portraits of Marie Antoinette, lived in exile after the fall of the monarchy, while Adélaide Labille-Guiard supported the Revolution and painted images of such revolutionaries as Madame Roland and Robespierre.

On balance, the Revolution was not a good time for great art as patronage dried up and political concerns took the place of leisure activity. But the Revolution made possible the flowering of a new kind of popular culture as revolutionaries enthusiastically joined in the creation of a political system stressing equality of rights and patriotism. Popular prints and cartoons commemorating or commenting on the momentous events immediately began to appear in cheap editions that poorer people could afford. New symbols were created to replace those of the monarchy and the church. Instead of a king as the embodiment of France, revolutionary pictures featured a female figure representing liberty, often sporting a Phrygian cap. This female figure also came to represent the republic and was even given a nickname, Marianne. This image still survives as the embodiment of the French nation.

With the demise of religion, the nation became the focus of loyalty, identification, and ceremony. A church in Paris was converted into a memorial for the great men of the nation, the Pantheon. The first man to be honored was Mirabeau in April 1791, followed shortly after by Voltaire, the implacable enemy of the church, whose remains were placed in the Pantheon in July 1791. Fittingly, this memorial site was given a name from ancient history. The classical (and pagan) past was frequently invoked by speakers, and Marianne and other allegorical figures were depicted in classical dress. From the ancients, Frenchmen were supposed to learn devotion to and sacrifice for the nation. People were instructed in these new values through images, plays, speeches, and patriotic festivals.

The festivals were also occasions for the people to participate and to develop their own patriotic traditions. At the first Festival of Federation in 1790, those who came to prepare the grounds of the Champ de Mars for the ceremony sang a new song, "Ça ira" (things will work out), expressing their optimism about the future. But even at that early date, the lyrics included threats to hang aristocrats from lampposts. As the monarchy gave way to a republic, the violent language against the enemies of the Revolution became more pronounced. One popular song, "La Carmagnole," praised the sound of the cannon.

By the time of the Terror, profound changes had taken place in society. In their desire for equality, *sans-culottes* rejected the habits of polite society and looked at all upper-class people with suspicion. Anything reminiscent of the nobility or the Ancien Régime was considered dangerously counter-revolutionary. True revolutionaries were expected to wear simple garb (in contrast to the elaborate wardrobes in fine materials of the Ancien Régime) and don the revolutionary Phrygian cap and the tricolored cockade. They refused to use the old titles of address, such as "monsieur" or "madame" (which denoted subservience), insisting instead that all people be called merely "citizen" or "citizeness." The formal "vous," which indicated respect for superiors, gave way to the egalitarian "tu" when speaking to another. A great word of opprobrium was "aristocrat," applied to anybody who put on airs, whether bourgeois or noble, and whose political philosophy deviated from strict equality. The intensity of the suspicion against "aristocrats" was magnified by the dangers of war and by the need to save the country at all costs.

THE WAR AND THE CIVIL WAR

As the Committee of Public Safety consolidated its power in the fall of 1793, it began to make progress with the two greatest challenges it faced, the war against foreign enemies and the civil war at home. Even before the Terror was organized, the French armies defeated the British and the Dutch at the battle of Hondschoote (not far from the English Channel) on September 6, 1793. Later considered a turning point in the war, this victory seemed unsatisfactory at the time, because, although Dunkirk had been saved, the French general in charge, Houchard, did not follow up aggressively and the armies of the enemy were allowed to escape. Fearing that Houchard was not up to the task before him, the Committee decided to remove him. But they could not merely announce that the general was incompetent, because, having appointed him, they too would look incompetent. Besides, Houchard was the first commoner to command the armies, and they did not want to give the impression that only noble officers could be successful. So Houchard was sacrificed to the need to maintain confidence in the government and in the army. He was accused of being a traitor, sent before the Revolutionary Tribunal, and guillotined.

The next commoner named to command proved to be quite competent, eventually rising to become a Napoleonic marshal. Jourdan was a young man who had fought in the American Revolution and was committed to the Revolution. He was ably backed by Carnot on the Committee of Public Safety, who was doing everything in his power to find clothing and arms for the ill-equipped army, now expanded by the new recruits brought in by the *levée en masse.* Jourdan won the battle of Wattignies on October 15–16, opening the way into Belgium. Successes occurred on other fronts as well. The Austrians were pushed out of Alsace in the east and the Spanish retreated in the south.

The French government was also scoring successes in the civil war in fall 1793. Representatives on mission, dispatched to put down the federalist revolts that still bedeviled the republic, came with the full authority of the Convention and could appoint different local authorities to maintain allegiance or requisition everything that the armies needed. For example, Couthon, a member of the Committee of Public Safety, went to his home territory, the department of the Puy de Dôme in Auvergne, along with two other members of the Convention, to raise troops to help put down the revolt in nearby Lyon. While he was in Puy de Dôme, Couthon removed the government of the department and joined eagerly in the establishment of a new form of natural religion to replace Catholicism. Although Couthon's rhetoric could be as sanguinary as any revolutionary's, his methods were more circumspect than others, and only seven people died during the Reign of Terror in the department of the Puy de Dôme.

The vengeance on Lyon exacted a much higher price in lives. The federalist revolt in Lyon had run its course, and the republican army that had been besieging the city easily marched into Lyon on October 9. But the Committee of Public Safety was not satisfied by mere victory. They wanted to destroy the rebellious city and use it as an example to others. On October 12, they had the Convention pass a decree ordering the complete destruction of the city of Lyon: "There shall remain only the homes of the poor, the houses of patriots who have been led astray or proscribed. . . . The collection of houses left standing shall henceforth bear the name of Ville-Affranchie" (the Liberated City).[13] Couthon found these orders uncongenial and managed to be recalled to Paris. He was replaced by men with less delicate scruples about the use of violence: Collot d'Herbois (a member of the Committee of Public Safety) and Joseph Fouché. Collot, whose Hébertist sympathies dictated strong prejudices against the upper classes for preying on the poor, was eager to wreak vengeance on the inhabitants of the city. He did not believe that any reliable patriots remained.

The climax of the violence in Lyon came in early December when several hundred people were marched out of the city to an open place where graves had already been dug for them and were mowed down by cannon ("cannonades"). Those who were not killed by the initial barrage were then dispatched by soldiers with swords standing nearby. This method having proved not only distasteful to the soldiers, but also impractical because of problems associated with the mass graves, the revolutionaries continued the executions of traitors by using the guillotine, which was slower but still effective. By April 1794, almost two thousand inhabitants of Lyon had been executed, about a tenth of the total death sentences handed out during the Reign of Terror. When Fouché heard the news that the British had been forced out of the port of Toulon on the Mediterranean and that it was once again in French hands, he wrote to Collot: "Tears of joy stream in my eyes and flood my soul . . . We have only one way of celebrating victory. This evening we send two hundred and thirteen rebels under the fire of the lightning-bolt."[14] Fouché, later famous as Napoleon's cynical and unscrupulous police chief, was at this earlier date caught up in the revolutionary fervor and seemed to believe sincerely that the gruesome work he embraced with such zeal would bring future happiness to France.

The vengeance in the west of France was even worse. The Vendéan army was defeated by the republicans at Cholet in the middle of October 1793. The disorganized Vendéan army, accompanied by their families and other refugees, next headed toward the English Channel, having heard that the king of England, George III, had issued a manifesto promising them aid. However, coordination was lacking and when they reached the port of Granville, no British ships were in sight, because the British had no idea where they were supposed to meet up with the Vendéans or when. Granville was ably defended by the republicans, and the Vendéans retreated south, back toward the Loire. The two sides clashed in the streets of Le Mans. After that defeat, the retreating Vendéans were pursued and killed by the republican army. Men, women, and children were cut down indiscriminately to prevent their rising in revolt again. The republicans finally finished off the remnants of the Vendéan army at the battle of Savenay on December 23, 1793. The victorious general announced his triumph to the

Committee of Public Safety: "I have crushed children beneath my horses' hooves, and massacred the women, who thus will give birth to no more brigands . . . We take no prisoners, they would need to be given the bread of liberty, and pity is not revolutionary."[15]

An organized program to root out supporters of the rebellion was established with a special court (a military commission) to supplement the other courts. More than half of all death sentences during the Terror were handed down in the Vendée. Impatient with the slow pace of the executions, Carrier, the representative on mission in Nantes, came up with the idea of emptying the prisons under cover of darkness, tying up the prisoners, and loading them onto barges, which were taken to the middle of the Loire River. A hole was then cut in the barges so that all on board would drown. Although these so-called *noyades* (drownings) were not ordered by the Committee of Public Safety, when the committee heard about them they did not chastise Carrier (he was eventually recalled for not following the orders of the Committee on other matters). The numbers killed in the *noyades* (perhaps two thousand) seem insignificant, however, when put into the larger context of the Vendée deaths.[16] For the killing was not over in the Vendée. In the spring of 1794, republican armies (the notorious "infernal columns") swept across the region, killing potential rebels of all ages and both sexes and burning everything in their path. An exact figure for deaths is, of course, impossible to compute. Responsible estimates range from 150,000 to 250,000 rebels dead. But the republicans suffered as well. It is not unreasonable to estimate that all told perhaps 400,000 French people lost their lives in the brutal wars of the Vendée.

THE ATTACK ON THE FACTIONS

The Parisian *sans-culotte* movement reached its height during the Year II, the Year of the Terror. *Sans-culottes* demanded equality in society and popular sovereignty exercised through direct action of the people, not through elected representatives. They justified their intervention at key points in the Revolution by these beliefs. *Sans-culottes* expected to have an important role in political affairs. Each section in Paris elected an assembly that organized committees to manage the local area, oversee the National Guard, and watch for suspicious individuals. The sections also watched over the government and the army and intervened if officials did not live up to their expectations. They believed they had the right to recall officials and reject laws of which they disapproved. The *sans-culotte* movement exercised its greatest power in September 1793, when Parisians invaded the Convention and forced the deputies to declare Terror and to accede to other demands. But the independent action of the *sans-culottes* was undermined by the centralization of the government. Local surveillance committees, for example, came under the control of the Committee of Public Safety along with other local agencies. The Jacobin Clubs, working under the direction of the Committee, also began to arrogate to themselves many of the functions of the sectional assemblies.

By early 1794, the Committee of Public Safety had assumed the powers of a dictatorship. The Convention obligingly reelected the members every month. But despite its power, the Committee still faced factional challenges from both the right and the left. When the government had been in the hands of the king and the aristocrats, challenging its power was revolutionary. But the government was now the Committee of Public Safety, and they believed they embodied the Revolution. To challenge their authority was to attack the Revolution itself.

On their left, the Hébertists, who still controlled important posts in the city administration and in the Cordeliers Club, were demanding more radical measures. In December 1793, their prospects improved when Collot d'Herbois returned to Paris after putting down the revolt in Lyon, eager to defend himself from accusations that his measures had been too extreme. On the other end of the political spectrum was a group disparagingly called "the Indulgents," which included the formidable revolutionary, Georges-Jacques Danton. The "Indulgents" questioned the necessity of further terror now that the Federalist revolts and the rebel army in the Vendée had been defeated.

Naturally, the Committee of Public Safety had no intention of relinquishing its power or of mitigating the Terror. Robespierre gave speeches on December 25 (5 Nivôse) and on February 5 (17 Pluviôse) in which he justified the need for a strong and stable government, argued against a premature dismantling of the Terror, and warned the factions to fall into line. In the speech of December 25, Robespierre explained that a sort of dictatorship was needed while the republic was being founded:

> The aim of constitutional government is to preserve the Republic. The aim of revolutionary government is to found it.
>
> The Revolution is the war of liberty against its enemies. The constitution is the rule of liberty when victorious and peaceable. . . .
>
> Constitutional government is chiefly concerned with civil liberty, revolutionary government with public liberty. Under constitutional rule it is almost enough to protect individuals against the abuses of public

power; under revolutionary rule the public power is obliged to defend itself against all the factions that attack it.[17]

Both moderation and extremism, he argued, were dangerous to a revolutionary government. Enemies of the country could take advantage of either faction for their own purposes. Indeed, Robespierre believed that foreign countries were fomenting divisions among the revolutionaries. If the revolutionaries were disunited, their enemies could defeat the Revolution. Any criticism of the government was now deemed unpatriotic.

Meetings at the Jacobin Club were especially stormy in January 1794, as the two factions attacked each other. Robespierre tried to temper the quarrels by suggesting that the members spend several meetings discussing "the crimes of the English government and vices of the British constitution." But focusing on the evils of their foreign enemies could paper over the factional disputes only temporarily. On February 5, Robespierre again addressed the Convention to explain the principles of political morality that should guide them. In this speech he conjured up a republic that, once the Revolution had triumphed, would promote all virtues and allow republicans to live together in a just and prosperous country.

> We wish an order of things where all low and cruel passions are enchained by the laws, all beneficent and generous feelings awakened; where ambition is the desire to deserve glory and to be useful to one's country. . . .
>
> We wish to substitute in our country morality for egotism, probity for a mere sense of honor, principle for habit, duty for etiquette, the empire of reason for the tyranny of custom, contempt for vice for contempt for misfortune, pride for insolence, large-mindedness for vanity, the love of glory for the love of money . . . that is to say, all the virtues and miracles of the Republic for all the vices and puerilities of the monarchy.
>
> We wish in a word to fulfill the course of nature, to accomplish the destiny of mankind, to make good the promises of philosophy, to absolve Providence from the long reign of tyranny and crime. May France . . . become the model to the nations, the terror of oppressors, the consolation of the oppressed, the ornament of the universe. . . . That is our ambition. That is our aim.

Building on the ideas of the *philosophes*, Robespierre asserted that a republic had to be built on the principle of virtue. But, he continued, "If the basis of popular government in time of peace is virtue, the basis of popular government in time of revolution is both virtue and terror: virtue without which terror is murderous, terror without which virtue is powerless."[18] Until the infant republic was established, terror was a necessity to protect it from its enemies. But for Robespierre, terror was not merely a temporary expedient in a time of emergency. It was a means to create a race of virtuous people who would be able to sustain the republic and create a moral world. Unfortunately, this meant getting rid of all those who were not true republicans or who were not virtuous enough. True revolutionaries did not worry about this because the virtuous "people" who incarnated the general will would be spared. All others who led the "people" astray or who corrupted them were considered enemies or foreigners who should be purged from the nation. This speech naturally brought fear to many hearts. How could anybody be sure that they were pure enough to meet this new definition? When would the terror end?

The speech of February 5 served a political purpose, warning the two factions that criticized the Committee of Public Safety to fall into line. Both factions had advocates in the Committee of Public Safety, and their quarrels threatened the unity of the committee. And if they did not stand together, they might lose their power. The Hébertists were calling for the elimination of the moderates and accusing the Committee of being too lenient with them. A food shortage and economic crisis in the spring gave new life to the *sans-culotte* movement and made the danger of an Hébertist uprising seem all too real to the Convention.

On March 13, Saint-Just (in the name of the committee) gave a report to the Convention entitled "Report on the factions of foreign inspiration, and on the conspiracy plotted by them in the French Republic, to destroy representative government by corruption, and to starve Paris." His speech not only set out to show that all evils besetting them were of "foreign inspiration," he also sought to prove that those who criticized the government and talked about insurrection were against the people, because the current government was the people. "Every party is then criminal, because it is a form of isolation from the people and the popular societies, a form of independence from the government. Every faction is then criminal, because it tends to divide the citizens; every faction is criminal because it neutralizes the power of public virtue."[19] Factions, he concluded, were a criminal attack upon the sovereignty of the people. That night Hébert was arrested. Another eighteen individuals, including several foreigners, joined him before the Revolutionary Tribunal. All were condemned to death (except for a woman who was pregnant) and were guillotined on March 24.

Having attacked the faction on the left, the government now was in danger of falling under the influence of the "Indulgents" and finding themselves accused in turn of "moderatism." To prevent this and to get rid once and for all of the factions, on March 29 the two committees issued warrants for the arrest of the moderates, including Danton and other members of the Convention. The decision was dangerous and controversial. One member of the Committee of Public Safety, Lindet, refused to sign the warrant, as did one member of the Committee of General Security. In attacking Danton, they were attacking one of the stalwarts of the Revolution.

After the fall of the king, Danton gave a speech before the Commune on September 2, 1792, urging volunteers to enlist. His call has served as a rallying cry throughout French history, most notably in World War I. "The tocsin that will ring is no signal of alarm; it is sounding the charge against the enemies of the nation. *Pour les vaincre, Messieurs, il nous faut de l'audace, encore de l'audace, toujours de l'audace et la France est sauvée!*" (To defeat them, sirs, we must dare, dare again, and go on daring, and France will be saved.)[20] Danton's fiery speeches earned him a following in the Convention and saved him when suspicion arose that he was involved in Dumouriez's treason.

Throughout his career, Danton was pursued by rumors of accepting money from various sides, including Orléans, the British, and the French royal family. In his analysis of these charges, the historian Norman Hampson concluded that Danton's rapid increase in wealth was probably due to accepting bribes. Hampson stressed Danton's pragmatism rather than ideological fervor, calling him a kind of political boss whose tendency to compromise and arrange things was suspect in a time of revolution. Revolutionaries, especially Robespierre, approached issues as stark moral choices between good and evil. Danton, too, was forced to adopt this kind of language. But his usual tactic, according to Hampson, was "sweetening moderate policies by dressing them up in violent language."[21]

Although Robespierre and Danton had been political confederates in the past and still seemed to be cooperating in December 1793 and January 1794, Robespierre lost confidence in Danton and questioned his political behavior. Even Robespierre's enemies believed in the accuracy of the nickname Robespierre had been given: "The Incorruptible." Billaud-Varenne said that Robespierre "was able to have so much ascendance over public opinion . . . because he ostentatiously showed the most austere virtues, the most absolute dedication and the purest principles."[22] To the "Incorruptible," Danton's devotion to the republic seemed lukewarm and therefore dangerous.

In the fall of 1793, Danton had turned down reelection to the Committee of Public Safety and had retired for a month to his estates in the Aube (most likely purchased with bribes) to recuperate from an illness.

When he returned, he openly advocated a relaxation of the Terror, which he believed was no longer necessary. Even more problematic from Robespierre's point of view was that Danton continued loyally to support his old confederate, Fabre d'Eglantine, who had been arrested for corrupt financial dealings. Robespierre hoped to preserve the unity of the Committee of Public Safety by sacrificing some of the "Indulgents" so that neither faction would be seen to triumph. He probably would have spared Danton, but Danton insisted on protecting his old friend Fabre. Danton and Robespierre met privately a few times in the spring of 1794 to try to iron out their differences, but without success. Danton's political maneuverings and enjoyment of life could no longer coexist with Robespierre's narrowing political orthodoxy and devotion to virtue, as he understood the word.

Unusual care was taken in the preparation for the trial of Danton and the other prisoners, because the Committee of Public Safety feared that Danton's great persuasive powers might sway the jurors and the judges to let him off. On the second day of the trial (April 3), Danton dominated the proceedings with a long peroration, loud enough to be heard outside the chamber. The prisoners demanded that a long list of witnesses be called, including several representatives and Robespierre himself. The Committee immediately went to the Convention to report that the accused were insulting the court and that the Committee had discovered a plot in the prisons to revolt, rescue those on trial, and murder the members of the Committee. In light of these serious (and invented) dangers, the docile Convention agreed that prisoners who insulted the court could be removed from the judicial chamber. On April 5, having called no witnesses on either side, the jury agreed that they had heard enough to make up their minds and found all except one of the prisoners guilty. As he was led to the guillotine, Danton is supposed to have urged his executioners, "Above all, don't forget to show my head to the people: it's worth seeing."[23]

THE GREAT TERROR

In his speech to the Convention justifying the arrests of the "Indulgents," Saint-Just had assured the representatives that with the demise of the factions, all traitors had been uncovered and purges would end. In fact, the number of arrests and guillotinings went up dramatically in the next few months. During this time the Committee of Public Safety gathered ever more power to itself. They eliminated the ministries and replaced them with commissions under their control (thus doing away with even the fiction of the separation of legislative and executive power). They created their own police service, which now rivaled the Committee of General Security. There was no question now that the Committee of Public Safety exercised dictatorial powers. But they still had to be reelected by the Convention every month.

The Committee of Public Safety might have been a political dictatorship, but it was not a socialist one. They relaxed price controls, giving manufacturers an opportunity to make more profits. Some historians who argue that the government of the Terror was heading toward a socialist regime point to the Ventôse Decrees. At the end of February and beginning of March (8 and 13 Ventôse), Saint-Just introduced into the Convention legislation to distribute property to the poor. But the purpose of the legislation was not so much to make the poor more prosperous as to punish traitors by taking away their property. The Ventôse Decrees were impractical economically because the land taken away from politically suspect persons in rural areas was of no use to the urban poor, its intended beneficiaries. The legislation might have had a political purpose, to ease the discontent of the *sans-culottes* during the economic crisis of the spring and to mollify them for the arrest of the Hébertist leaders. In any case, the Committee of Public Safety fell from power before the legislation could be put into effect, and the alleged "socialist" intentions of its members cannot be proved from the Ventôse Decrees.

The announced aim of moral regeneration of the population was furthered by legislation to create an educational system (not implemented before the demise of the Convention). The Convention fostered unity by outlawing any language except French and promoted decency by urging people not to use obscene language. They censored plays and enlisted artists to produce works that extolled the goals of the government. As a culmination of their campaign of moral regeneration, the Convention authorized the creation of a civic religion, The Cult of the Supreme Being. On May 7, Robespierre introduced the legislation with a speech entitled, "On the principles of political morality."

Although it was the work of many people, the legislation on the cult perfectly summarized Robespierre's hope that religion could be a unifying rather than a divisive force in society, and that a civic religion would be an acceptable substitute to Christianity to provide a moral basis for society. "Immorality," he declared, "is the basis of despotism, as virtue is the essence of the Republic." Robespierre's speech once again extolled the wonders of the French nation: "The French people appear to have outstripped the rest of the human race by two thousand years; one might even be tempted to regard them as a distinct species among the rest. Europe is kneeling to the shadows of the tyrants whom we are punishing. . . . Europe cannot conceive of life without kings and nobles; and we cannot conceive of it with them."[24] The Convention decreed that festivals would be held on each *décadi* to promote various civic virtues (for example, justice, modesty, courage, heroism). On one of those *décadis*, a special Festival of the Supreme Being would be held. As it happened, that special festival was scheduled for 20 Prairial (June 8, 1794).

Designed by the artist David (who was at that time a member of the Committee of General Security), the festival on June 8 brought delegations from each of the sections of Paris to the Tuileries Gardens to a ceremony presided over by the members of the Convention. As president of the Convention, Robespierre gave a speech (more like a sermon) on the blessings that God had bestowed upon a people who sought freedom. A symbolic figure of atheism was then set on fire, and as it succumbed to the flames an image of wisdom appeared instead. There followed a grand procession (complete with cavalry, bands, and a float) to the Champ de Mars, where an artificial mountain had been created. To the sound of trumpets, the huge gathering joined in song and momentarily forgot (or pretended to forget) the privations that they suffered and the factional disputes that divided them.

Despite Saint-Just's promises, the demise of the Dantonists did not bring an end to factions. And now Robespierre's enemies questioned the prominence he had been given in the Festival of the Supreme Being, accusing him of using the new cult to become a dictator. In late May, two individuals attempted to assassinate Robespierre and Collot d'Herbois. Though each had acted alone, fear of a plot made it possible for the Committee of Public Safety to push through a law that made executions for political crimes even easier.

Judicial authority had been centralized on May 8, when provincial revolutionary courts were abolished and all political cases were put under the jurisdiction of the Revolutionary Tribunal of Paris. With the passage of the Law of 22 Prairial (June 10, 1794), the Revolutionary Tribunal was given more discretion in deciding cases. The court was to pursue "enemies of the people." Suspect actions were broadly defined to include impeding supplies, calumniating patriotism, attacking the unity of the Republic, deceiving the people, or spreading false news. Almost anybody could fear falling victim to such vaguely defined crimes. Furthermore, the only penalty the Revolutionary Tribunal could mete out was death. The accused was either guilty and would be executed or innocent and would be freed. Written proofs and witnesses were no longer necessary, and prisoners were not allowed lawyers.

As soon as the court was convinced of guilt or innocence, it could move on to the verdict.

The Law of 22 Prairial marked the beginning of the era known as the "Great Terror." Between June 10 and July 27 (when Robespierre fell from power) the pace of executions increased dramatically. Between March 1793 and June 1794, an average of three people per day had been executed under orders of the Revolutionary Tribunal. During the Great Terror more than thirty per day were executed. The problem of overcrowded jails was solved by instituting mass trials. On June 16, a group of seventy-three prisoners who had no ties to each other were tried together. In Paris, the profile of the person falling victim to the Terror was changing. Although priests, nobles, and middle-class people had been executed in large numbers earlier in the Terror, they had presumably been found guilty because of actual involvement in counter-revolutionary activity. In the last days of the Terror, the proportion of priests among the victims rose from 7 percent to 12 percent and the proportion of nobles from 8 percent to 20 percent. The upper-middle class was also being disproportionately targeted. The terror, historian Hugh Gough concluded, "was developing into a social war" against the rich and religious.[25]

The dramatic increase in the number of executions during the Great Terror was occurring when the French armies were enjoying great success in the field. The historian T. C. W. Blanning warns us not to attribute French success to greater devotion to the cause on the part of the French soldiers or to higher motivation among soldiers fighting a nationalistic war (an argument often heard). Instead, he believes that the main reason for French success was the ability the revolutionary authorities had to commandeer the resources of the country for the war effort. In February 1793, the army numbered 361,000. By January 1794, it had increased to 670,900, and by June to 893,000. The numbers would be even larger in the fall. The allies, by contrast, managed to put only about 200,000 troops in the field in 1794. With its ability to control the economy for war, the Committee of Public Safety directed the armaments industry to increase the production of muskets. By spring of 1794, the French were producing as many muskets as the rest of Europe combined.

Ancien Régime warfare had to be adapted to the new circumstances. Unable to afford and unable to manage the logistical nightmare of supplying food for such a large force from central depots, the Convention now expected the troops to provide for themselves by living off of the land, in other words, looting conquered areas. No longer tied to depots, the French army could now maneuver with great speed. The Convention solved the problem of the lack of experience of the new recruits by decreeing the *amalgame* in January 1794. New recruits and experienced regular soldiers were to be mixed together in amalgamated units. The soldiers were now better trained. They were also better led. Men with talent and years of service whose promotion under the Ancien Régime had been halted by their lack of noble status could rise to high positions. The soldiers, who were beginning to be less suspicious of their officers, and the officers, who were experienced and able, worked together more effectively. The generals were motivated by patriotism, but also by fear. They knew that failure might mean a death sentence. In 1793, seventeen generals were guillotined, and in 1794, sixty-seven generals were put to death.

The French army used their superior numbers effectively by going on the attack. Many of the characteristics of military campaigns that are often considered innovations of Napoleonic warfare were actually pioneered by the revolutionary armies. They had already begun the conquest of Europe and the policy of requisitioning what they needed from conquered areas. Success, of course, must be understood by looking at both sides. The French also won because the allies (always eyeing each other suspiciously) did not work together well and were prone to disperse their troops, which gave the larger numbers of French soldiers a distinct advantage. The result was that the French armies were making progress on several fronts by the middle of 1794. On June 26, they defeated the Austrians at the battle of Fleurus (the British had refused to support their allies) and by early July, the French were occupying Belgium.

THE FALL OF ROBESPIERRE

The Terror could no longer be justified by pressing military necessity. But putting a stop to it was not going to be easy, because any expression of criticism of the Committee of Public Safety or support of moderate measures would be characterized as treason. What brought an end to the Committee's dictatorship was division within its own ranks. The government had confronted enemies before, but they now no longer faced them as a united group. The Committee of General Security resented the senior committee's appropriation of its police powers and the lack of consultation over the Law of 22 Prairial. Since the death of Danton, many representatives feared that they might be targeted next. If Danton could be accused of treason, then anybody could. Had the Committee of Public Safety stood together, they might have weathered the storm. But they now began to suspect each other. Robespierre had a bitter falling out with Billaud and Collot d'Herbois. They all sought support outside the Committee. Robespierre and his friends could count on the Commune, while Billaud and Collot had allies in the Convention.

Robespierre hurt his own position by staying away from Committee meetings for about a month. Finally, on 8 Thermidor (July 26), he gave an ill-considered speech to the Convention, threatening enemies on all sides (including members of the great committees, but without naming names), and talking darkly of conspiracies against the republic. Not knowing who was being targeted, all his enemies on the right and on the left now joined to destroy him. That night Robespierre sought the support of the Jacobin Club. When Collot and Billaud saw that the Jacobin Club came down on Robespierre's side, they spent the rest of the night making plans with members of the Convention for the following day.

The next morning, 9 Thermidor (July 27), the Convention (by prearrangement) refused to allow Saint-Just to speak. Billaud accused Robespierre of intending to destroy the Convention. When Robespierre tried to defend himself, the Convention shouted, "Down with the tyrant!" The chaotic session, in which Robespierre was not able to make himself heard, voted for the arrest of Robespierre, Couthon, and Saint-Just. Augustin Robespierre asked to be included in the fate of his brother, and Le Bas in the fate of his friend Saint-Just (who was engaged to marry Le Bas's sister). These five men were taken into custody on the floor of the Convention. However, the jailers refused to accept the prisoners, and the sympathetic Commune government (reorganized with Robespierre supporters since the execution of Hébert) took them to the Hôtel de Ville, calling on the National Guard to come to their aid. This was the perfect moment for the people of Paris to rise in defense of their hero. But they did not. Discouraged and disillusioned, the Parisian *sans-culottes* had no wish to protect the members of the Committee of Public Safety who had not supported their economic goals and who had stifled the direct democracy on which the *sans-culotte* movement thrived. The followers of Hébert were not likely to save Robespierre. The Convention decreed that the five men were outlaws, thus permitting their execution without a trial.

That night Le Bas committed suicide, the paralyzed Couthon fell down a flight of stairs, and Augustin Robespierre injured himself jumping out of a window. Robespierre also tried to commit suicide with a pistol, but managed only to wound himself grievously in the jaw. On the night of 10 Thermidor (July 28), the four surviving prisoners were guillotined, along with about eighteen members of the Commune government who had supported them. Over the next two days, eighty-three supporters of Robespierre from the Commune and from the Jacobin Club were also sent to the guillotine. The fall of Robespierre marked the end of the Terror, although nobody realized it at the time and most of those who brought about his fall did not intend to end it.

WHY THE TERROR?

One of the perennial questions in the history of the French Revolution is why the Terror occurred. Conservatives believe that a Revolution founded on violence and chaos, rejecting the restraints of religion and tradition, was bound to lead to excesses. Writers sympathetic to the Revolution explain the Terror as the result of "circumstances." To save the country from external war and civil war, the government resorted to drastic measures. The results, though not attractive, saved the Revolution from the forces that threatened it. A modern view, most prominently identified with the historian François Furet, argues that the rhetoric the early revolutionaries used to justify the Revolution would lead them inexorably to more radical measures that would culminate in the Terror. Each of these views can be supported by evidence, but each also has problems.

The conservative explanation that Terror was to be expected when societies reject tradition and authority has the longest history. It was first enunciated in a work by Edmund Burke written in November 1790, several years before the actual Terror. His *Reflections on the Revolution in France* quickly became famous, in part because he foresaw the violent nature of the Revolution and because he had a simple explanation for what was going wrong. He blamed the Enlightenment for undermining respect for the institutions of the past. Change, he believed, needed to take place slowly, otherwise it would lead to chaos. All societies, Burke argued, needed to be founded on religion, which provides wholesome restraints on the vanity and sinfulness of human beings. Without such restraints, individuals will go astray. No human beings are wise enough to create an entirely new society, he believed. It is much safer to build on the tried and true institutions of the past. For conservatives, the Terror was to be expected because the goals of the Revolution from the beginning rejected the past and created totally new (and untested) institutions. In response to this view, one could argue that the Revolution was not very violent in the early years and that the new institutions had found wide acceptance in the country. The Terror came later and was not necessarily a direct result of the beginning of Revolution.

Supporters of the Revolution responded to the conservative criticism by blaming the Terror on the opponents of the Revolution. The revolutionaries were forced to violent measures to protect themselves from determined adversaries. "Circumstances" dictated the Terror. The argument from circumstance runs afoul of the actual chronology of events. By the spring of 1794, the period of greatest danger for the country was over. The civil war in the Vendée had been defeated, the federalist revolt had been put down, and foreign armies had retreated from French soil. Despite the improving circumstances, the Terror did not end. It would not reach its height until after the passage of the Law of 22 Prairial on June 10, 1794. By then, calls had been made (most notably by Danton and his followers) to mitigate the rigors of the Terror on the grounds that it was no longer needed to save the country. So circumstances alone cannot explain the Terror.

Robespierre, who is often portrayed as the very incarnation of the Revolution, provided a justification of the Terror in his famous speech on February 5. In it he proclaimed that during a time of revolution, terror and virtue were linked. Terror was needed, not merely to defeat the professed enemies of the nation, but to rid the country of evil in order to create a new nation of worthy people. He identified himself with the Revolution and with the people. At one point he declared, "I am not the courtier, nor the moderator, nor the tribune, nor the defender of the people, I am the people myself!"[26] Deeply influenced by the ideas and the example of Rousseau, Robespierre believed the people to be good. He believed as well that a republic had to be based on virtue. Therefore, if the republic were to survive, all hints of corruption and compromise had to be rigorously expunged from the body politic. The general will, Rousseau had famously declared, could not err, but it could be misled. Robespierre was haunted by the fear that ambitious individuals would lead the country astray. He persistently sought to unearth the conspiracies that threatened the republic and to unmask the traitors disguised as patriots.

Robespierre had not begun his career as an advocate of violence. Indeed, he had in 1791 supported the abolition of the death penalty. By 1794, however, he had embraced violence, execution, and purges as the only ways to create a new, more virtuous nation that could defeat its enemies. He argued not that terror should be adopted as an expedient, but rather that terror would lead to virtue. His espousal of the Cult of the Supreme Being was another way to inculcate virtue in the country. Unlike Danton, who saw terror as a mere instrument of state to face an emergency, Robespierre saw terror as essential to the ultimate goals of the Revolution. He would not compromise. He held on to terror, even as those around him began to doubt its wisdom, to fear its excesses, or to worry that they would be the next targets of its violence. And as he became more and more isolated from his colleagues and the people he claimed to love so much, he lost political support.

When his enemies arrested him on July 27 (9 Thermidor), the crowds who had adored him in the past did not come to his defense. Those now in power justified his execution by placing the blame for the terror on Robespierre and the confederates who died along with him. To clear themselves of responsibility (and, indeed, many of Robespierre's enemies had much more blood on their hands than he), they accused him of being the villain, of being a dictator who had misled them. Their judgment has stuck because the winners get to write the histories and because Robespierre often served as the spokesperson of the Committee of Public Safety. His words and speeches have endured, and with them his reputation as the dictator of the Terror.

More recently, the historian François Furet, agreeing that circumstances alone cannot explain the Terror, has sought its origins in the rhetoric of the revolutionaries. He argued that the Terror was the inevitable outcome of the radical language used to justify the Revolution. Although the early goals of the Revolution may have been moderate, the arguments used to support them were dangerous because they emphasized the general will, the unity of the nation, and the need to exclude those who were not part of the nation. Therefore, basing itself on this view of the general will, the Committee of Public Safety would not tolerate any criticism of its policies because that would undermine its power and the will of the people. Anybody who expressed dissenting opinions was assumed to be an enemy of the people—thus the horrifying logic of the Terror. It could not be stopped because if you showed doubts about it, those doubts were proof that you were a traitor or in the pay of the enemy.

The problem with this view of the Terror is that it assumes (as does the conservative view) that ideas alone gave rise to it. But at any time, ideas of many kinds exist in a political system. Barry Shapiro has demonstrated that in the early years of the Revolution the humane strains of Enlightenment reformist ideas held sway. The political ideas emphasized during the Terror were not the only ones available to the revolutionary leaders. Ideas alone cannot adequately explain the Terror. But when war was declared, the nature of the Revolution changed inexorably. The early defeats in the war made possible the overthrow of the king, conscription led to civil war in the Vendée, fear of traitors and enemies brought an end to political pluralism, and the need to mobilize the country for war resulted in a dictatorship. So "circumstances" cannot wholly explain the Terror, but it cannot be understood without taking them into account. Without the war, the Revolution would have been quite different, emergency measures might not have been accepted, and the Terror might not have occurred.

9

THERMIDOR AND THE DIRECTORY

The men who engineered the removal of Robespierre from the Committee of Public Safety had little in common except their hatred of the famous man. Most wanted the Terror to continue. Others wanted to ease the Terror. In fact, once the unity of the Committee of Public Safety had been broken, the Convention was able to exert its authority over the committees again, and the result was a weakening of the dictatorship and an end to the Terror. Getting rid of Robespierre had been justified by calling him a dictator and by blaming him for the Terror. Having used that argument, the members of the Convention then had to distance themselves from the policies of the committee.

Although their argument that Robespierre was the sole mastermind of the Terror is not true, the accusation has stuck. Because Robespierre fell during the month of Thermidor, the period after the fall of Robespierre is known as the Thermidorian Reaction (in politics, a reactionary movement is one that goes back to the way things were before). During this period of a little over a year, the Convention continued to rule France, but their policies were far less radical than before. The aim of Conventionnels, however, remained the same: to create a republican form of government for France and win the allegiance of the population to the republic. After writing a new constitution, the Convention gave way in October 1795 to a government known as the Directory.

THERMIDORIAN REACTION

On the day following the execution of Robespierre and his confederates, the Convention began the process of dismantling the institutions of the

Terror. They decreed that a quarter of the members of each of the committees had to retire each month. Immediately, Prieur de la Côte d'Or and Jean Bon Saint-André were removed and Tallien and Thuriot (both Montagnards who had been instrumental in Robespierre's fall) took their places. On August 1, the Convention repealed the Law of 22 Prairial and later that month released those who were languishing in jail as a consequence of that law. They abolished other instruments of the Terror as well. The Revolutionary Tribunal was reorganized, and the representatives on mission lost many of their powers. The Paris Commune government, so closely associated with Robespierre, found its powers taken over by the Convention. The dreaded neighborhood surveillance committees were shut down. In November 1794, the Convention ordered the Paris Jacobin Club to be closed. Carrier, the man who had come to epitomize the excesses of the Terror for the *noyades* in the Vendée, was sent before the Revolutionary Tribunal in late November and executed on December 16. Surviving representatives who had protested against the purge of the Girondins were once again allowed to sit in the Convention.

The Convention, recognizing that many of the institutions of the Terror were hated, especially by people in rural areas, found it politically expedient to do away with them. The Terror could no longer be justified as an extraordinary measure needed in wartime, because the armies of the Republic were winning and the civil war had been defeated. After the purges of the Terror, no significant revolutionary leaders remained to rally the crowds to revolutionary action. Instead, the movement was in the opposite direction. Prisoners arrested during the Terror were now released and were eager to seek revenge on those who had persecuted them.

People who had resented the burden of being forced to be virtuous and who felt oppressed by life under a regime of fear now experienced an overwhelming sense of relief. Young people wanted to enjoy themselves. Instead of constant attention to political questions, they devoted themselves to eating, gambling, and dancing. They rejected the simplicity of dress that had been favored under the Terror and adopted extravagant costumes (of classical inspiration for the women). These young people, dubbed *Les Incroyables* (incredible ones) or *Les Merveilleuses* (their female counterparts: the marvelous ones), were more likely to attack radicals than to follow them. Royalists once again felt free to make their feelings known. Elegant young royalists (often called *Muscadins*) roamed Paris attacking symbols of Revolution, destroying artificial mountains, and breaking busts of Marat.

Economic problems did not disappear with the political relaxation. After a cold, wet summer in 1794, the harvest was bad. In November the

Figure 9.1. Fashionable people during the Directory. The cartoonist has exaggerated the extravagant styles affected by pleasure-starved people after the Terror ended. The emphasis on fashion was the antithesis of the Jacobin desire to regenerate the French people by creating virtuous citizens devoted to republican simplicity and willing to make sacrifices for the nation. Courtesy of the Division of Rare and Manuscript Collections, Cornell University Library.

Convention allowed goods to be imported freely, but this free-trade policy did not work well with the price-fixing of the Maximum. The Maximum was difficult to enforce, and people were ignoring it in local markets and charging the market price for goods. Hoping that doing away with the Maximum would solve the problems of scarcity and ultimately stop the slide in the value of the assignat, on December 24, 1794, the Convention abolished the Maximum, with the provision that the government might still requisition goods for the army at the lower prices. Foreign trade resumed, but no longer held down by the Law of the Maximum, prices for all commodities rose sharply. Between the beginning of 1795 and the month of March, the cost of butter doubled and the cost of meat went up by 500 percent. In Paris, food was rationed, but there was not enough to go around.

During this difficult economic period, the government faced enormous financial hardships. Taxes were not coming in, and the government's costs went up along with the inflation of prices. The government hoped to raise funds by selling the remaining *biens nationaux* and then retiring the assignats that were submitted as payment in order to reduce inflation. But the need for funds was so great that they continued to print assignats, thus creating a universal lack of confidence in paper money. Assignats became essentially worthless.

The crisis over food grew progressively worse over the bitterly cold winter and led to two uprisings in Paris in the spring of 1795. In both, women once again played a major role, as they usually did when the issue was the need to provide for their families. On 12 Germinal (April 1, 1795), a crowd of unarmed people invaded the Convention demanding bread and the Jacobin Constitution of 1793. The Convention was able to call on the National Guard of the more prosperous districts to put down the uprising. The famine (the worst of the revolutionary period) spawned food riots in many places throughout the country, even though the government managed to bring in large shipments of food from abroad.

Another uprising took place in Paris on 1 Prairial (May 20, 1795), with crowds again demanding bread and the establishment of constitutional government under the Jacobin constitution. The food crisis was so serious that many of those participating hoped for the return of the Terror. One participant declared: "Under Robespierre, blood ran and we had bread; today blood does not run and we don't have any bread, and we ought to make some blood flow to get some."[1] The purges of the Terror had deprived the popular movement of its effective leaders, making it easier for the Convention to put down the uprising and regain control. The handful of Montagnard deputies who sympathized with the insurrection were arrested and condemned to death. Troops were sent into the rebellious neighborhoods, and the whole event was blamed on foreign agitation and terrorists disguised in women's clothes. The effectiveness of Parisian uprisings seemed to be at an end. The Convention, unlike the monarchy earlier, showed itself willing to use the army against the people of Paris to put down disorder.

Violence continued to threaten stability, however, because the surviving moderate and royalist victims of the Terror (released from prison in the autumn of 1794) now sought vengeance on their persecutors. Terrorists were hunted down and lynched, especially in the south of France where the "White Terror" raged in the first part of 1795, leading to perhaps two thousand deaths. The relaxation of Terror brought a resurgence of rebellion in the west as well. There, in addition to the revival of the royalist and Catholic army in the Vendée, another anti-republican movement, known as

Chouannerie, also held sway. Strongest in the area north of the Loire, Chouans were draft-dodgers, former Vendéan soldiers, or anti-republican agitators who had never really put down their weapons. They maintained themselves in armed bands by robbery and other crimes and by constant harassment of the republicans in a sort of guerrilla warfare. The government had trouble telling the difference between ordinary criminals and insurgents intent on bringing down the regime. Crime was a persistent problem during this period. It was often difficult to determine whether a crime had been committed for pecuniary gain or to avenge previous political wrongs. If the government were to remain in power, it needed to bring order and stability to the country, whatever the source of disorder was.

In the spring of 1795, the government was able to get some rebels to put down arms by promising freedom of religion. On February 21, 1795, the Convention declared that the government would no longer provide financial support to the church and decreed the separation of church and state. They allowed freedom of all religions, but ceremonies were to be held indoors without any public demonstrations or processions, and clerical dress was forbidden. The result was a resurgence of Catholicism throughout the country, as villages took back control of their local churches and began to revive religious practices. Women, who had been especially important in maintaining the clandestine exercise of religion and in hiding refractory priests, once again took the lead in reestablishing regular worship. The goal of the government, still strongly anti-Catholic, had not been to set off a religious revival, but that is what happened.

The reaction against the Terror and republicanism was so strong that there was even talk of the reinstitution of the monarchy. Louis XVII, as the son of Louis XVI was called by devoted royalists, still languished in prison after the guillotining of both of his parents. He died there (apparently of natural causes) on June 8, 1795, making his uncle, the Comte de Provence, heir to the throne. Under the name Louis XVIII, he issued a statement from exile in Verona at the end of June declaring his devotion to the institutions of the Ancien Régime, to the complete restoration of the Catholic religion, and to vengeance against regicides. Such intransigence, of course, would prevent his coming to power, but it did indicate the reviving confidence of royalists and their threat to the republican regime. On June 27, émigrés, with the financial support of the British, landed a military expedition at Quiberon Bay in Brittany. Lack of coordination with royalists within France doomed the attempt, which was easily crushed by the troops of General Hoche.

CONSTITUTION OF THE YEAR III

Faced with dangers from both royalists on the right and uprisings on the left, the committees of the Convention endeavored to create a constitution that would not allow either extreme to come to power. Inspired in part by the Constitution of 1791, the Constitution of the Year III (1795) began with a declaration of rights augmented by a declaration of duties. Having decided to do away with universal male suffrage, their declaration pointedly omitted the clause proclaiming equality. Like the Constitution of 1791, the Constitution of the Year III dictated a rigorous separation of powers. The executive was to appoint and oversee the ministers, who could not be dismissed by the legislative power.

The danger that a single-house legislature could become dictatorial had been amply demonstrated by the period of the Terror. No longer afraid that the nobility would dominate an upper house, the authors of the new constitution created a two-house legislature. They guarded against radicalism by restricting voting for the legislature to the well-to-do. A large number of men qualified for the primary assemblies: all male citizens twenty-one years old who met residency qualifications and paid taxes. But these men only chose electors who in the final electoral colleges would choose the representatives. The higher age and tax-paying qualifications of the electors meant that only about thirty thousand men were eligible. However, there were no property qualifications for those elected as representatives. The lower house, called the Council of Five Hundred, initiated and debated bills, which were then sent for the required approval of the upper house, the Council of Elders (Anciens). To ensure responsible behavior, a member of the smaller Council of Elders (only 250 members) was required to be at least forty years old and to be a married man or a widower. One-third of each house would stand for election each year.

The authors of the constitution tried to solve the problem of the executive power (which had bedeviled the revolutionaries all along) by an original idea. An elected president might too easily become a monarch (what if a Bourbon were elected?), so they decided to put the executive power in the hands of a Directory of five men with experience in government. The Elders would choose the Directors, one of whom was to retire every year.

The constitution was easily approved when submitted to the voters. But an additional provision (the so-called Two-Thirds Decree) proved extremely controversial. Remembering the ill-advised self-denying ordinance passed by the Constituent Assembly that did not allow any of its members to sit in the Legislative Assembly (thus depriving it of experienced legislators), the Convention decreed that two-thirds of the new councils must be composed of representatives from the Convention. They were motivated, of course, by a desire to stay in power, and they were worried as well that, because of the resurgence of royalism, republicans might be defeated. The measure was understandably unpopular, especially among the monarchists, who now echoed revolutionary rhetoric by claiming that it frustrated the will of the people. Those Conventionnels retained in the new assemblies were derisively called *les perpétuels* (the perpetual ones).

Not long before the Convention gave way to the new councils, the royalists rebelled against this republican ploy by provoking an uprising in Paris. On October 5, 1795 (13 Vendémiaire), the more prosperous sections on the Right Bank whose citizens tended to support constitutional monarchy declared themselves in rebellion and sent some 25,000 insurgents to overturn the new constitution and the former Jacobins who, through the Two-Thirds Decree, were ensuring their continuation in power. The Convention managed to save itself by releasing prisoners to fight against the royalists and by calling on the aid of the army. A young general, Napoleon Bonaparte, was in charge of putting down this rebellion. Napoleonic legend recalls that his orders to use artillery, the famous "whiff of grapeshot," quickly dispersed the crowds and the threats to the Convention. In fact, the fighting went on for most of the day and left hundreds dead. The government of the Directory, which took power on October 27, became more and more dependent on the support of the army.

The Directory period tends to be slighted in histories of the Revolution, in part because it falls between two dramatic periods, the Terror and the Napoleonic era. Yet the Directory accomplished a great deal and was the most long-lasting of the governments during the First Republic. Its bad reputation resulted in part from the contention of the Bonapartists later that Bonaparte's seizure of power had saved France from chaos. Once again (as we saw in the case of Robespierre), the winners wrote the histories and interpreted the past in the most favorable light for themselves. The Directory, faced with many problems, nonetheless made progress on economic matters, got the debt under control, and stabilized the taxation system. They created a professional bureaucracy, bringing together officials from the Ancien Régime as well as those from the revolutionary period. Although they accomplished much administratively, politically the Directory was on quite shaky ground. They were unable to bring stability to France, and the attempt to do so undermined the rule of law. War or preparations for war continued throughout the entire period.

POLITICS UNDER THE DIRECTORY

The leaders of the Directory have a reputation for corruption and intrigue. That reputation, although deserved by some, is somewhat exaggerated. It is important to remember that our perception is colored by the fact that the Directory was criticized by both the right and the left. But corruption certainly existed during this period, as speculators made fortunes from *biens nationaux*, those who provided goods to the armies used their connections with government officials to make themselves rich, and generals looted conquered lands. More important than corruption in explaining the demise of the Directory was its failure to live up to its avowed intention of establishing a representative system and the rule of law. In order to stay in power, the Directors resorted to manipulating and voiding elections and to putting down violence by extraordinary measures, thereby violating the constitution and the hopes for a genuinely representative government.

The first five Directors were Carnot (the former member of the Committee of Public Safety, who continued his work on the military);[2] Reubell (a lawyer from Alsace who had served in the Estates General and had been a Montagnard in the Convention); Letourneur (a military man who had served on the Committee of Public Safety after the fall of Robespierre and who worked closely with Carnot); La Révellière-Lépeaux (who belonged to neither the Mountain nor the Girondins, but left the Convention at the purge of the Girondins and returned in the spring of 1795); and Barras (a nobleman who had been on military expeditions to India, was elected to the Convention, and helped to bring down Robespierre). Of these men, Barras, who served throughout the entire time of the Directory, certainly merits the reputation for corruption and unscrupulous behavior. He lived ostentatiously and enjoyed the society of the salons of Paris with its prominent hostesses like Madame Tallien, Josephine de Beauharnais, and Juliette Récamier.

The Directors established their headquarters at the Luxembourg Palace. They set about trying to solve the problems of the disorganization of local government (election of local officials was revived) and the deplorable state of the finances. Although they had put down the Vendémiaire uprising, royalist demonstrations continued and conservative newspapers once again made an appearance. Soon, the Directory also had to face a threat from the left. In 1796, a man named Babeuf, who had taken the revolutionary first name of "Gracchus" (after a Roman republican), created a new kind of political movement. Recognized by some Marxists in modern times as the first true socialist of the French Revolution, Babeuf had become an expert on the seigneurial system during the Ancien Régime and advocated the equal distribution of landed property.

His "Conspiracy of the Equals" attracted only a small group. He realized that for his revolt to succeed, he would need the support of former Jacobins. He therefore announced as his program, not property redistribution, but rather establishing a government under the Constitution of 1793. Lacking money, a network of affiliates, or much support in the cities, the conspiracy would probably have failed in any case, even if it had not been denounced by a police spy in its midst before it could be launched. The government used the occasion to attack Jacobinism in general, arresting many who did not even know Babeuf. Several were deported; Babeuf and an associate were guillotined. The Jacobin movement survived the attack by rejecting conspiracy, accepting the Constitution of the Year III, and becoming a parliamentary opposition.

To give themselves time to become well established in office, the authors of the Constitution of the Year III had directed that the annual renewal of the first third in the councils (originally chosen in October 1795) would be delayed until spring of 1797. The interest in those elections was high, with some towns having rival newspapers to support the republican and the royalist sides. Although royalists were not at all united on goals (some were strict absolutists and supporters of Louis XVIII, others wanted a limited constitutional monarchy with perhaps the son of the Duc d'Orléans as the monarch), they cooperated to win elections. Meeting at a house in the rue de Clichy and therefore known as the "Club de Clichy," moderates and royalists financed newspapers and promoted their candidates in the provinces. For the first time, candidates were allowed to put themselves forward before the election, and voters were encouraged to turn out, although the response was better in towns than in rural areas. The result was a decisive defeat for the republicans and the Directory. Only 13 out of 216 former members of the Convention were elected. The new deputies included a substantial number of royalists, who were able to appoint Barthélemy (the candidate of the right) to replace Letourneur as the new Director. The victory of the right was in large part a vote for peace.

The electoral victory of the right emboldened royalists throughout the country. Fearful that after reducing the threat of the Jacobins the Directory was about to succumb to the royalists, three of the Directors decided to void many of the elections, on both the national and local level. Carefully planned in cooperation with the army, the coup d'état of Fructidor (18 Fructidor, September 4, 1797) annulled elections in forty-nine departments, removing 177 representatives. On the night of September 4, General

Augereau (sent to Paris from Bonaparte's army in Italy) ordered troops into the chambers of the assemblies and arrested royalist deputies, fifty-three of whom were deported. The Director Carnot fled and the recently appointed Barthélemy was deported. Both of them had opposed the coup. The coup was followed by the so-called Fructidor terror in which royalists were removed from office throughout the country and those suspected of fomenting insurrection were arrested. The coup of Fructidor put an end to the experiment in constitutional government. The Directory had now made clear that they governed, not by the consent of the people in open elections, but by the support of the army.

RELIGION AND EDUCATION UNDER THE DIRECTORY

The fall of Robespierre brought an end to the Cult of the Supreme Being with which he had been closely identified. This new civic religion that the Convention had created to mold citizens for the reinvigorated nation had not had a chance to win many converts. When the Terror no longer buttressed the attack on the church, a revival of Catholicism occurred in many parts of France.

Between 15 and 25 percent of the clergy had emigrated during the Revolution, and many more were in hiding or imprisoned. In the absence of priests, lay people, especially lay women, learned to take over many responsibilities, teaching religion to their children, reading the Bible, and relating the lives of the saints. They had to continue to do so under the Directory. In some parts of France, as we have seen, Catholicism was strongly allied with royalist and anti-republican political views. But a devotion to Catholicism usually survived even in areas that were strongly republican. Inspired by the rhetoric of freedom of the Revolution and by techniques of organization learned in the political struggles, parishes petitioned authorities to allow churches to reopen and justified the revival of religion in the name of freedom. They insisted that one could be both a good republican and a good Catholic at the same time.

Radical revolutionaries, who had hoped that the state could take the place of religion in the lives of the people, contemplated their failure with disappointment. The problem, they came to believe, was the influence of women, who were irrational, easily swayed by priests, and incapable of understanding the benefits of a reasoned republicanism. The image of fanatical women under the control of the local priest, used to great effect in the late nineteenth century to deny women the vote, was born in the era of the

Revolution. But, of course, both women and men could have good rational reasons for rejecting the demands of the Revolution, which had disrupted their traditional way of life, caused economic hardships, and forced young men to leave home to fight (and die) in distant lands. The Revolution, by closing down religious orders, had destroyed charitable and educational institutions on which ordinary people depended. In the autumn of 1794, when former nuns, brothers, and priests were released from the prisons and those in hiding began to emerge cautiously, they once again took up their charitable work, founding new orders and reviving old ones. Emigré clerics slowly began to return. They stepped in to fill the void left by the decision of the impecunious Directory in October 1795 to abandon its financial commitment to hospitals and charities. The government now expected private charity to fund health care and provide for the poor.

Refractory clergy returned bitterly opposed to the republic and its institutions. But another group of churchmen, the priests of the constitutional church that had been created by the Civil Constitution of the Clergy in 1791, still hoped to reconcile Catholicism and the republic. During the period of Dechristianization, most (perhaps 22,000 out of 28,000) had been forced to resign or to cease saying mass. But one bishop had never abandoned his post. Henri Grégoire (usually known as Abbé Grégoire) began in late 1794 to organize the surviving constitutional bishops into a group called the United Bishops.

Although they had the support of neither the government nor the papacy, they set about resurrecting the institutions of the constitutional church. They retained the controversial elective principle, but with the provision that only members of the church could vote. Despite the odds against them, the constitutional church at first managed to re-create a church hierarchy in most areas of France. They called themselves the Gallican Church and authorized the celebration of mass in French rather than Latin. But the Gallican Church, which was strongest in urban areas, steadily lost adherents to the refractory priests. In rural areas women especially boycotted the new church in favor of the old. Still, the efforts of Grégoire meant that the constitutional church had to be taken into account when Napoleon Bonaparte negotiated with the pope for the reintroduction of an official Catholicism in France in 1801.

The policy of the Directory toward religion constantly changed as political circumstances changed. When the Directory worried about resurgent Jacobinism, they were more tolerant of Catholics. On the other hand, after the Fructidor coup of 1797, which annulled royalist elections, a wave of repression against Catholics followed. But throughout the period, the official policy of the Directory was anti-Catholic, in part because they feared that Catholics in cooperation with émigrés would bring down the republic. The government tried (rather unsuccessfully) to enforce observance of the *décadi* rather than Sunday and promoted republican festivals. They gave their blessing to a new civil religion called Theophilanthropy, a form of Deism that was designed to promote proper morality for a republic. At its height after the coup of Fructidor of 1797, it offered simple ceremonies with readings from many traditions, including ancient Greek texts, Confucius, and the Koran. Its dry intellectual tone appealed only to a few in the cities, and the government soon abandoned support because most of the adherents were die-hard Jacobins.

The government also sought to promote right-thinking through education. Reviving educational projects that went back to Condorcet's draft law from the spring of 1792, they hoped to replace predominantly religious instruction with secular schools staffed by non-clerics. Although they had little success at the elementary level, the Directory did manage to set up schools at the secondary level. Every department was to have an Ecole Centrale (Central School) that would provide scientific, secular, and utilitarian education on the model of Enlightenment philosophy. Local teachers under the supervision of departmental committees used the resources of libraries in former convents or religious institutions to support their instruction. Although with varying degrees of success, these schools were prospering under the Directory. Napoleon Bonaparte did away with them to create instead his system of lycées, which were more centralized, promoted military values, concentrated on preparing government officials, and were far less independent.

The anti-Catholic policy of the Directory was startlingly clear in its treatment of the Church in areas conquered by its armies. The French confiscated church property and reorganized the churches. The Directory rejected any suggestion of finding an accommodation with Pope Pius VI. As French armies marched through the Italian peninsula, they took territory from the Papal States to incorporate into the Cisalpine Republic that the French had created. The French treated the pope harshly, forcing him to pay fines and to cede works of art that were shipped back to France. In 1798, an invading army proclaimed a republic in Rome and took the pope prisoner. He died in French hands in Florence in 1799. In 1801, his successor, Pius VII, was able to negotiate an agreement with Napoleon Bonaparte, who hoped to make his authority more secure by defusing the religious battles in France. This agreement, called the Concordat, once again made Catholicism an official (though not the exclusive) religion of France.

WAR, FOREIGN POLICY, AND GENERALS

The armies were no longer the large revolutionary masses of the Year II. The troops had become professionals who obeyed their officers and maintained order as directed by the government in power. To preserve the republic, the Directory needed to create stability and order within the country. But the more it relied on the military to put down violence, crime, and insurrection, the less the government could claim to be maintaining the rule of law.

The Directory period was dominated by war. Despite the broad sentiment for peace that had been demonstrated in the elections of 1797, the Directory depended too much on the profits of war to be able to put an end to it. The generals were the great heroes of the age, whose stature propped up the Directory. War made the generals rich, powerful, and famous. The age of the "nation in arms" and the "citizen soldier" seemed to be over. Instead of defending the Revolution at home from the threat of monarchical Europe (the justification for war earlier in the decade), the armies had now become the instruments of French imperialism as they embarked on the conquest of foreign lands.

French armies were doing well in the wars because the allies were hampered by different goals and distrust of each other. In the east, Catherine the Great consolidated Russia's control of its portions of the partition of Poland (see chapter 6). She hoped Prussia and Austria would exhaust themselves in fighting against the French. Great Britain, whose interests in northern Europe were threatened by French expansion, needed allies. But the only power committed to the war against France was Austria, in part because that country's financial difficulties dictated staying in the war to receive subsidies from Great Britain. Austria faced many problems in foreign policy, the most important being the wish to keep Prussia from assuming dominance over the smaller German states.

By the fall of 1794, Prussia wanted peace. The French conquest of Holland threatened to spread revolution into northern Germany, and Prussian resources were already exhausted. The Prussians were convinced even further for peace after the third partition of Poland in 1795 when, with Russia and Austria, it took a share of Polish lands. Having achieved this important goal, Prussia saw no reason to continue fighting and negotiated a peace with France at Basel in April 1795. Other countries also sued for peace: the Dutch in May and the Spanish in July. Having defeated the Dutch, the French transformed that country into a republic, named the Batavian Republic, that was organized on the same principles as the French

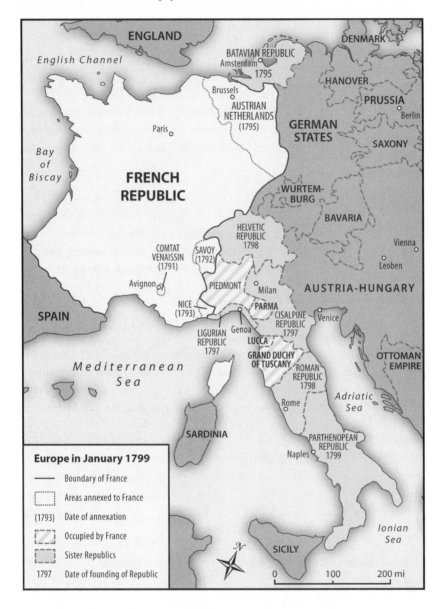

Republic. Belgium, now firmly in French hands, was incorporated into and administered as part of France.

France's opponents at the end of 1795 were Great Britain, Austria, and the small kingdom of Piedmont-Sardinia, on France's southern border. Great Britain regretted the French domination of Belgium because of its strategic location on the English Channel. They also feared that with both

Belgium and the Netherlands in French control, France would take advantage of the Dutch navy to transform itself into a formidable naval rival. Austria, which had owned Belgium (the Austrian Netherlands) before the French Revolution, was not content to lose it without compensation. Because Belgium was so far from Vienna, Austria would have been pleased to exchange Belgium for Bavaria. But Prussia objected to that exchange, because Austria would thereby obtain more territory within the German-speaking countries of the Holy Roman Empire.

In 1795, the Austrian position was rather precarious. They participated in the last partition of Poland, receiving some Polish lands. But the demise of Poland actually hurt Austria's strategic position. Austria now faced a strong Russian state without Poland as a buffer. Austria was locked in struggle with an enlarged Prussia (which had also gotten a share of the Polish lands) over which country would dominate the Holy Roman Empire. And its only substantial ally was Great Britain, which did not help its cause very much because Great Britain recognized that Austria had no choice but to continue the alliance. Austria exercised considerable influence on the Italian peninsula, where several ruling families looked to them for guidance and where Piedmont-Sardinia was an ally. But even in the Italian peninsula, Austria was threatened by the French. France had already annexed Savoy in 1792 and Nice in 1793. And French troops were poised to move south in 1796 under the command of Napoleon Bonaparte.

Born Napoleone Buonaparte in Corsica in 1769 to a minor noble family, Bonaparte (despite his Italian heritage) was French because Corsica had fallen into French hands shortly before his birth. He prepared for his military career by studying in French military academies and had specialized in the artillery. Bonaparte happened to be at the right place to help in the recapture of Toulon in December 1793, which put an end to the federalist revolt there and was rewarded by being made a brigadier general. He was twenty-four years old. He came to the attention of Augustin Robespierre (brother of the more famous Robespierre), who was representative on mission in the area. Bonaparte accompanied Augustin back to Paris, just in time to witness Robespierre's fall. His Jacobin connections landed Bonaparte in jail, but he was soon released. He helped the Convention put down the Vendémiaire uprising in October 1795 and thus ingratiated himself with the leaders of the Directory. In March 1796 he was appointed commander of the Army of Italy.

For the campaign of 1796, the Directory planned two theaters of operation: Germany and Italy. They hoped to keep Austria tied down in both places so that it could not concentrate its armies. They were also preparing an invasion of Ireland as soon as the navy could be brought up to the level of providing suitable transport. They envisioned a fatal blow to the British when the Irish would rise to support the French and when British anti-war sentiment would put pressure on the government to end the struggle with France. However, to fight the British they needed a navy. On the other hand, the British, dominant at sea, needed another power to provide an army to fight the French on the continent. Britain helped finance the land war on the continent, but did not contribute many troops to the effort because it lacked a large army. On the Rhine, two French armies under General Jourdan and General Moreau faced the troops of Archduke Charles of Austria. The Directory intended for this to be the main theater of operations, but Bonaparte soon changed that. Even though he had a much smaller army, the campaign in Italy came to dominate events.

For the campaign beginning in April 1796, Bonaparte planned to move up from the Riviera and cut the connection between the Piedmontese and the Austrian armies. After defeating the Piedmontese, he would then push the Austrians east out of Italy and join the victorious French armies from the Rhine as they forced the Austrians to retreat. They could then dictate peace terms at Vienna. The plan worked at first as Piedmont sued for peace. The fighting continued in the area of the quadrilateral fortresses, a group of forts that guarded the passes over the Alps, and the French armies also moved south to take over papal lands. The French army surrounded the city of Mantua, where an Austrian army was holed up, waiting for the siege to be lifted by their fellow Austrians. The fighting continued throughout the fall of 1796. Mantua finally capitulated in February 1797, and the French armies moved on toward Vienna. But Bonaparte, assuming that the armies on the Rhine were not making progress, signed preliminaries of peace at Leoben (some one hundred miles short of Vienna) in April 1797.

The Directory's aims in Italy had been to get money from the country and to use lands conquered there to exchange for Belgium, in order for France to gain a secure title to Belgium. But in the peace of Leoben, Bonaparte showed that he was pursuing his own foreign policy. Instead of using Italian territory as negotiating chips, Bonaparte had created the Cispadane Republic in northern Italy in October 1796, which proved problematic during the negotiations for peace. Bonaparte could no longer offer Milan to Austria in exchange for Belgium. Instead he proposed that the Austrians take Venice, an independent state that was not at war. Using the excuse of revolts occurring there, Bonaparte sent troops in to overthrow the government and carved up the territory, part of it going to Austria. Bonaparte then redrew the map of Italy to create the Cisalpine Republic out of the Cispadane Republic and the territories captured from Venice and the pope. Like the Batavian Republic, the Cisalpine Republic was a so-called sister republic, organized on the model of French republican institutions and completely subordinate to France. Several explanations have been given for Bonaparte's actions. Perhaps he wished to create a sympathetic regime to ensure that his army would be supplied. Perhaps he was indeed devoted to republican institutions and wanted to see the principles of self-determination spread to Italy (although this seems unlikely as he had little confidence that the Italians would create stable republican regimes). More likely, he coveted his own empire in Italy. In any case, the campaign of 1796–1797 had left France in control of northern Italy.

Bonaparte's conduct shows that he was acting on his own and not following the orders and plans of the Directory. The Directors were losing control of their generals and of foreign policy. The final peace treaty, the Treaty of Campo Formio, was not signed until October 18, 1797. The Austrians delayed negotiations because they hoped that the victory of moderates and royalists committed to peace in the elections in France in the spring of 1797 would force the Directory to make a more conciliatory gesture toward peace and give more concessions. But after the coup of Fructidor (on September 4, 1797) when royalist elections were annulled, they saw that they had no choice but to sign the final treaty. The Treaty of Campo Formio, though not as harsh as it might have been, was nonetheless a defeat for Austria. They had to recognize the Cisalpine Republic, which was nothing more than a satellite of France (it had to supply troops when France went to war and its economy was under French control). The treaty opened the way for further French encroachments on the Italian peninsula at the expense of Austrian influence there. The French acquisition of territory in the Rhineland demonstrated that Austria was not able to protect the principalities within the Holy Roman Empire either. Some of the states of the Holy Roman Empire (notably Württemberg and Bavaria) now sought security in alliances with France.

During 1797, negotiations between France and Great Britain did not come to anything. Neither power was willing to give up the struggle nor believed that it had to. France was winning the war on the continent, and Great Britain had many hopes for continued success in the naval colonial wars. During the Terror, the French had poured many resources into trying to build up their navy. However, the lack of skilled sailors, the enormous expense of building ships, shortage of building materials, and the defeat in a naval battle on June 1, 1794 (Ushant, called by the British "the

Glorious First of June") put the British ahead in this sector of the war. They took advantage of their superiority by trying to take over the French colonies in the West Indies.

The slave rebellion that had broken out in the French colony of Saint-Domingue in 1791 (see chapter 6) had spread throughout the colony. The French government finally responded in the summer of 1792 by sending troops and commissioners to rally the free people of color to its side and put down the slave rebellion. However, by the time these forces arrived, the Revolution of August 10 had dethroned Louis XVI and had established a republic. Some white planters fled from the chaos. Others opposed the Jacobins and fought them in the name of the deposed king. Seeking help from the English forces in the Caribbean, these white planters hoped to reestablish themselves in positions of authority and to preserve the slavery system. By early 1793, the French had declared war on the British, and the cooperation of the planters with the British made them traitors in the eyes of the Jacobins in the Convention.

Great Britain was not the only power trying to take advantage of the situation. The Spanish, whose colony shared the island of Hispaniola with the French colony of Saint-Domingue, sought an alliance with the former slave armies. In February 1793, Sonthonax, the Convention's envoy in Saint-Domingue, wrote home to France urging the Convention to do something for the slaves in hopes of getting them on the side of France. He stressed the danger of losing the colony entirely. The Convention, despite its avowed devotion to equality and freedom, did nothing for the slaves. Sonthonax decided to act on his own to get the support of slaves for France by offering them freedom. But the leaders of the army of former slaves rejected the offer and continued to fight against the French.

Toussaint Louverture now emerged as an important leader in Saint-Domingue. A former slave himself, Louverture was committed to preserving freedom for the former slaves. At first he cooperated with the Spanish, but then he began negotiating with the French as well. The former slaves hesitated to throw their lot in with the French because in 1793 it looked as if the French were about to be defeated by the combined forces of Europe. The British, who intended to pay for the war with the riches of the Caribbean, landed in Saint-Domingue in September 1793, and in early 1794 they captured two other French colonies, Guadaloupe and Martinique.

In the midst of this crisis, when France seemed about to lose its colonial empire, the Convention in Paris finally acted. On February 4, 1794, the Convention declared the emancipation of all the slaves. They did so, not because there had been a growth of antislavery sentiment in France, but

Figure 9.2.   Toussaint Louverture. Because no drawing from life was ever made, the images of the Haitian leader varied widely from one engraving to another. This image appeared in a book published in 1805, A *Historical Account of the Black Empire of Hayti,* by Marcus Rainsford. The British author probably met Toussaint Louverture during his travels in Haiti. This sympathetic portrait of the general shows him with military plans in one hand and a sword in the other. (In order to discourage theft, the library that originally owned this book placed its stamp in a prominent place in all of the illustrations.) Courtesy of Special Collections Library, Penn State University.

rather in hopes of saving the West Indian islands for France. The emancipation decree of the radical Convention was not destined to last long. Evidence that no profound shift had occurred in attitudes toward slavery in France is provided by the actions of Napoleon Bonaparte. When he came to power he felt no hesitation in trying to take back control of the West Indian islands and reenslave the people. He was able to do so in Guadeloupe and Martinique. Martinique had been in British hands and reverted to France in 1802 at the Peace of Amiens. But in Saint-Domingue the army, under the capable direction of Toussaint Louverture, had not only prevailed over the French, it had also conquered the rest of the island from the Spanish and controlled it all.

When Bonaparte sent an army to Saint-Domingue in 1801, the French encountered a determined foe and difficult circumstances. One historian wrote, "After one artillery barrage of a fort the black defenders began singing French revolutionary patriotic songs causing the French troops to doubt their purpose: 'our soldiers looked at each other questionably; they seemed to say: 'Are you our barbaric enemies? Are now we the only soldiers of the Republic? Have we become servile political instruments?'"[3] The French army was defeated by the resistance of the black and colored troops and by the depredations of yellow fever. So Haiti became an independent country, the only example of a completely successful slave revolt. Toussaint, meanwhile, still hoping to find a way for a free Haiti to be a part of a French empire, was negotiating with French envoys. They captured him by trickery in 1802 and sent him to France, where he died in prison in 1803.

EGYPT AND THE SECOND COALITION

Napoleon Bonaparte was rewarded for his successes in Italy in 1796 and 1797 by being named the head of the "Army of England," which was still being organized for an invasion. Fearing that an invasion was neither practical nor likely to lead to much glory, General Bonaparte persuaded the Directory to send the army to invade Egypt. Bonaparte had been making a name for himself in Paris by associating with prominent intellectuals and getting elected to the Mathematical Section of the National Institute (the republic's version of the academies first established by Cardinal Richelieu to promote learning). The Directors were happy to remove this potentially troublesome political figure from Paris and consented to his proposal, though they worried about sending the army so far away.

The motives for Bonaparte's grand scheme have been much debated. As a Corsican, perhaps he was more interested in the Mediterranean than in northern Europe. Perhaps he was trying to acquire an empire for himself. There is some evidence that he was making plans to establish a permanent colony in Egypt. He seems to have been taken with the adventures of Alexander the Great and might have been planning to emulate him, with Egypt only the first step in the creation of an eastern empire. He justified the intervention by arguing that striking at Egypt would be a way of striking at England's empire by disrupting routes to the east. He might have considered a much more convenient target for striking at England: the kingdom of Hanover in northern Germany. George III was both king of England and king of Hanover. But Hanover did not offer the opportunities for glory that Egypt did.

Whatever the reasons for Bonaparte's choice of targets, the expedition had momentous and long-lasting consequences. It might have been picturesque, but it proved disastrous as a foreign policy, creating the unlikely alliance of Russia and the Ottoman Empire. As the sovereign of the territory in northern Africa, the Ottoman Empire responded to this unprovoked act of aggression by declaring war. Other European powers also now joined with the Ottoman Empire and England to create the Second Coalition. While Bonaparte was away from France, this coalition turned the tide in the war and began defeating French armies in Europe, thus hurting the prestige and popularity of the Directory and eventually providing an excuse for Bonaparte's seizure of power. In intellectual terms, the expedition created great advances in the subject of Egyptology when the French discovered the Rosetta stone, the key to reading ancient Egyptian hieroglyphics. The most long-lasting result of the French expedition was the sense of resentment that it created among people in the Middle East, who put it on a par with the Crusades as an example of European aggression against Islam. The Ottoman Empire was traditionally a French ally, and France was not at war with them when the invasion began.

The French expedition of three hundred ships sailed from Toulon on May 19, 1798, and managed somehow to escape destruction by the British navy. The British, aware that ships were being gathered but not knowing their target, sent a navy under the command of Admiral Nelson into the Mediterranean to find the fleet and destroy it. The French headed first for the island of Malta, which they easily captured from the remnants of the Knights of Saint John, a former crusading order dating back to the Middle Ages. On June 18, the fleet set sail from Malta. Admiral Nelson assumed that they would go directly from Malta to Alexandria, so he headed toward that city. The French fleet, which was much slower than the British, evaded them by going first to Crete. Nelson, not finding the French at Alexandria, next searched for them at Crete. When the French arrived in Egypt at Aboukir Bay, to the east of Alexandria, they discovered that the British had left only a few hours earlier. Quickly disembarking the soldiers in the middle of the night for fear that Nelson would return, Bonaparte then ordered them to march across the desert to attack Alexandria, which they easily captured on July 2, 1798.

Although Egypt was nominally under the sovereignty of the Ottoman Empire, the local ruling elite was composed of a special group known as Mamelukes. Originally created in the thirteenth century when the sultan bought boys from the Caucasus mountains to form the elite of his army, they gained control of Egypt and founded their own dynasty. They continued to rule there even after the conquest of Egypt by the Ottoman Turks in 1517, replenishing their population periodically by purchasing boys from the Caucasus or the Balkans who were trained as warriors. Although the Mamelukes were known as skillful fighters, they were no match for the more advanced technology of the French soldiers. At the Battle of the Pyramids, near Cairo on July 21, 1798, the French won a decisive victory and took control of Egypt. A few days later, however, on August 1, 1798, Nelson almost completely annihilated the French fleet at Aboukir Bay, leaving the French army with no means of returning to France.

The invasion of Egypt brought together the Second Coalition against the French. Great Britain, of course, was still in the war and was now joined by the Ottoman Empire. After the death of Catherine the Great in late 1796, Russia had been ruled by her son, Paul I, who hoped to avoid becoming involved in the European wars. But he was worried about the seemingly insatiable conquests of the French revolutionary regime, and Russia naturally feared greater French power in the eastern Mediterranean. Paul, who saw himself as the defender of the Knights of Malta, finally joined the coalition after the Knights were attacked. Naples took advantage of the weakened French position in Europe (in 1798 and 1799 revolts broke out in several of the territories conquered by the French) by attacking the French-sponsored republic in Rome, without success. The French occupied Naples and transformed it into the Parthenopean Republic. Austria also joined the coalition, hoping that with the additional aid of the Russians, it would be able to invade France and overthrow the Directory.

After consolidating his power in Egypt (where a rebellion had broken out against the invaders), Bonaparte next turned his attention to preventing the British and the Turks from combining their forces. He led his army north, to the area then known as Syria (what is today called Israel and Palestine). At Jaffa on March 7, 1799, the French were victorious over the Turks, but the aftermath of the battle discredited the victory, as the French massacred three thousand Turkish prisoners on the grounds that they did not have the troops to watch over them nor supplies to take care of them. The French army was beginning to suffer from infection by the plague. They next attempted to take the fortress at Acre. After besieging it for two months, Bonaparte finally retreated in May when he learned that the British were transporting a Turkish army to Egypt. When Bonaparte left on the costly Syrian campaign he had thirteen thousand men. He returned to Cairo with fewer than eight thousand and immediately had to confront the Turkish army, a force of twenty thousand men. The French dealt them a crushing blow at the battle of Aboukir on July 25, 1799.

From the British Bonaparte received copies of newspapers that he had been unable to see because of the British blockade of Egypt. He learned about the desperate conditions of the French army in Europe and the unpopularity of the French government, and saw that an opportunity existed for him there. He sailed for France, leaving his army behind in Egypt. On October 13, 1799, the news reached Paris that Bonaparte had landed in southern France.

BRUMAIRE

While Bonaparte was busy in Egypt, the Second Coalition had been making gains against the French, pushing them back on all fronts. The French troops, spread over a vast territory across Europe, were unable to defend such a large area successfully. They also suffered from a lack of manpower, with some of their best troops in Egypt. The Directory hoped that more men would be available soon when the new conscription law went into effect. Passed in September 1798, the Jourdan law made all Frenchmen aged twenty to twenty-five eligible for the draft each year, with the twenty-year-olds to be chosen first, and the rest if needed. The first call was for 200,000 men.

Although the allies had the numerical advantage, they waited until the Russians could join them to begin the campaign of 1799. The French, therefore, launched the first attack. The Directory's plan was to advance on several fronts. But their low numbers immediately led to trouble. General Jourdan refused to take responsibility for the defeats of his army in Germany and resigned his command. In Italy, where the bulk of the French army was concentrated, the allied armies under the command of Russian General Suvorov conquered Milan and Turin. By the end of June, the French armies were in full retreat from Italy. Historian T. C. W. Blanning remarked that Suvorov had "in just 2 months . . . conquered Italy more quickly and completely than had Bonaparte in 1796."[4] In Switzerland, meanwhile, the Austrians defeated the French and took control of the Alpine passes between Germany and Italy. Along with the defeats of the French armies came revolts against the French occupiers, especially in Belgium, the Rhineland, and southern Italy.

The military defeats in the spring of 1799 brought about another political crisis in Paris. The Directory had managed to remain in power by continuing to overturn the will of the people as expressed in elections. In the elections of 1798 (Year VI), the voters had sent large numbers of extreme Jacobins to the two councils. The response of the government was to void some elections and replace those elected with their own supporters (the coup of 22 Floréal, Year VI—May 11, 1798). The elections in the spring of 1799 (Year VII) again saw the victory of men on the left, eager to resurrect a Jacobin style of government and mobilize the country to face the dangers of war. Essential for understanding the events of 1799 was the choice of Sieyès as the replacement for the retiring Reubell. Sieyès had never approved of the constitutional provisions of the Directory and was bent on bringing about changes in the government. He was able to do so because the councils, in response to the poor military situation, forced changes in the makeup of the Directory that actually benefited his plans.

For the first time, the legislature brought about a coup against the Directors. On June 17, they annulled the election of the Director Treilhard on the grounds that it had been illegal because he had too recently left the legislature. In his place they chose a pro-Jacobin, Gohier, who ended up siding with Sieyès's plans for change. Then, on the next day (June 18–30 Prairial), the councils threatened two other Directors (Merlin de Douai and La Réveillière-Lépeaux) with impeachment, thus forcing them to resign. The coup of 30 Prairial put in office General Moulin and Roger Ducos, who gave their support to Sieyès in his attempt to transform the government. When Sieyès engineered this change in the coup of Brumaire, it seemed to many French citizens as merely another in this line of illegal moves by which the politicians had managed to keep themselves in office. But it turned out to be fundamentally different.

In June, the councils continued their attempts to shore up the war effort by decreeing that all men eligible for the draft (aged twenty to twenty-five) would be called up immediately. They also instituted a forced loan on rich people. The area occupied by French armies was now so limited that they could no longer live off the foreigners. These measures naturally caused resistance. The councils responded by the Law of Hostages on July 12, 1799, which permitted the arrest of relatives of émigrés in areas that were causing disturbances. Predictably, the royalist areas in the Vendée rose in revolt once again. The Directors were faced with dangers from both the left and the right.

The French armies began to make some progress in the autumn, forcing the allies out of the Batavian (Dutch) Republic and Helvetic (Swiss) Republic by the end of September. Wishing to take advantage of the army's renewed success, Sieyès was determined to put through his plans for a coup to transform the government. Amendment of the constitution would take too long, he believed. However, to change the institutions by force would require the collaboration of the army and a general. Sieyès's first choice to assume the role (General Joubert) had died in battle in Italy in August. Another likely candidate (Jourdan) was rejected because he was a Jacobin. Moreau declined the honor, suggesting instead that Sieyès talk to Bonaparte, who had just landed in southern France on October 9. Not realizing that their objectives were fundamentally different and underestimating the general's considerable political skills, Sieyès negotiated with Bonaparte to join him and his colleagues in the coup.

The justification for the illegal measures was the threat of a Jacobin uprising in Paris. On November 9, 1799 (18 Brumaire), the Council of Elders voted to move the councils to the old royal palace at Saint-Cloud where they would be free from harassments by the crowds in Paris. Bonaparte was named commander of the troops in the area to protect the government. His role was supposed to be minor, to look statesmanlike while the councils were pressured to do the confederates' bidding. On November 10 (19 Brumaire), the councils were told that all of the Directors had resigned and that they should transfer authority to Bonaparte and his associates. Rather then meekly obeying, however, the councils refused to act. Impatient with the delay, Bonaparte appeared before the Council of Elders to issue threats of armed intervention, a tactic not likely to win their support. He followed that unwise endeavor with another potentially disastrous scheme. He decided to go before the Council of Five Hundred. The deputies were now alarmed at what was going on, and a free-for-all ensued as they converged upon Bonaparte and began beating him. Although he managed to escape, the situation was deteriorating rapidly, with the Five Hundred threatening to declare Bonaparte an outlaw.

The savior of the day was General Bonaparte's brother, Lucien Bonaparte, who was the leader of the Council of Five Hundred. He and

Napoleon appeared before the troops, and Lucien told them that the council faced an uprising by some of the members, who, according to Lucien, were in the pay of England and were brandishing daggers against their fellow deputies. He begged for their help. Napoleon, meanwhile, was bleeding, having been scratched in the face during the earlier confrontation. The troops responded to protect their commander and to save the country from foreign agitators. As they entered the council rooms to force out the recalcitrant deputies, the legislators fled, jumping out of the windows in some cases. Those remaining acquiesced to the demands, giving power to a provisional executive of three Consuls (Sieyès, Roger Ducos, and Bonaparte) who would exercise power while a committee wrote a new constitution for France.

The country responded with almost complete indifference. The coup of Brumaire looked like another of the maneuvers by which the factions had been keeping themselves in power for the past five years. But some people recognized that a new factor had been added. Immediately after the coup Benjamin Constant warned Sieyès of the danger of working with Bonaparte. Constant feared the republic would not survive in the hands of "a man who talks only of himself" and who had the support of "the generals, the soldiers, the aristocratic population," and those who admired power.[5] Indeed, Bonaparte made certain that the new constitution would provide him with a great deal of authority. To solve the problem of the executive power, the new government would have three consuls (hence the name of the government, the Consulate). Sieyès had assumed that the First Consul would be a sort of figurehead and that the real work would be done by the other two. Bonaparte changed this by giving the First Consul the predominant position and leaving the other two as merely advisers. Felix Markham, a biographer of Napoleon, has called this a second coup d'état. The men who brought about the Brumaire coup had not envisioned anything of this sort emerging from it. Bonaparte managed to fashion the new constitution to make himself, not the legislatures or the other consuls, the real ruler of France. He was able to stay in power by defeating the foreign enemies of France, by putting down the factional strife within the country, and by establishing a sort of dictatorship. In 1804, he converted the remnants of the republican form of government into an empire with himself as the new Emperor Napoleon I.

CONCLUSION

Although violence and political conflicts between the revolutionaries and their opponents continued, the rise of Bonaparte was the beginning of the end of the revolution. He would abandon the attempt to rule by constitutional means and employ military force to exert control over the country. The French Republic survived for a few years, but Bonaparte's coming to power can be conveniently seen as the end of the Revolution in France. Under Bonaparte, liberty was sacrificed for order as he created a regime that emphasized stability and foreign empire. The heady days of the Revolution when French revolutionaries believed that a new regime could be created that would transform society and regenerate human beings was over.

But France was not the same. Socially and politically the nation that emerged at the end of the revolutionary decade had been transformed. Napoleon stopped the Revolution in France by paying more attention to stability than to issues such as rights, liberty, and equality that had consumed the revolutionaries. But he knew that the French people would not forget the gains of the Revolution. While bringing back nobility, reintroducing censorship, and stressing authority, Napoleon carefully maintained the fiction that his government rested on the will of the people. The elaborate government structure of the Consulate and the Empire (designed to channel power into the hands of one man) was ostensibly based on universal male suffrage. He allowed elections and consulted the will of the people through plebiscites. He created a nobility, but it was explicitly open to all who carried out extraordinary services to the state. The Revolution had created a new idea of a properly organized political and social system. When the Bourbons returned, their government, too, had to include representative institutions.

In many ways the Napoleonic empire dismantled revolutionary institutions within France. But the Napoleonic empire abroad had revolutionary consequences. As the French armies moved out to conquer territory in Europe, the rest of Europe felt the effects of the Revolution as it succumbed to French authority or transformed its own societies to harness the resources needed to fight the French.

The lives of ordinary French citizens were no longer the same. The state now took a greater role in education, in local administration, and in justice. The most isolated peasant had felt the weight of the national government through more efficient taxation, religious policy, and conscription. People developed a new sense of the nation as young men left their villages to form a part of a national army and then marched off to the far corners of Europe. Their participation in the wars gave them a renewed commitment to the nation and a sense that France had an important role to play in the world.

The revolutionary decade had long-lasting effects on the French nation. The Revolution delayed France's economic development as war siphoned off resources. France would have to wait until the 1840s to embark on the kind of industrial expansion that was already taking place in England. The Revolution brought into the open social conflicts that had been kept in check under the Ancien Régime. Indeed, the Revolution made those social divisions even worse. The struggles over religion created animosities that survived throughout the nineteenth century. The competing ideologies of the revolutionary era were not forgotten. They have continued to animate political debate in France and around the world to the present. The final word on the meaning of the French Revolution is still to be written.

CHRONOLOGY

ANCIEN RÉGIME

1713	*Unigenitus*
1748	Publication of Montesquieu, *De l'Esprit des Lois*
1751	Beginning of publication of *Encyclopédie*
1756–1763	Seven Years' War
1762	Publication of Rousseau, *The Social Contract*
1771	"Maupeou Revolution" closes parlements

REIGN OF LOUIS XVI (UP TO 1788)

1774	**Louis XVI becomes king**
	Turgot liberalizes grain trade
	Parlements are reinstated
1776	Turgot dismissed, replaced by Necker (1777)
1778	France allies with United States of America
1781	Ségur Ordinance
	Battle of Yorktown
	Necker's *Compte rendu*
	Joly de Fleury replaces Necker
1783	**Peace of Paris**
	Calonne appointed controller general
1785	Affair of the Diamond Necklace
1787	
February 22	**Assembly of Notables begins**
April	Calonne dismissed, replaced by Loménie de Brienne

249

August 14	Parlement of Paris exiled to Troyes
September	Dutch crisis
November	Edict of Toleration
November 19	Royal Session of Parlement of Paris

1788

May 8	May Edicts to reorganize the courts
August 8	**Collapse of the Ancien Régime government,** Loménie de Brienne announces that Estates General will meet on May 1, 1789

ESTATES GENERAL AND BEGINNING OF REVOLUTION

1788

August 25	Loménie de Brienne resigns, Necker returns to office
September 25	Parlement of Paris says Estates General will follow "forms observed in 1614"
November 6	Second meeting of the Assembly of Notables begins
December 27	King decrees doubling of the Third Estate

1789

January	Abbé Sieyès, *What Is the Third Estate?*
January 24	King issues call for elections to Estates General
April	Réveillon riots in Paris
May 5	**Opening session of Estates General**
June 10	Third Estate offers "last invitation" to other two Estates
June 17	**Third Estate declares itself the National Assembly**
June 20	Tennis Court Oath
June 23	Royal Session
June 27	Louis XVI orders First and Second Estates to join the National Assembly
July 11	Necker is dismissed
July 14	**Fall of the Bastille**
July 20–August 4	Great Fear
August 4–5	**Night of August 4, abolition of feudal privileges**
August 10	Municipal authorities given control over National Guards and king deprived of command of army in the interior of the country

| August 11 | Passage of the August 4th Decrees |
| **August 26** | **Declaration of the Rights of Man and Citizen** |

NATIONAL ASSEMBLY

1789

September 10	Assembly decides on one-house legislature
September 11	Absolute veto defeated, king given a suspensive veto
October 1	Banquet for Flanders Régiment at Versailles
October 5–6	**October Days, king brought to Paris**
October 19	Constituent Assembly begins meeting in Paris
October 21	Decree on martial law
end of October	Distinction between active and passive citizen created
November 2	Property of the church "placed at the disposal of the nation"
November 7	Assembly decrees that no member may serve as minister of the king
December 19	Sale of church land is authorized, assignats created
December 24	Granting of civil rights to Protestants

1790

February 4	King appears at Assembly and greeted warmly
February 13	Monastic vows abolished
February 26	France reorganized into 83 departments
May 3	Redemption values of seigneurial obligations are set at 20–25 times their annual value
May 21	Paris reorganized into 48 sections
June 19	Titles of hereditary nobility abolished
July 12	**Civil Constitution of the Clergy**
July 14	Fête de la Fédération
August	Nancy Rebellion
August 16	Decree reorganizing the Judiciary
November 27	Decree requiring Clerical Oath
December 26	King approves Clerical Oath legislation

1791

April	Pope Pius VI condemns Clerical Oath
April 2	Death of Mirabeau
April 18	Crowds prevent king from going to Saint-Cloud for Easter

May 7	Refractory priests granted permission to use church buildings and celebrate mass
May 15	Free-coloreds given equal rights of citizenship as whites
May 16	"Self-denying ordinance" is passed
June 14	Le Chapelier Law
June 20	**Flight to Varennes, Royal Family leaves Paris around midnight**
June 21	King's flight stopped at Varennes
June 25	Royal Family returns to Paris
July 14	Second Fête de la Fédération
July 16	Assembly decrees that Louis XVI will be retained as king if he accepts the completed Constitution
July 17	**Massacre of the Champ de Mars**
August	Slave revolt in Saint-Domingue
August 27	Declaration of Pillnitz
September 12	Annexation of Avignon
September 13	Louis XVI accepts the Constitution
September	Olympe de Gouges, *Declaration of the Rights of Woman and Citizen*

LEGISLATIVE ASSEMBLY

1791

October 1	Legislative Assembly opens
October 14	Louis XVI calls on émigrés to return
November 9 and 29	Assembly passes decrees against émigrés and non-juring priests; Louis XVI vetoes both measures
December 14	Louis XVI announces to Assembly that he has issued an ultimatum to elector of Trier to disperse émigrés

1792

March 1	Death of Leopold II of Austria; he is succeeded by his son Francis II
March 10–23	Appointment of Girondin ministry
April 20	**France declares war against Austria**
April 28	French armies invade Austrian Netherlands
May 27	Legislative Assembly passes decree for deporting refractory priests

June 8	Legislative Assembly passes decree establishing a camp of *fédérés* near Paris
June 10	Roland sends threatening letter to king (read at Legislative Assembly on June 13)
June 13	King dismisses Girondin ministry
June	Marshall Luckner leads French army into Austrian Netherlands
June 18	Lafayette's letter calling on suppression of Jacobins read at Legislative Assembly
June 19	King vetoes decrees regarding refractory priests and *fédérés*
June 20	**Invasion of the Tuileries**
June 28	Lafayette addresses Legislative Assembly
July 11	Assembly declares a state of emergency (*la patrie en danger*)
July 14	Fête de la Fédération
July	Army and commissioners sent to Saint-Domingue to put down slave insurrection
July 28	News of Brunswick Manifesto reaches Paris
August 6	Demonstrators at Champ de Mars call for king to be deposed
August 8	Assembly refuses to impeach Lafayette
August 10	**Insurrection overthrows Louis XVI**
August 19	Prussian and Austrian armies invade France
August 26	News of fall of Longwy reaches Paris
September 2	News of surrender of Verdun reaches Paris
September 2–6	**September Massacres**
September 20	Law establishing civil registers of deaths and births and allowing divorce
September 20	Battle of Valmy

NATIONAL CONVENTION (UP TO SEPTEMBER 1793)

1792

September 20	**First meeting of National Convention**
September 22	Convention proclaims Year I of the Republic
October 2	Creation of Committee of General Security
October 10	Brissot expelled from Jacobin Club

November 6	French defeat Austrians at battle of Jemappes
November 19 and	
December 15	Propagandist Decrees
December 10	King's trial begins

1793

January 21	**Louis XVI is guillotined**
February 1	France declares war on Great Britain and Holland
February 24	Convention establishes conscription to raise 300,000 troops
March	Rebellion in the Vendée begins
March 10	Revolutionary Tribunal created
March 18	French defeat at Neerwinden
March 21	Decree creating local committees of surveillance
April 5	Dumouriez defects to the enemy
April 6	Creation of Committee of Public Safety
April 13	Convention votes to bring Marat to trial
April 24	Marat's trial before Revolutionary Tribunal
May 4	Law of the Maximum
May 31	Uprising demands the arrest of the Girondins
June 2	***Journée* of June 2, purge of Girondins from the Convention**
June 10	Legislation on dividing common lands
June	"Federalist" revolts begin
July 10	Danton fails to be reelected to Committee of Public Safety
July 13	Marat assassinated
July 17	Seigneurial dues abolished without compensation
July 27	Robespierre elected to Committee of Public Safety
August 23	**Proclamation of *levée en masse***
September 2	News reaches Paris that Toulon had been handed over to the British

REIGN OF TERROR

1793

| **September 5** | ***Journée* of September 5, Terror declared "the order of the day"** |

September 8	French defeat British and Dutch at battle of Hondschoote
September 17	Law of Suspects
September 22	Year II begins
September 25	Committee of Public Safety takes united front before criticism of Convention
September 29	General Maximum
October 5	Revolutionary calendar is adopted
October 10	Declaration that government will be "revolutionary until the peace"
October 12	Convention decrees destruction of Lyon (retaken by republican army on October 9)
October 16	Battle of Wattignies
October 16	Marie Antoinette executed
October 30	Convention outlaws women's political clubs
November 10	Festival of Reason in Notre Dame in Paris
December 4	**Law of 14 Frimaire or Law of Revolutionary Government**
December 23	Army of the Vendée defeated at Savenay
1794	
January	Fabre d'Eglantine, Hérault de Séchelles, and others arrested
February 4	Convention declares emancipation of all slaves
February 5	**Robespierre's speech on "the principles of political morality"**
February 26 and March 3	Laws of Ventôse (8 and 13 Ventôse)
March 13	Arrest of the Hébertists (guillotined on March 24)
March 29–30	Arrest of Danton and the "Indulgents" (guillotined on April 5)
May 7	Cult of the Supreme Being is authorized
June 8	Festival of the Supreme Being
June 10	**Law of 22 Prairial, beginning of the "Great Terror"**
June 26	Battle of Fleurus
July 27	**Robespierre and his associates arrested (9 Thermidor)**
July 28	Robespierre, Couthon, Saint-Just, and others guillotined (10 Thermidor)

THERMIDOR AND THE DIRECTORY

1794

August 1	Repeal of the Law of 22 Prairial
September 22	Year III begins
November 12	Jacobin Club of Paris ordered closed
December 24	Maximum abolished

1795

January	Third partition of Poland
April 1	**Popular uprising of 12 Germinal**
April 5	Treaty of Basel, peace between France and Prussia
May 20	**Popular uprising of 1 Prairial**
June 8	Death of Louis XVII, Comte de Provence assumes title of king as Louis XVIII
August 22	Constitution of Year III completed
September 23	Year IV begins
October 5	Royalist uprising of 13 Vendémiaire
October 27	**Directory government begins**

1796

March	Bonaparte named head of army of Italy
May 10	Babeuf arrested
September 22	Year V begins

1797

April	Elections of Year V
April 18	Bonaparte signs preliminaries of peace with Austria at Leoben
May 20	Barthélemy chosen Director
May 27	Babeuf executed
September 4	**Coup d'état of Fructidor (18 Fructidor)**
September 22	Year VI begins
October 18	Treaty of Campo Formio between France and Austria

1798

May 11	Coup of 22 Floréal, voiding elections of Year VI
May 19	French expedition for Egypt sails from Toulon
July 21	Battle of the Pyramids
August 1	Nelson decisively defeats French fleet at Aboukir Bay
September 5	Jourdan Law establishing conscription
September 22	Year VII begins

1799

Spring	Elections of Year VII won by the left, Sieyès named a Director
March 7	Victory of French over Turks at Jaffa
Spring–Summer	French army defeated in Italy
June 18	Coup of 30 Prairial, Councils force change of Directors
July 12	Law of Hostages
July 25	Victory of French over Turks at battle of Aboukir
September 23	Year VIII begins
October 9	Bonaparte lands in France
November 9	Councils moved to Saint-Cloud (18 Brumaire)
November 10	**Coup d'état of Brumaire brings Bonaparte to power (19 Brumaire)**

NOTES

INTRODUCTION

1. Arthur Young, *Travels in France during the Years 1787, 1788 & 1789*, ed. Jeffry Kaplow (New York: Anchor Books, 1969), p. 131.
2. Thomas Paine, "Rights of Man," in *Collected Writings*, ed. Eric Foner (New York: Library of America, 1995), p. 537.

CHAPTER 1

1. Voltaire, *Letters on England* (New York: Penguin Books, 1980), Letter XIII.
2. Rousseau, *The Social Contract; and, Discourses*, translated and introduced by G. D. H. Cole (London: Everyman's Library, 1973), p. 177.

CHAPTER 2

1. Michael Kwass, *Privilege and the Politics of Taxation in Eighteenth-Century France: Liberté, Égalité, Fiscalité* (Cambridge, UK: Cambridge University Press, 2000), p. 45.
2. Colin Jones, *The Great Nation* (London: Penguin Books, 2003), p. 33.
3. Jones, *The Great Nation*, p. 263.
4. John Hardman, *Louis XVI: The Silent King* (London: Arnold, 2000), p. 39.
5. Robert D. Harris, *Necker: Reform Statesman of the Ancien Régime* (Berkeley: University of California Press, 1979), p. 184.
6. William Doyle, *Origins of the French Revolution*, 3rd edition (Oxford: Oxford University Press, 1999), p. 50.
7. Jean Egret, *The French Prerevolution, 1787–1788*, trans. Wesley D. Camp (Chicago: University of Chicago Press, 1977), p. 2.

8. Doyle, *Origins*, p. 53.

9. Egret, *Prerevolution*, p. 6.

10. Egret, *Prerevolution*, p. 21.

11. Egret, *Prerevolution*, p. 34.

12. Egret, *Prerevolution*, p. 49.

13. T. C. W. Blanning, *The French Revolutionary Wars, 1787–1802* (London: Arnold, 1996), p. 19.

14. Egret, *Prerevolution*, p. 111.

15. Bailey Stone, *The French Parlements and the Crisis of the Old Regime* (Chapel Hill: University of North Carolina Press, 1986), p. 90.

16. Timothy Tackett, *Becoming a Revolutionary: The Deputies of the French National Assembly and the Emergence of a Revolutionary Culture (1789–1790)* (Princeton, NJ: Princeton University Press, 1996), p. 80.

CHAPTER 3

1. John Hardman, *The French Revolution: The Fall of the Ancien Régime to the Thermidorian Reaction, 1785–1795*, Documents of Modern History (London: Arnold, 1981), p. 70.

2. Jean Egret, *The French Prerevolution, 1787–1788*, trans. Wesley D. Camp (Chicago: University of Chicago Press, 1977), p. 197.

3. Egret, *Prerevolution*, p. 214.

4. John Hall Stewart, *A Documentary Survey of the French Revolution* (New York: Macmillan Company, 1951), pp. 42–56.

5. Stewart, *Documentary Survey*, p. 31.

6. Timothy Tackett, *Becoming a Revolutionary: The Deputies of the French National Assembly and the Emergence of a Revolutionary Culture (1789–1790)* (Princeton, NJ: Princeton University Press, 1996), p. 35.

7. George V. Taylor, "Revolutionary and Nonrevolutionary Content in the Cahiers of 1789: An Interim Report," *French Historical Studies* 7 (1972): 494.

8. Michael P. Fitzsimmons, *The Night the Old Regime Ended: August 4, 1789, and the French Revolution* (University Park: The Pennsylvania State University Press, 2003), p. 101.

9. Tackett, *Becoming a Revolutionary*, p. 140.

10. Tackett, *Becoming a Revolutionary*, p. 141.

11. Tackett, *Becoming a Revolutionary*, pp. 147–48.

12. Stewart, *Documentary Survey*, p. 88.

13. Stewart, *Documentary Survey*, pp. 89–98.

14. Barbara Luttrell, *Mirabeau* (Carbondale: Southern Illinois University Press, 1990), p. 128.

15. Arthur Young, *Travels in France during the Years 1787, 1788 & 1789*, ed. Jeffry Kaplow (New York: Anchor Books, 1969), p. 131.

16. George Rudé, *The Crowd in the French Revolution* (Oxford, UK: Clarendon Press, 1959), pp. 57–58.

17. T. C. W. Blanning, *The French Revolutionary Wars, 1787–1802* (London: Arnold, 1996), p. 28.

18. Louis XVI speaking to Axel von Fersen, quoted in Munro Price, *The Road from Versailles: Louis XVI, Marie Antoinette, and the Fall of the French Monarchy* (New York: St. Martin's Press, 2003), p. 249.

19. Georges Lefebvre, *The Great Fear of 1789*, trans. Joan White (New York: Vintage Books, 1973), p. 18.

20. Fitzsimmons, *Night*, p. 14.

21. Fitzsimmons, *Night*, p. 16.

22. Stewart, *Documentary Survey*, p. 107.

23. Egret, *Prerevolution*, pp. 108–9.

CHAPTER 4

1. The American Bill of Rights had no influence on the Declaration of the Rights of Man because it had not yet been written.

2. Quotes are from Dale Van Kley, ed., *The French Idea of Freedom: The Old Regime and the Declaration of Rights of 1789* (Stanford, CA: Stanford University Press, 1994), pp. 1–3.

3. Camille Desmoulins, *Les Révolutions de France et de Brabant*, no. 1, p. 1. My translation.

4. Malcolm Crook, *Elections in the French Revolution* (Cambridge, UK: Cambridge University Press, 1996), p. 13.

5. Crook, *Elections*, p. 38.

6. Ted W. Margadant, *Urban Rivalries in the French Revolution* (Princeton, NJ: Princeton University Press, 1992), p. 94.

7. John Hall Stewart, *A Documentary Survey of the French Revolution* (New York: Macmillan Company, 1951), pp. 111–12, 258–59.

8. Madame de Staël, *Considérations sur la Révolution Française*, edited by the Duc de Broglie and the Baron de Staël (Paris: Charpentier, 1862), accessed online ARTFL—my translation.

9. Saul K. Padover, *The Life and Death of Louis XVI* (New York: Pyramid Books, 1963), p. 118.

CHAPTER 5

1. John Hall Stewart, *A Documentary Survey of the French Revolution* (New York: Macmillan Company, 1951), p. 176.

2. Munro Price, *The Road from Versailles: Louis XVI, Marie Antoinette, and the Fall of the French Monarchy* (New York: St. Martin's Press, 2003), p. 153.

3. Timothy Tackett, *When the King Took Flight* (Cambridge, MA: Harvard University Press, 2003), p. 102.

4. Stewart, *Documentary Survey*, p. 206.

5. Stewart, *Documentary Survey*, pp. 205–10.

6. Stewart, *Documentary Survey*, p. 240.

7. Tackett, *Flight*, p. 147.

8. Tackett, *Flight*, p. 201.

9. Barry Shapiro, "Self-Sacrifice, Self-Interest, or Self-Defense? The Constituent Assembly and the 'Self-Denying Ordinance' of May 1791," *French Historical Studies* 25 (Fall 2002): 641.

CHAPTER 6

1. Munro Price, *The Road from Versailles: Louis XVI, Marie Antoinette, and the Fall of the French Monarchy* (New York: St. Martin's Press, 2003), p. 223.

2. *Archives Parlementaires* 34: 223–24. My translation.

3. Tackett says 150 affiliated with Jacobins and 170 with Feuillants out of around 750 deputies. Timothy Tackett, "Conspiracy Obsession in a Time of Revolution: French Elites and the Origins of the Terror, 1789–1792," *American Historical Review* 105 (June 2000): 709.

4. M. J. Sydenham, *The Girondins* (London: University of London, 1961), p. 208.

5. John Hall Stewart, *A Documentary Survey of the French Revolution* (New York: Macmillan Company, 1951), p. 273.

6. Nigel Aston, *Religion and Revolution in France, 1780–1804* (Washington, DC: The Catholic University of America Press, 2000), p. 180.

7. Quoted in Georges Lefebvre, *The French Revolution from Its Origins to 1793*, trans. Elizabeth Moss Evanson (New York: Columbia University Press, 1962), p. 217.

8. M. J. Sydenham, *The French Revolution* (New York: Capricorn Books, 1966), p. 91.

9. Geoffrey Cubit, "Robespierre and Conspiracy Theories," in *Robespierre*, edited by Colin Haydon and William Doyle (Cambridge, UK: Cambridge University Press, 1999), p. 80.

10. Laura Mason and Tracey Rizzo, *The French Revolution: A Document Collection* (Boston: Houghton Mifflin, 1999), p. 161.

11. Sydenham, *The French Revolution*, p. 97.

12. Mason and Rizzo, *Document Collection*, p. 162.

13. Lefebvre, *French Revolution from Its Origins*, p. 218.

14. T. C. W. Blanning, *The Origins of the French Revolutionary Wars* (London and New York: Longman, 1986), p. 104.

15. Stewart, *Documentary Survey*, p. 246.
16. Stewart, *Documentary Survey*, p. 260.
17. Blanning, *Origins of the French Revolutionary Wars*, p. 119.
18. Gita May, *Madame Roland and the Age of Revolution* (New York and London: Columbia University Press, 1970), p. 116.
19. Malcolm Crook, *Elections in the French Revolution* (Cambridge, UK: Cambridge University Press, 1996), p. 30.
20. Sarah Maza, *Private Lives and Public Affairs* (Berkeley, CA: University of California Press, 1993), p. 168.
21. Maza, *Privates Lives*, pp. 209–10.
22. Mason and Rizzo, *Document Collection*, pp. 110–13.
23. Laurent Dubois, *Avengers of the New World: The Story of the Haitian Revolution* (Cambridge, MA: Harvard University Press, 2004), p. 105.
24. Mason and Rizzo, *Document Collection*, pp. 168–70.

CHAPTER 7

1. John Hall Stewart, *A Documentary Survey of the French Revolution* (New York: Macmillan Company, 1951), p. 234.
2. Robespierre, speech of December 3, 1792, *Regicide and Revolution: Speeches at the Trial of Louis XVI*, edited with an introduction by Michael Walzer (Cambridge, UK: Cambridge University Press, 1974), p. 131.
3. Walzer, *Regicide*, p. 138.
4. Colin Jones, *The Longman Companion to the French Revolution* (London: Longman, 1988), p. 192.
5. Alison Patrick, *The Men of the First French Republic* (Baltimore: The Johns Hopkins University Press, 1972), p. 1. My translation.
6. Stewart, *Documentary Survey*, p. 403.
7. Louis R. Gottschalk, *Jean Paul Marat: A Study in Radicalism* (Chicago: University of Chicago Press, 1967), p. 97.
8. Gottschalk, *Marat*, p. 160.
9. R. R. Palmer, *Twelve Who Ruled* (Princeton, NJ: Princeton University Press, 1941), pp. 32–33.
10. Georg Büchner, *Danton's Death* (1835), in *Complete Plays and Prose*, translated by Carl Richard Mueller (New York: Hill and Wang, 1963), p. 19.

CHAPTER 8

1. John Hall Stewart, *A Documentary Survey of the French Revolution* (New York: Macmillan Company, 1951), p. 473.

2. Geoffrey Best, *War and Society in Revolutionary Europe 1770–1870* (Montreal: McGill-Queen's University Press, 1982), p. 63.

3. "The 'Manifesto' of the Enragés. Jacques Roux before the Convention, 25 June 1793," in John Hardman, ed., *The French Revolution: The Fall of the Ancien Régime to the Thermidorian Reaction 1785–1795* (London: Edward Arnold, 1981), pp. 172–73.

4. R. R. Palmer, *Twelve Who Ruled* (Princeton, NJ: Princeton University Press, 1941), p. 45.

5. Palmer, *Twelve Who Ruled*, p. 52.

6. Stewart, *Documentary Survey*, pp. 477–78.

7. Palmer, *Twelve Who Ruled*, p. 71.

8. Stewart, *Documentary Survey*, p. 480.

9. Palmer, *Twelve Who Ruled*, p. 126.

10. Laura Mason and Tracey Rizzo, *The French Revolution: A Document Collection* (Boston: Houghton Mifflin, 1999), pp. 234–35.

11. Nigel Aston, *Religion and Revolution in France, 1780–1804* (Washington, DC: The Catholic University of America Press, 2000), p. 187.

12. Palmer, *Twelve Who Ruled*, p. 121.

13. Palmer, *Twelve Who Ruled*, p. 156.

14. Palmer, *Twelve Who Ruled*, p. 175.

15. David Andress, *The Terror: The Merciless War for Freedom in Revolutionary France* (New York: Farrar, Straus & Giroux, 2005), pp. 247–48.

16. Figures on *noyades* are from Palmer, *Twelve Who Ruled*, p. 222; other figures are from Colin Jones, *The Longman Companion to the French Revolution* (London: Longman, 1988), pp. 115–21, and from Hugh Gough, "Genocide and the Bicentenary: The French Revolution and the Revenge of the Vendée," *The Historical Journal* 30, no. 4 (Dec. 1987): 987.

17. Palmer, *Twelve Who Ruled*, p. 264.

18. Palmer, *Twelve Who Ruled*, pp. 275–76.

19. Palmer, *Twelve Who Ruled*, p. 291.

20. Norman Hampson, *Danton* (New York: Holmes & Meier, 1978), p. 81. My translation.

21. Hampson, *Danton*, p. 118.

22. David P. Jordan, *The Revolutionary Career of Maximilien Robespierre* (Chicago: University of Chicago Press, 1985), p. 40.

23. Hampson, *Danton*, p. 174.

24. George Rudé, ed., *Robespierre*, Great Lives Observed series (Englewood Cliffs, NJ: Prentice-Hall, 1967), pp. 69, 70.

25. Hugh Gough, *The Terror in the French Revolution* (New York: Palgrave, 1998), p. 58.

26. David P. Jordan, "The Robespierre Problem," in *Robespierre*, edited by Colin Haydon and William Doyle (Cambridge, MA: Cambridge University Press, 1999), p. 22.

CHAPTER 9

1. Albert Soboul, *The Sans-Culottes; the Popular Movement and Revolutionary Government, 1793–1794*, trans. Rémy Inglis Hall (Garden City, NY: Anchor Books, 1972), p. 45.

2. Carnot replaced Sieyès, who refused to serve when he was elected.

3. Nigel Aston, *The French Revolution, 1789–1804: Authority, Liberty, and the Search for Stability* (Houndsmill, UK: Palgrave Macmillan, 2004), p. 248.

4. T. C. W. Blanning, *The Origins of the French Revolutionary Wars* (London: Longman, 1986), p. 237.

5. James Livesey, *Making Democracy in the French Revolution* (Cambridge, MA: Harvard University Press, 2001), p. 234.

SELECT BIBLIOGRAPHY

Listed are books in English that were especially helpful in writing this book or that are recommended for further reading. Although they are grouped by chapter, many books were sources for more than one chapter.

GENERAL HISTORIES

Aston, Nigel. *The French Revolution, 1789–1804: Authority, Liberty and the Search for Stability*. European History in Perspective. Basingstoke, Hampshire, UK: Palgrave Macmillan, 2004.

Bosher, J. F. *The French Revolution*. New York: W. W. Norton, 1988.

Doyle, William. *The Oxford History of the French Revolution*. 2nd ed. Oxford, UK: Oxford University Press, 2002.

Lefebvre, Georges. *The French Revolution from Its Origins to 1793*. Translated by Elizabeth Moss Evanson. London: Routledge and Kegan Paul and New York: Columbia University Press, 1962.

———. *The French Revolution from 1793–1799*. Translated by John Hall Stewart and James Friguglietti. London: Routledge and Kegan Paul and New York: Columbia University Press, 1964.

Schama, Simon. *Citizens: A Chronicle of the French Revolution*. New York: Knopf, 1989.

Sutherland, D. M. G. *The French Revolution and Empire: The Quest for a Civic Order*. Malden, MA: Blackwell Publishing, 2003.

SOURCES FOR DOCUMENTS

Censer, Jack R., and Lynn Hunt. *Liberty, Equality, Fraternity: Exploring the French Revolution*. University Park: The Pennsylvania State University Press, 2001. This book includes a CD-ROM with documents and images. See also the website for this book, http://chnm.gmu.edu/revolution.

Hardman, John, ed. *The French Revolution: The Fall of the Ancien Régime to the Thermidorian Reaction, 1785–1795*. Documents of Modern History. London: Edward Arnold, 1981.

Mason, Laura, and Tracey Rizzo. *The French Revolution: A Document Collection*. Boston: Houghton Mifflin Company, 1999.

Stewart, John Hall. *A Documentary Survey of the French Revolution*. New York: Macmillan, 1951.

DICTIONARIES

Furet, François, and Mona Ozouf. *A Critical Dictionary of the French Revolution*. Translated by Arthur Goldhammer. Cambridge, MA: Harvard University Press, 1989.

Jones, Colin. *The Longman Companion to the French Revolution*. London: Longman, 1988.

Scott, Samuel F., and Barry Rothaus, eds. *Historical Dictionary of the French Revolution, 1789–1799*. 2 vols. Westport, CT: Greenwood Press, 1984.

UNDERSTANDING THE FRENCH REVOLUTION

Kaplan, Steven. *Farewell, Revolution*. Ithaca, NY: Cornell University Press, 1995.

Paine, Thomas. "Rights of Man" in *Collected Writings*, edited by Eric Foner. New York: Library of America, 1995.

Young, Arthur. *Travels in France during the Years 1787, 1788 & 1789*, edited by Jeffry Kaplow. New York: Anchor Books, 1969.

CHAPTER 1

Bosher, J. F. *French Finances, 1770–1795: From Business to Bureaucracy*. Cambridge, UK: Cambridge University Press, 1970.

Burke, Edmund. *Reflections on the Revolution in France*. Oxford, UK: Oxford University Press, 1993.

Chartier, Roger. *The Cultural Origins of the French Revolution*. Translated by Lydia G. Cochrane. Durham, NC: Duke University Press, 1991.

Jones, Colin. *The Great Nation: France from Louis XV to Napoleon*. London: Penguin Books, 2003.

Jones, P. M. *The Peasantry in the French Revolution*. Cambridge, UK: Cambridge University Press, 1988.

Kwass, Michael. *Privilege and the Politics of Taxation in Eighteenth-Century France: Liberté, Égalité, Fiscalité*. Cambridge, UK: Cambridge University Press, 2000.

Matthews, George T. *The Royal General Farms in Eighteenth-Century France*. New York: Columbia University Press, 1958.

Maza, Sarah. *The Myth of the French Bourgeoisie: An Essay on the Social Imaginary, 1750–1850*. Cambridge, MA: Harvard University Press, 2003.

Murphy, Orville T. *The Diplomatic Retreat of France and Public Opinion on the Eve of the French Revolution, 1783–1789*. Washington, DC: The Catholic University of America Press, 1998.

Stone, Bailey. *The Genesis of the French Revolution: A Global-Historical Interpretation*. Cambridge, UK: Cambridge University Press, 1994.

———. *Reinterpreting the French Revolution: A Global-Historical Perspective*. Cambridge, UK: Cambridge University Press, 2002.

Van Kley, Dale. *The Jansenists and the Expulsion of the Jesuits from France, 1757–1765*. New Haven, CT: Yale University Press, 1975.

———. *The Religious Origins of the French Revolution from Calvin to the Civil Constitution, 1560–1791*. New Haven and London: Yale University Press, 1996.

CHAPTER 2

Best, Geoffrey. *War and Society in Revolutionary Europe 1770–1870*. Montreal: McGill-Queen's University Press, 1998.

Blanning, T. C. W. *The French Revolutionary Wars, 1787–1802*. London: Arnold, 1996.

Blaufarb, Rafe. *The French Army, 1750–1820: Careers, Talent, Merit*. Manchester, UK: Manchester University Press, 2002.

Doyle, William. *Origins of the French Revolution*. 3rd ed. Oxford, UK: Oxford University Press, 1999.

Echeverria, Durand. *The Maupeou Revolution: A Study in the History of Libertarianism, France 1770–1774*. Baton Rouge: Louisiana State University Press, 1985.

Egret, Jean. *The French Prerevolution, 1787–1788*. Translated by Wesley D. Camp. Chicago: University of Chicago Press, 1977.

Fraser, Antonia. *Marie Antoinette: The Journey*. New York: Anchor Books, 2002.

Hardman, John. *Louis XVI*. New Haven: Yale University Press, 1993.

———. *Louis XVI: The Silent King*. London: Arnold, 2000.

Harris, Robert D. *Necker: Reform Statesman of the Ancien Régime*. Berkeley: University of California Press, 1979.

Horn, Jeff. *The Path Not Taken: French Industrialization in the Age of Revolution, 1750–1830*. Cambridge, MA: MIT Press, 2006.

Jones, P. M. *Reform and Revolution in France: The Politics of Transition, 1774–1791.* Cambridge, UK: Cambridge University Press, 1995.

Murphy, Orville T. *The Diplomatic Retreat of France and Public Opinion on the Eve of the French Revolution, 1783–1789.* Washington, DC: The Catholic University of America Press, 1998.

Padover, Saul K. *The Life and Death of Louis XVI.* New York: Pyramid Books, 1963, originally published 1939.

Riley, James C. *The Seven Years War and the Old Regime in France: The Economic and Financial Toll.* Princeton, NJ: Princeton University Press, 1986.

Schroeder, Paul W. *The Transformation of European Politics, 1763–1848.* Oxford, UK: Clarendon Press, 1996.

Stone, Bailey. *The French Parlements and the Crisis of the Old Regime.* Chapel Hill: University of North Carolina Press, 1986.

Swann, Julian. *Politics and the Parlement of Paris under Louis XV, 1754–1774.* Cambridge, UK: Cambridge University Press, 1995.

CHAPTER 3

Fitzsimmons, Michael P. *The Night the Old Regime Ended: August 4, 1789, and the French Revolution.* University Park: The Pennsylvania State University Press, 2003.

Godechot, Jacques. *The Taking of the Bastille, July 14th, 1789.* Translated by Jean Stewart. New York: Scribner, 1970.

Hyslop, Beatrice Fry. *A Guide to the General Cahiers of 1789.* New York: Columbia University Press, 1936.

Lefebvre, Georges. *The Coming of the French Revolution.* Translated by R. R. Palmer. Princeton, NJ: Princeton University Press, 1967.

———. *The Great Fear of 1789: Rural Panic in Revolutionary France.* Translated by Joan White. New York: Vintage Books, 1973.

Markoff, John. *The Abolition of Feudalism: Peasants, Lords, and Legislators in the French Revolution.* University Park: The Pennsylvania State University Press, 1996.

Rudé, George. *The Crowd in the French Revolution.* Oxford, UK: Clarendon Press, 1959.

Scott, Samuel F. *The Response of the Royal Army to the French Revolution: The Role and Development of the Line Army, 1787–1793.* Oxford, UK: Clarendon Press, 1978.

Sewell, Jr., William H. *Rhetoric of Bourgeois Revolution: The Abbé Sieyes and What Is the Third Estate.* Durham, NC: Duke University Press, 1994.

Shapiro, Gilbert, and John Markoff. *Revolutionary Demands: A Content Analysis of the Cahiers de Doléances of 1789.* Stanford, CA: Stanford University Press, 1998.

Tackett, Timothy. *Becoming a Revolutionary: The Deputies of the French National Assembly and the Emergence of a Revolutionary Culture (1789–1790).* Princeton, NJ: Princeton University Press, 1996.

Wick, Daniel L. *A Conspiracy of Well-Intentioned Men: The Society of Thirty and the French Revolution*. New York and London: Garland Publishing, 1987.

CHAPTER 4

Crook, Malcolm. *Elections in the French Revolution*. Cambridge, UK: Cambridge University Press, 1996.

Fitzsimmons, Michael P. *The Remaking of France: The National Assembly and the Constitution of 1791*. Cambridge, UK: Cambridge University Press, 1994.

Gottschalk, Louis R., and Margaret Maddox. *Lafayette in the French Revolution through the October Days*. Chicago: University of Chicago Press, 1969.

———. *Lafayette in the French Revolution from the October Days through the Federation*. Chicago: University of Chicago Press, 1973.

Margadant, Ted W. *Urban Rivalries in the French Revolution*. Princeton, NJ: Princeton University Press, 1992.

Shapiro, Barry. *Revolutionary Justice in Paris, 1789–1790*. Cambridge, UK: Cambridge University Press, 1993.

Van Kley, Dale, ed. *The French Idea of Freedom: The Old Regime and the Declaration of Rights of 1789*. Stanford, CA: Stanford University Press, 1994.

Waldinger, Renée, Philip Dawson, and Isser Woloch, eds. *The French Revolution and the Meaning of Citizenship*. Westport, CT: Greenwood Press, 1993.

CHAPTER 5

Andress, David. *Massacre at the Champ de Mars: Popular Dissent and Political Culture in the French Revolution*. Suffolk, UK: The Royal Historical Society, 2000.

Aston, Nigel. *Religion and Revolution in France, 1780–1804*. Washington, DC: The Catholic University of America, 2000.

Gough, Hugh. *The Newspaper Press in the French Revolution*. London: Routledge, 1988.

Kates, Gary. *The Cercle Social, the Girondins, and the French Revolution*. Princeton, NJ: Princeton University Press, 1985.

Kennedy, Michael L. *The Jacobin Clubs in the French Revolution*. 3 vols. Princeton, NJ: Princeton University Press, 1982–1999.

Luttrell, Barbara. *Mirabeau*. Carbondale: Southern Illinois University Press, 1990.

Popkin, Jeremy D. *Revolutionary News: The Press in France, 1789–1799*. Durham, NC: Duke University Press, 1990.

Price, Munro. *The Road from Versailles: Louis XVI, Marie Antoinette, and the Fall of the French Monarchy*. New York: St. Martin's Press, 2003.

Tackett, Timothy. *Religion, Revolution, and Regional Culture in Eighteenth-Century France: The Ecclesiastical Oath of 1791*. Princeton, NJ: Princeton University Press, 1986.

———. *When the King Took Flight*. Cambridge, MA: Harvard University Press, 2003.

CHAPTER 6

Bertaud, Jean-Paul. *The Army of the French Revolution: From Citizen-Soldiers to Instrument of Power*. Translated by R. R. Palmer. Princeton, NJ: Princeton University Press, 1988.

Blanning, T. C. W. *The Origins of the French Revolutionary Wars*. London: Longman, 1986.

Dubois, Laurent. *Avengers of the New World: The Story of the Haitian Revolution*. Cambridge, MA: Harvard University Press, 2004.

Godineau, Dominique. *The Women of Paris and Their French Revolution*. Translated by Katherine Streip. Berkeley: University of California Press, 1998.

Hufton, Olwen H. *Women and the Limits of Citizenship in the French Revolution*. Toronto: University of Toronto Press, 1992.

May, Gita. *Madame Roland and the Age of Revolution*. New York: Columbia University Press, 1970.

Maza, Sarah. *Private Lives and Public Affairs: The Causes Célèbres of Prerevolutionary France*. Berkeley: University of California Press, 1993.

Mitchell, C. J. *The French Legislative Assembly of 1791*. Leiden, Netherlands: E. J. Brill, 1988.

Sydenham, M. J. *The Girondins*. London: The Athlone Press, 1961.

CHAPTER 7

Forrest, Alan. *The Soldiers of the French Revolution*. Durham, NC: Duke University Press, 1990.

———. *Paris, the Provinces and the French Revolution*. London: Arnold, 2004.

Germani, Ian. *Jean-Paul Marat: Hero and Anti-Hero of the French Revolution*. Lewiston, NY: E. Mellen Press, 1992.

Godechot, Jacques. *The Counter-Revolution: Doctrine & Action, 1789–1804*. Translated by Salvator Attanasio. New York: Howard Fertig, 1971.

Gottschalk, Louis R. *Jean Paul Marat: A Study in Radicalism*. Chicago: University of Chicago Press, 1967.

Hanson, Paul R. *The Jacobin Republic under Fire: The Federalist Revolt in the French Revolution*. University Park: The Pennsylvania State University Press, 2003.

Patrick, Alison. *The Men of the First French Republic: Political Alignments in the National Convention of 1792*. Baltimore: The Johns Hopkins University Press, 1972.

Reinhardt, Steven G., and Cawthon, Elisabeth, eds. *Essays on the French Revolution: Paris and the Provinces.* College Station: Texas A&M University Press, 1992.

Walzer, Michael, ed. *Regicide and Revolution: Speeches at the Trial of Louis XVI.* Cambridge, UK: Cambridge University Press, 1974.

CHAPTER 8

Andress, David. *French Society in Revolution 1789–1799.* Manchester, UK: Manchester University Press, 1999.

———. *The Terror: The Merciless War for Freedom in Revolutionary France.* New York: Farrar, Straus & Giroux, 2005.

Furet, François. *Interpreting the French Revolution.* Translated by Elborg Forster. Cambridge, UK: Cambridge University Press, 1981.

Gough, Hugh. *The Terror in the French Revolution.* New York: Palgrave, 1998.

Hampson, Norman. *Danton.* Oxford, UK: Basil Blackwell, 1978.

Haydon, Colin, and William Doyle, eds. *Robespierre.* Cambridge, UK: Cambridge University Press, 1999.

Hunt, Lynn. *Politics, Culture, and Class in the French Revolution.* Berkeley: University of California Press, 1984.

Jordan, David P. *The Revolutionary Career of Maximilien Robespierre.* Chicago: University of Chicago Press, 1985.

Kennedy, Emmet. *A Cultural History of the French Revolution.* New Haven, CT: Yale University Press, 1989.

McManners, John. *The French Revolution and the Church.* New York: Harper & Row, 1969.

Ozouf, Mona. *Festivals and the French Revolution.* Translated by Alan Sheridan. Cambridge, MA: Harvard University Press, 1988.

Palmer, R. R. *Twelve Who Ruled.* Princeton, NJ: Princeton University Press, 1941.

Rudé, George. ed. *Robespierre.* Great Lives Observed series. Englewood Cliffs, NJ: Prentice-Hall, 1967.

———. *Robespierre: Portrait of a Revolutionary Democrat.* New York: Viking Press, 1975.

Slavin, Morris. *The Hébertistes to the Guillotine: Anatomy of a "Conspiracy" in Revolutionary France.* Baton Rouge: Louisiana State University Press, 1994.

Soboul, Albert. *The Sans-Culottes; the Popular Movement and Revolutionary Government, 1793–1794.* Translated by Rémy Inglis Hall. Garden City, NY: Anchor Books, 1972.

CHAPTER 9

Brown, Howard G. *Ending the French Revolution: Violence, Justice, and Repression from the Terror to Napoleon.* Charlottesville: University of Virginia Press, 2006.

Desan, Suzanne. *Reclaiming the Sacred*. Ithaca, NY: Cornell University Press, 1990.

Herold, J. Christopher. *Bonaparte in Egypt*. New York: Harper & Row, 1962.

Lefebvre, Georges. *The Thermidorians and the Directory*. Translated by Robert Baldick. New York: Random House, 1964.

Livesey, James. *Making Democracy in the French Revolution*. Cambridge, MA: Harvard University Press, 2001.

Lyons, Martyn. *France under the Directory*. Cambridge, UK: Cambridge University Press, 1975.

———. *Napoleon Bonaparte and the Legacy of the French Revolution*. New York: St. Martin's Press, 1994.

Markham, Felix. *Napoleon*. New York: Signet, 1966.

Woloch, Isser. *Jacobin Legacy: The Democratic Movement under the Directory*. Princeton, NJ: Princeton University Press, 1970.

———. *The New Regime: Transformations of the French Civic Order, 1789–1820s*. New York: W. W. Norton, 1994.

INDEX

ABOUT THE AUTHOR

Sylvia Neely is associate professor of history at Pennsylvania State University. She holds a BA from Duke University, an MA from New York University, and a PhD in history from the University of Notre Dame. She has taught courses on the French Revolution for many years at Penn State, Saint Louis University, and Indiana University–Purdue University at Fort Wayne. Professor Neely is the author of *Lafayette and the Liberal Ideal, 1814–1824: Politics and Conspiracy in an Age of Reaction* and of other publications on the revolutionary era in France and the United States. Her current project is a study of Lafayette's career during the French Revolution.